YOUR MINDFUL COMPASS:

BREAKTHROUGH STRATEGIES FOR NAVIGATING LIFE/WORK RELATIONSHIPS IN ANY SOCIAL JUNGLE

Andrea M. Schara

ISBN: 061592879X
ISBN-13: 978-0615928791

CONTENTS

For my son and daughter:
E. Martin Schara IV and Michelle Schara Mauboussin
and their families

Basic relationship patterns, developed for adapting to the parental family in childhood, are used in all other relationships throughout life.
- Murray Bowen, M.D.

IN GRATITUDE

I am deeply grateful to Murray Bowen. A revolutionary thinker and pioneer, Murray Bowen (1913–1990) was the first psychiatrist to develop a theory of human behavior based on the family as an emotional unit. Bowen demonstrated this in his own family encouraging others, like this author, to alter one's participation in the ongoing system, allowing change to take place.

Bowen believed in me when I was struggling, gave me a hand up, accepted me into postgraduate training at the Georgetown University Family Center despite my having only two years of college, and then allowed me to take photos in exchange for tuition to various symposiums. After four years of family systems theory training, he hired me to work at the Georgetown University Family Center as the audio visual (A/V) coordinator, saying it was easier to teach me the A/V role than teach an A/V expert Bowen theory.

I quickly recognized that what Bowen said was so far from mainstream psychiatry, that taping him and listening to the tapes again and again would be the only way to grasp this totally new way of thinking. A/V coordinator was perfect for me. As a teacher Bowen was at times direct and challenging. Using metaphors, paradox, and even slights of hand as a Zen master might, he delivered his out-of-sync, interrupting messages. (Each of us has our way of seeing things, our perceptual blindness, our way of getting along with others, and our beliefs as to how the world is. How does anyone interrupt these, allowing another to think differently?)

Bowen once took my arm and, pointing to a couple, asked in his Socratic way: "What are these people doing? Who is in charge? How do you know?" The first time I heard him speak to an audience he peppered his talk with unanswerable questions: "How do you de-twitch people? How is what you do with people different from what you might do to calm animals down? Do you know what you are up against in yourself and in relating to your multigenerational family? How about the challenges with your friends and loved ones? Are you ready for the kiss of togetherness?"

Bowen challenged me to deal with tricks—his and others. Like an imp he was watching, smiling, getting upset, and never explaining what he was up to. He explained himself in books, letters and videotapes. Writing about the role of a coach in being outside the emotional system, he explained how such a position allowed one to teach, give suggestions and tell personal stories without forcing, preaching, or believing he knew the "right way."

Demonstrating with his own life what it takes to be a lifelong participant-observer, he was quick to challenge and "jam people up." "Let's see what you can do" seemed to be his mantra. He was constantly putting others into some kind of an alliance, while separating himself out as different. Bowen would say, "I am listening to you." Yes, listening to you but not agreeing with you. Bowen made people uncomfortable unless they could stand-alone and did not need approval for their ideas. He was challenging people to rise up and take a stand to say what they would and would not do, to define more of a Self. Who knows what research questions were on his mind as he interacted with you? But when his blue eyes were twinkling and he was looking at you, you knew that questions and unusual, what I call "non-linked" behavior responses, were about to be unleashed in your direction.

An endlessly curious researcher of human behavior, Bowen watched many others and me. We were part of the human parade on a multigenerational train ride. Bowen rode alongside family after family, inserting a question here, a story there, just to see how people would react—if they would grow or get off the train. Sometimes he might throw a pearl and another time some coal. Ready or not, "relationship stuff" was always coming your way.

Toward the end of his life I traveled with him because of his serious physical limitations. Perhaps my family position as an oldest daughter of brothers favored by grandparents, plus luck, allowed me to figure out how to relate well enough, especially to his wife and family. I appreciated this opportunity more than any words can convey.

Bowen would not approve of my explanation of Family Systems theory, of how I have managed myself, coached others or have written this book. Approval was at the bottom of his list as to what was important. Figuring out the right kind of challenge fascinated him, often leading to his highlighting the creative ways people developed to overcome or wiggle out of intense problems.

Watching, reading, and listening to Bowen, I was often struck with his ability to observe the human condition and take an action based on his theory to stay interested and connected while separating himself out from the others. As with us all he had his own issues and peculiarities but his real gift was to point us in a direction to see what we had not seen about the human and the mechanisms of family life under pressure. His lasting, jarring question, "How come you cannot see what is right in front of you?" is as important and as unanswered today as it was back then.

I designed this book in his memory to do for others what he did for me: To enable motivated individuals be more for Self, to have a few systems ideas, to grasp a deeper understanding of our link with other social species and to really see how social systems function. The future is uncertain. But what is certain is that we will always need to understand how to manage ourselves and to see the impact of our very social relationships on each other.

Andrea Schara and Murray Bowen at Walter Reed Studio, 1987

INTRODUCTION & OVERVIEW OF CHAPTERS I-XIV

We are all painfully blind to relationship processes which are generated by the larger system to control its members. The larger unit has to survive. The individual is often expendable. However, the human has the ability to see the social pressure and to then gain some degree of independence from the constraints of these ancient social systems. In this day and age we are born into an accepted view of relationship dynamics, which is an individual centric view of the world. To see how systems function to pressure us, requires a dose of systems knowledge as an antidote to our social blindness. Knowledge will not matter unless it is personal. Therefore, this book only gives you a peek into a deeper understanding of how systems regulate the individual members in both subtle and brutal ways. If you use a Mindful Compass to navigate through the social constraints, then this knowledge becomes yours. I have combined both personal and coaching ideas to give you my best understanding of Bowen Theory. The Mindful Compass is designed to enable you to build a knowledge pathway through any social system. We can learn from success and also from frustration or even failure to navigate and then correct our view of social systems. Being able to relate well to others can impact the lives of future generations and is well worth the effort to understand and learn a new way to relate to difficult people and/ or challenging situations. There is freedom in developing a Mindful Compass and learning how to alter your part in these sensitive and sometimes reactive relationship systems. It is, overall, hard to comprehend how we are automatically "controlled" by ancient emotional processes. It is easier to see once one begins to develop a deeper understanding of both one's multigenerational family life and Bowen theory. The interactions with Bowen, to challenge and to think for self and to keep learning and questioning, were useful in altering my automatic responsiveness. Therefore, I pass this knowledge on to others as best I can.

Introduction to Bowen Theory 101

Murray Bowen, M.D. was the first psychiatrist to hospitalize members of nuclear families for two or more years at the National Institute of Mental Health (the first whole family was admitted at the very end of December 1955 and the last family left December 31, 1958). Bowen studied relationships in families as family members dealt with a schizophrenic family member. Observing interactions, not diagnosing individuals, led to his development of the eight interlocking concepts. These concepts explain how the various parts of the family system function. He explained that two forces influence the human— one for "togetherness," encouraging people to think alike and to go along with others and the other, a counterbalancing force for individuality, to be all for Self. Differentiation represents the observation that there is a middle way—to be for Self and to be for others. Bowen "coached" people to be aware—to see and manage Self in the emotional system. The family as a unit is a different way to understand and deal with human behavior. The real source of healing was in one's family system itself. When under the influence of "togetherness" forces, people are reactive and more regulated by the group. By enabling people to see what they are up against, to be more neutral and to find ways to develop the skills to be better able to relate well during turbulent times, people can increase their functioning. Few things are harder but more worthwhile than this effort to be a Self in a social group.

"Thinking Systems" - Developing Your Mindful Compass

There are ways to enable people to broaden their thinking to become better observers of the many ways each of us is a part of a social system and often unduly influenced by that social system. When times are tough, going along can lead us into quagmires. A Mindful Compass allows us to know the obstacles to change. By using the compass one can develop a deeper Self with a capital S. Otherwise, people respond automatically, as a small self (a reaction to others or following automatic programming). Through interacting mindfully, people build a more mature Self and in so doing encourage maturity and less dependency throughout the family. This has important implications for the future evolution of the family as a system.

Action for Self and Resistance as Natural

In describing the Mindful Compass the first two points are (1) the ability to take ACTION and to define one's vision and (2) to deal with the RESISTANCE one faces to being more of a Self in any system. **To change, one has to be able to reduce anxiety (response to real or imagined threat) and see the emotional systems as it is, a natural force. This enables one to develop a less reactive and more differentiated Self.** The trip through the social jungle is fraught with challenges. We can all be duped into giving in to please others or into backing down when it comes to articulating and clarifying one's viewpoints. A family leader calibrates a personal compass by questioning and clarifying the world around him or her, establishing principles for being a more mature self, and becoming less sensitive to the emotional forces in the multigenerational family and in other social systems.

Systems Knowledge and Standing Alone

The last two points on the Mindful Compass are (3) the ability to use KNOWLEDGE to connect meaningfully with others and (4) the ability to STAND ALONE and be more separate. Knowledge enables us to stand alone, to be more objective and strategic, to welcome and endure emotional challenges, and to understand deeply the reason for taking on issues in one's family or work place. In achieving this different way of relating, one grants freedom to another to be the way the other is, while still holding each individual responsible for his or her actions. People have the ability to act in ways to get beyond the emotional road blocks, to know cut off individuals in their extended family, to get beyond the multigenerational gossip problems, to reduce stress in interactions, to relate from curiosity rather than from a need for social approval or to command or control others. Changing self to be more of one's best Self requires seeing the system, increasing knowledge, and lowering reactivity, while interacting with others or even thinking about others. This and more can lead to the building of one's emotional backbone.

The Usefulness of Developing Your Mindful Compass

Family or workplace "rules" are not unlike the rules of other mammalian social groups or even ant colonies. Interactions determine how the mind/brain/body is influenced, which leads individuals to function in specific roles for the group. Humans are sensitive to one another. This sensitivity can run the gamut from being totally independent to being totally dependent on others. (Bowen called this "fusion," indicating the primitive nature of our association whereby two function as one.) Differentiation allows individuals to become more of a Self. We live in some degree of fusion and dependence with others. These overlapping relationships, where people are not sure what they stand for, or sometimes who they are, are the result of fusion. One can humorously refer to this as con-fusion or our life as scrambled eggs. We are somewhere in a scrambled mix of others' ideas and opinions. We are not yet well defined, and therefore we are vulnerable to becoming more scrambled.

Substantial life energy is devoted to figuring out social relationships. Our brain no longer has to focus on the lions and tigers in the social jungle, but instead must manage complex relationships. Unwanted, intrusive, and unavoidable social interaction can drive even fairly social creatures mad. And we are vulnerable to sticking with ineffective "rules" (or the status quo), especially when threatened. Aware leaders can identify system-level problems and effectively use knowledge to alter their participation in social systems.

Understanding Triangles in the Social Jungle

Contrary to popular opinion, scientific facts show how triangles are the most stable alliance between people. Triangles consist of two individuals who agree with each other, while a third individual is on the outside. Such alliances can both manage anxiety by promoting scapegoating, or triangles can allow an outside person to change the dynamic for the better in that three-person system. If one person can remain neutral while relating to the other two as individuals and avoid taking sides, the other two will be able to resolve conflict. This is the basis for mediation and marital counseling. One-on-one relationships tend to collapse. Enter the "triangled one," who can reduce anxiety of the twosome for better or worse. Such alliance building occurs in colonies of bacteria and in learning. Triangles often determine social rank. You can see this at the dinner table. When tension is high there is more gossip, taking sides or blame. If one person is neutral and does not

8

take sides, then triangles can enable problem solving simply because of that neutrality and refusal to take sides. Interlocking triangles occur as more and more people are drawn into a conflict and begin to take sides. People can be drawn in and not take sides and form alliances to do productive work, too. Therefore it's important to understand the functioning of triangles as anxiety absorbers or as ways to generate more cooperative behavior. Knowledge of triangles helps individuals understand anxiety and how it can be managed mindfully.

Reducing Con-fusion at Home and Work: Getting to Know Your Extended Family

Knowledge of Self, family and others in social systems is the key to change. By focusing on self and seeing how one's family has managed challenges over the generations, we can see the impersonal nature of emotional process. In seeing the system, people are far better observers and can relate more effectively to each individual. Knowledge of history enables us to redirect anxiety and to appreciate differences. As one is able to know others in the family, one is automatically freer of the projections and gossip of the past. A mature leader can listen to others without reacting automatically by communicating his or her thinking and what he or she will do in a variety of ways, some of which can be shocking. A Mindful Compass can be more important than an automatic compass. This effort to be more defined in a social group has a multigenerational payoff. It is this capacity to see relationship dynamics and alter how one functions in them that result in solving system-level problems more effectively.

Relationship Blindness and the Evolving Brain

The emotional system, with its ancient mechanisms, does not function well on automatic pilot if one is trying to manage Self in our modern jungle. When one is faced with emotional issues, how does one become more rational and factual? The tigers are everywhere now. In today's social jungle, we react to traffic jams as though they were tigers. Our primitive brain is over-reactive to threats, especially when we do not "see the system." We have in common with reptiles the most primitive instincts—mating, defense of territory, and giving in to the dominant ones. The instinctual brain areas are not in direct communication with the more cognitive part of the

9

brain. Therefore, in the sending of signals and the recognition of old clues, one is never sure which part of our brain is in charge of our actions. The brain, after the fact, explains it all to us as though it acted in our best interest. But did it? Or is your brain just singing the multigenerational instinctual song? The brain produces justifications for taking actions to increase comfort, which decreases maturity. Not being able to reflect on the long-term consequences of our actions reduces our ability to know one another and to solve problems. Our blindness to the impact we have on one another can be a result of our brains' short-term orientation. In this brave new world, there is no one to blame, there are no simple solutions, but there are many ways to be observant and creative in our ability to see and to respond to one another. We are all vulnerable to being blinded by our investment in our own way of doing things, and it is a risk to become more aware of the social jungle and our part in it.

The Rise of Systems Thinking in the Social Sciences

There is a payoff for those willing to examine the social research to understand the way the human brain is set up to perceive the environment, and how that then influences decision making. We are prejudiced and can easily be blindsided by innocent or manipulative stories parading as facts. In addition, linear (i.e., 1, 2, 3) thinking can encourage us to make poor decisions. Reality becomes a "social reality" under pressure. The social group itself may need to become more oriented to providing ways to develop perceptual independence in its members. One can understand the way the human brain is set to react or to more rationally predict the future. Sorting out reactivity from rationality will be key to any kind of orderly transition during chaotic times. There can be catastrophic consequences when applying short-term, cause-effect thinking to an impending challenge. We all have some access to a "bubbling sea" of systems information, but our tendency towards cause-effect thinking influences (in this case negatively) our ability to anticipate and respond realistically to the potential challenges that are likely to occur. We can understand how systems work. Leaders can learn to see the automatic focus on the weak and vulnerable and courageously interrupt this negative focus on others. For this skill to become more widespread, leaders need to find others who are aware of the possibility of runaway, primitive thinking and/or relationships traps. By being more aware of others and the impact they have on us and we on them, leaders can better adapt during times of great change.

Writing Your Story: Learning and Reflecting

As a leader, changing one's Self to deal with problems rather than trying to force others to change, requires building one's emotional backbone. Writing or telling a story about one's life can help people gain greater objectivity and even find ways to put a positive spin on difficult events. Research notes how journaling strengthens immune cells. Exploring and writing about one's family is a workout, but these exercises in "the multigenerational emotional gym" will build your emotional backbone. Those willing to undertake the task of building family relationships increase their resilience and emotional backbone.

The potential payoff for gaining knowledge about both family history and the process of building or repairing relationships gives us a stronger relationship base for future generations. Building more compassionate relationships may overturn some of an individual's most cherished beliefs. This is a small price to pay to live in a less emotionally driven world. We are too easily swayed by emotional appeals and social relationships. It requires discipline to understand others and our deeper self and to communicate, despite rejection.

What does it take to be a self in any system?

Just as no one ant can build an ant colony, no one person can create for him or herself all that is needed for survival. We are dependent on the work of others for our food, water, clothes, education and protection, among other things. By cooperating, we benefit. Therefore, the pressure to fit in is enormous and can intrude on our equally deep urges to become our unique selves. The emotional system consists of instincts and all kinds of psychological mechanisms. It is an automatic guidance system. Our biology is over reactive to threats. Anxiety degrades relationships. We can see how it works in the way people behave when there are stressors in the system. Anxious people are more likely to maintain a negative or overly positive focus on others, neither of which is realistic. Relationship changes, exercise, mindfulness training, neurofeedback and many other efforts, which can help one to manage anxiety and integrate new knowledge, can redirect anxiety and maintain the courage to be one's best Self.

By "reorganizing" Self, an individual can find ways to also set others free from any automatic and anxious focuses. By taking an action stance, more for Self rather than following the dictates of the emotional system, we promote the ability of others to do the same. Leading by example may take longer.   However it is a more solid commitment to respecting others and focusing on how to relate well to them.

Learning from Other Living Systems

From ants to humans there may be general laws organizing the nature of all emotional systems. Looking at ants you see that if you remove a few from one job, such as searching for food, there is a seemingly automatic compensation. The colony decreases the rate at which ants assume the tasks of removing garbage or defending the nest in order to "force" more into searching for food. Without much of a brain, ants know what the others in the colony are up to and adjust their role automatically.

Neither humans nor ants need much of a brain to pick up signals about the needs of the group or colony and what we need to do for them in the moment. We are shifting in response to others without knowing. The brain is multilayered, evolutionarily designed, and connects us with other mammalian and reptilian species. Because of the "design" of the brain, it is very difficult to become aware of deep emotional states in one's own brain or self. We honor those who can perceive the environment more accurately.

Social Pressure and the Ability to Redirect Anxiety

Stanley Milgram demonstrated how people's obedience to authority is automatic, even when it leads to the potential death of innocent people. He was curious as to how interactions in the social group lead to an event like the Holocaust. The research shows that a majority of people will do harm to others based on a command from an authority figure, even if that command goes against a value not to harm others. How can good and normal people be so blind to the consequences of their behavior? Solomon Asch showed that one-third of people would alter their perceptions as to the length of line, so as to go along with a social group that formed only an hour previously. Last but not least, logic is of little use when people are vulnerable to emotional guidance. You may only intensify emotions with logic. Therefore, the ability to understand and use emotionality to both communicate and understand others is a skill that has a significant impact on both individuals and social groups.

Bowen described a road map allowing us to understand how to be a more separate and well-defined individual, with all the costs and benefits of so doing. If using a Mindful Compass does confer an adaptive response, then we should see more leaders who are aware of the system and the process involved in changing Self.

Interviews

Dr. Bowen's idea that being able to separate out a more principled, mature Self, while staying in contact with others (the process of differentiation of self), was a natural phenomenon. People could figure out the emotional system intuitively, experiment and know how to lead.

I wondered whether leaders could explain how they were able to separate out from the pressures in their social systems - to be better defined in relationship to the important people in their family or at work. Would they tell me what it took to be a Self and stand apart from the group? Would they tell me how others would automatically oppose the growth of a "leader?"

To answer these questions I asked friends for names of people they considered natural and mature leaders. I interviewed ten, all of whom were local leaders. None had any knowledge of Bowen Theory or were famous or well-known beyond their communities.

They are people who have made a difference in some area of society, telling us fascinating stories of leading under conditions of uncertainty. Each individual reflected on what they have been up against in trying to move forward through the social jungle.

Our brains are designed for storytelling as part of how we have interacted over the generations. We tell stories as a way to learn from the past. This playful activity integrates the higher and lower parts of the brain. Stories promote our ongoing ability to cooperate for basic survival needs, gather resources, pass on values and raise children.

CHAPTER I
BOWEN FAMILY THEORY 101

I begin with a short overview of family systems theory developed by Murray Bowen, M.D., because my fundamental thinking about leadership comes from Bowen Theory. This book is about becoming a more effective, principle-based, mature leader who is less subject to the whims and pressures of the social group. Any of us can become this kind of a leader—either by default or by desire—by designing a *Mindful Compass* to guide us as we develop and implement our goals. All of us are already equipped with an *automatic compass* that guides us in how to react to the emotional messages in the social group. Simply because of the way our brain has been built to be overly sensitive to changes in the environment and clues from the social group, we react often without awareness much less thought. Leaders can increase the ability to develop their own *Mindful Compass* and thereby lead by self-defined principle and, when necessary, identify and override their reactive thoughts, feelings and behaviors.

In order to highlight the difference between one's automatic self and a Self who is making an effort to be more mindful, I have chosen to highlight the difference between the automatic and the mindful by using a capital S for the Self that is making an effort to override the automatic self when deemed necessary. There is a self that functions well on automatic. This automatic self may also be susceptible to becoming blindsided too. Therefore, I have designated the automatic self with the lower case s.

A Mindful Compass requires a broad knowledge of Bowen's "Systems Thinking" to identify what is authentic and real about one's Self and how to build up one's emotional backbone and decrease the part of "self" that is mostly mired in automatic reactivity. There are many ways to grow one's Self up. One of them is by having a Mindful Compass, which allows us to understand our actions in the light of our multigenerational family relationships. The emotional field that connects the generations has an unseen influence on us. A systems viewpoint offers us a different way to understand and to then alter our sensitivity to those unseen influences. Our emotional backbone connects us to our evolutionary heritage and this grants us greater objectivity.

All of this intellectual work to understand our position in any system gives us a hand up in managing our reactive nature. Deep knowledge of our reactivity makes many of the things that happen to us feel far less threatening and personal. Objectivity increases our ability to rise above the reactivity both within us and from others and to then change and adapt well to situations we encounter daily. If one can understand the reasons to decrease reactivity and to define self to others, then one can take on the work involved. The goal is that, even when under pressure, one can be less reactive and less controlled by the surrounding relationship system and therefore, paradoxically, be both separate from and a real resource to others in any social system.

Murray Bowen, M.D. (1913–1990), the first psychiatrist to develop a theory of human behavior from a natural systems perspective.

Following medical training, Murray Bowen served five years of active duty with the Army during World War II, from 1941-1946, serving in the United States and Europe and rising from Lieutenant to Major. Before the war, he had been awarded a fellowship in surgery at the Mayo Clinic that was to begin after military service. However, as a result of his wartime experiences, Bowen changed his interest from surgery to psychiatry. Instead of going to the Mayo Clinic he studied psychiatry at The Menninger Clinic in Topeka, Kansas.[1]

From 1946–1954, Bowen read extensively about biology and evolution, while simultaneously running research projects at the Menninger Clinic. Freud, he thought, had not made the leap to finding a scientific way of conceptualizing human behavior. Bowen began to observe an interactional world, leading to his development of an entirely different perspective on human behavior. Convinced that the only way to be free to think differently about the human condition was to move into research, he accepted a clinical director's position at the National Institute of Mental Health (NIMH). Over a five-year period, eighteen families with a schizophrenic member were studied while living on an inpatient unit. After that project ended in 1959, he joined the faculty of the Georgetown University School of Medicine.[2] It was here that he developed Bowen Family Systems Theory.[3] This theory of human behavior views the family as an emotional unit and uses Systems Thinking to describe the complex interactions in the unit.

Bowen believed that the emotional systems (instincts, behavioral patterns, and brain mechanisms) that govern human relationships have evolved over millions of years. He postulated that differentiation (level of emotional maturity) among family members produced variation, as individuals became more or less mature from one generation to the next. Less mature people are unable to grow away from others and are more dependent in many subtle ways. For example, the automatic focus on blaming others for the challenges life presents to us increases when differentiation among family members becomes progressively lower. Clinical symptoms appear in the family members, who are negatively and sometimes positively focused on, such as the one with the special talent or the most loving. In both cases there is an unrealistic focus that transmits the anxiety. Consider an extreme case where the parents imagine their child will be a famous golf player, no matter the child is mediocre at best. The pressure can be extreme to live up to expectations (and in some well-documented cases even to fall ill) when there is an intense, worried focus on one such individual. It is so very hard for anyone, who is in the middle of the situation, to see how the relationship pressure works.

The "focus on others" occurs automatically, intensifying family anxiety. We can see this as unrealistic expectations, concerns, or worry about others. By reorganizing the felt anxiety about others to focus on what Self can do (for Self), the anxiety calms down and people become more realistic. The "other focus," which can be seen in the development of symptoms, is on a continuum from mild to very intense. The tendency to over focus on others and to feel helpless is correlated with how isolated the family members have become, and the level of challenge the "problem" presents. However, once one individual begins to address his or her part in this family emotional process, the intensity can decrease, the symptoms will recede, and then more Self-directed development will proceed. This all takes time and a family leader willing and able to focus on Self rather than others is the mainstay of any such an effort.

There is considerable variability among individuals in any emotional unit or social group. Some members are more sensitive to stress and negativity and carry the symptoms, while others are relatively free from the kinds of sensitivity that produces symptoms. The freer ones can grow away from the dependencies during development and emerge as individuals able to stay in contact with the family in a more realistic and less emotionally driven way. The ability to function well in a group without as much reactivity to others can also be seen in how individuals function at work.

In every family there is someone who, even under pressure, is capable of seeing the way the system around them is working and can self-regulate, instead of being regulated by the group. To the degree that one person sees the reactivity in a more objective way and can control Self, there is less contagious anxiety for people to absorb. Family Systems Theory points to a way for any family unit to be able to grow, depending on the effort of aware and motivated people.

The usefulness of leadership is that one person can influence others in a positive way and then others in the group will be freer to also function for Self. There are fewer emotional entanglements as, one by one, people in the family learn to manage Self. Once one person begins to see how instinctually we are regulating one another this enables such individuals to participate more thoughtfully in all other social systems.

It is hard to see and understand that we live in emotionally regulated systems. Each of us is striving to be ourselves and at the same time we are being influenced by those around us. Bowen called these automatic processes the *force for togetherness* and the *force to be an individual*. The balance each individual strikes between these two forces influences may even determine one's level of emotional maturity.

How do individuals increase their awareness in order to see the family as an emotional unit? Is it easier to see this if we consider that over evolutionary time all social species have inherited mechanisms to distribute anxiety in automatic ways? People are usually totally unaware of the automatic nature of the emotional basis of their actions and reactions and tend to take things personally. We often think, "You are doing this to me." However, if an individual becomes aware of the system around him or her and is willing to define a Self by taking a stand and saying to others something along the lines of, "This is what I will and will not do," then the whole family can change. It may take time for the initial upset to pass and for the family to settle down. After all, defining a more separate Self can also create waves of reactivity, as you are no longer functioning in the way you once did.

Of course, if you are courageous enough to define a Self to a family member or someone who is important to you at work, then you will also realize that the others and you still live in a reactive world. In this very real, reactive world we feel the shifting of anxiety because others will get mad at you initially for saying or doing something "different" and you will experience this as unpleasant. This is one reason it takes awareness and strength, arising from one's inner convictions, to be a leader, who is willing to stand up for Self and to redirect the family or work system's anxiety.

When things begin to get stressful, aware leaders can see the flow of anxiety in the group building like a gathering storm. The process of spreading anxiety is impersonal. Once any of us can see the spreading of anxiety, we can begin to take the necessary precautions. Being aware of the approaching anxiety "storm" can make it easier to take a position to be more defined, just as one would prepare well for a thunderstorm.

Think of the spreading of anxiety as occurring because people are so connected. Perhaps you could even visualize a family as people attached to one another as if in a web. If one person changes his or her position in relationship to others, the web begins to alter its shape and a few seem to get more of the problems—the anxiety—which creates more trouble for some than for others. If one person can notice how people are impacting one another or how the web is put together, they can take the pressure off some or put the pressure on others. The direction of the anxiety and, therefore, the shape of the web, can be altered by those who can see the web in an impersonal way. There is no one to blame. Family dynamics are a part of life, part of our inheritance. Seeing this process over the generations a bit more objectively enables one to act more thoughtfully.

When stress hits a family or even a work relationship group, old patterns often re-emerge. If the leader can define him or her Self as to what he/she will or will not do, then people tend to settle down. This is one way leaders create change—by redirecting the focus onto individuals, who take responsibility for themselves and their part in the relationship system. People are not controlling and blaming others. They are more Self-defined. If one person has the knowledge and courage to change Self, a family system will slowly change.

The goal of "Family Systems Psychotherapy" is to increase individual family members' level of differentiation through the work of those who are motivated and capable of being in better emotional contact with the nuclear and extended family. This effort requires knowledge of the emotional system and implies a willingness to strengthen one's emotional backbone to manage and define Self in many close up or even distant family relationships.

The cornerstones of Bowen theory are the eight interlocking concepts influencing the counterbalance between togetherness and individuality. No one concept can be explained by another concept. No one concept can be eliminated or isolated from Bowen theory. Emotional, biological, and environmental influences are all factors that impinge on an individual's ability to adapt. Families have been emotionally organized units for hundreds of thousands of generations and the automatic mechanisms that run relationship dynamics in small groups have their own reasons for existence. The ability to see how emotional systems are organized in as neutral a way as possible gives us more freedom to be ourselves and to be less reactive towards those who, like us, are caught in the web of life.

The Eight Basic Concepts of Bowen Family Systems Theory

1. Levels of differentiation of self

"The level of differentiation is the degree to which one self fuses or merges into another self in a close emotional relationship. The scale has nothing to do with emotional illness or psychotherapy. There are low-scale people who manage to keep their lives in emotional equilibrium without developing emotional illness, and there are higher scale people who can develop symptoms under great stress." [4]

Families and social groups affect how people think, feel and act, but individuals vary in their susceptibility to "groupthink." Also, groups vary in the amount of pressure they exert for conformity. The less developed a person's "self," the more impact others have on his or her functioning and the more he or she tries to control the functioning of others.

Bowen developed a scale to measure differentiation of self. The scale has been seen as promising a way to measure functioning. No concrete scale to measure levels of differentiation of self has yet appeared. Bowen wrote it as a way to see the enormous variety in functioning. A system view considers the variation in functioning rather than focusing on diagnosing people. The descriptive scale considers human variation as spanning the following four quadrants.

0-25 – Here, there is very little to no ability to stand up for self. Mostly, one is reactive to levels of anxiety in the group and many decisions are made automatically to follow along or oppose others. Feeling "comfortable" dictates the life course.

25-50 – One can know the difference between facts and feelings, but intense and reactive feeling states combined with the levels of anxiety in the system, can degrade people's functioning. At this level of maturity, people can lose sight of important principles to guide decisions. When times are calm, people can use principles and think carefully about relationships and decisions. Principles can enable people to withstand the pressure to give in to relationship demands. This range is the quadrant where most of us function. "If the relationship system approves they can be brilliant students and disciples. If their expectations are not met, they assemble a pseudo-self in point-by-point opposition to the established order." [5]

50-60 – This is the area where one does know the difference between feelings and thinking. Therefore decisions are more thoughtful and relationships are calmer. These people can be principled and open with others. When opposed, they do not create great waves of reactivity. They are able to consider the long-term implications and are not overly defending Self against the attacks of others.

60-75 – People here are freer of the surrounding emotional system. They are clear on basic principles that direct behavior, can express beliefs without reactivity, and can find satisfaction in both emotional closeness and in goal-directed activity. They are more realistic about Self than those in the lower quadrants of the scale, who tend to automatically over or under evaluate self.

100 – This is an area towards which humans may evolve. 100 would be a perfect individual in emotional, cellular and physiological functioning. "It has not yet been possible to check the scale on extremely high level people, but my impression is that 75 is a very high-level person and that those above 60 constitute a small percentage of society." [6]

There are ways to raise one's level of basic maturity but it takes sustained effort to decrease the relationship sensitivity, given the way people are confused in relationships and are "fused" with one another. It is easy to say and hard to do – to increase the ability to be more aware of principles and to separate Self from others while being aware of the deep connection with others. Separating one's Self from the entanglements with others is the main discipline that one enters into as one begins to define who Self is, and what one will and will not do in relation to important others. In addition, our functioning is both inhibited and enhanced by many genetic-like psychological and physiological factors. The scale uses numbers to indicate the variation and the general markers for emotional maturity as to how people are able to handle anxiety and be more mature and principle-based individuals.

We can be aware that we are living in the middle of an emotionally primed, interactive relationship system. We can do better by knowing that our functioning is influenced by the surrounding social system. Especially during troubled times, it is crucial to increase our level of emotional maturity or differentiation and become better defined individuals, who are able to separate out from the pressure in the surrounding emotional systems. As this happens, gradually the system as a whole becomes more mature.

2. The nuclear family

This concept describes four relationship patterns to manage anxiety: 1) marital conflict, 2) dysfunction in one spouse, 3) impairment of one or more children, and 4) emotional distance. These mechanisms are automatically activated as anxiety and stress increase. As anxiety is absorbed, the history of sensitivity in relationships plays itself out and governs where problems are likely to develop in a family. Families tend to function at higher levels if they use many mechanisms and not just one. It is possible for people to become aware of the automatic nature of how we relate to one another and alter our behavior in them.

3. Family projection process

This concept describes the way parents transmit their emotional problems to a child. Some parents have great trouble separating from the child. They *imagine* how the child is. They do not have a realistic appraisal of the child. An extreme example would be that a child is born blind and the parents treat the child as though she or he can see. Parents unknowingly project the anxiety about self or their marriage onto the child by "worrying" about the child. Children often accept the projection of the anxiety and act out the projection so the parents' focus appears appropriate. The child is the symptom carrier for the parental anxiety. What an observer would see in a family that uses this mechanism to manage anxiety are the following behaviors: an intense focus on the child, very little focus on self, a need for attention and approval, confusion when it comes to realistic expectations for the child (and often for the adults), increasing blame on self or others, pervasive feeling of responsibility for others' happiness, and acting impulsively to relieve the anxiety of the moment. The bottom line—many of these kinds of feelings and verbal messages are about one person putting a "demand" on others to be more for them and less in favor of the other's ability to be more defined, a less automatic Self. As it becomes challenging to know "Where do I begin and end and where do you begin and end," here is where the mechanisms of fusion and confusion come to be played out. People can make assumptions about others, based on projection, partly because this is how the brain works.

4. Multigenerational transmission process

This concept describes how small differences in the levels of differentiation between parents and their offspring may lead, over many generations, to marked differences in functioning among the members of a multigenerational family. The way people relate to one another in one generation may create intense sensitivities, which are transmitted across generations. Some may drink in one generation and not in another, but the anxiety about drinking in one generation may manifest in another generation around drug use or other behaviors, e.g., eating disorders. People with more anxiety and less maturity can pressure others to make up for what has happened in the past and in doing so make people more vulnerable and even symptomatic.

A child's sibling position can be different from the child's functional position in one generation, which can have an impact on the next generation. For example, an oldest sibling is often in the functional position of being responsible for other siblings. If an oldest sibling falls ill, the functional position will have to shift to the next most able child. If the oldest is ill and cannot function well then the family may worry about the functioning of the oldest child in the next generation. In addition, a habit or a talent can remind parents of people they knew or have heard about in other generations. The association of one person with a memory of another person can conspire to decrease the ability of a child to develop a real identity in the family. "You **must** be a great chess player like your great grandfather was." This kind of projection can put a "demand" on the child to be what the other needs him to be. Love with such a demand can confuse children. Does the child want to be great or have ability for greatness? The potential of the child and the way family members relate to the child, along with his or her basic genetic inheritance, interact to shape the individual's level of maturity or "self."

5. Sibling position

Bowen Theory incorporates psychologist Walter Toman's work on sibling position. There are common characteristics of each sibling position. For example, oldest children tend to gravitate to leadership positions and youngest children often prefer to be followers, unless their parents disappointed them. Toman's research showed that spouses' sibling positions, when mismatched, often increase the chance of divorce.[7] There is a great deal to be learned about the influence over the generations when, for example, parents cannot understand a child as the parents are each the youngest in their family of origin and have no idea how to relate well to an oldest, even if it is their child. If the child is fortunate he or she may have some of the responsible traits of an oldest along with some of the fun loving nature of a youngest.

6. Triangles

A triangle is a three-person relationship system. It is considered the "molecule" of larger emotional systems because it is the smallest stable relationship system. A triangle can manage more tension than a two-person relationship as tension shifts among the three people in the triangle. Triangles can exert social control by the threat to put one person on the outside of a two-some or of a group. De-triangling occurs when, strategically, someone comes into a polarized situation and makes an effort to not take sides and relate well to each person. In mediation, we often see efforts to bring in an outsider when tension escalates between two individuals. Sometimes the mediator can relate to each side without taking sides. In this case the tension will resolve. Increasing the number of triangles by forming useful alliances (which do not polarize or blame people) can also stabilize spreading tension. Marital therapy uses the triangle to provide a neutral third party capable of relating well to both sides of a conflict.

7. Emotional cut off

People sometimes manage their unresolved emotional issues with parents, siblings, and other family members by reducing or totally cutting off emotional contact with them. This resolves nothing and risks making new relationships too important. In fact, *cut off* carries forward these unresolved emotional issues in one's family of origin into the nuclear families and other new relationships these individuals create.

8. Societal emotional process

This concept describes how the emotional system governs behavior on a societal level. The emotional system in society can promote progressive or regressive periods just as it does in a family.[8] The simplest description is that under stress the family members can be too nice or too mean. Parents that are too nice begin to give in to demands for short-term solutions to chronic problems. Just as in a family, leaders in society have a hard time identifying the nature of problems and a regression begins by giving in or

25

trying to solve big problems with little answers. Mechanisms that offer us ready solutions to increasing anxiety—conflict, distance, reciprocal functioning and illness—can absorb the increasing anxiety but only postpone solving the problems. People react to disharmony and demand more short-term solutions in order to be comfortable **now**. A regression is a return to an earlier period in development where there is less principle-driven behavior, some degree of giving in and seeking comfort, and perhaps overall less ability to recognize and respect individuals and to be able to cooperate. Since the arrow of time is always moving forward, new problems often demand new ways to adapt, forcing us into the discomfort zone.

CHAPTER II
"THINKING SYSTEMS" – DEVELOPING YOUR MINDFUL COMPASS

It is very challenging to be detached enough to observe just how the social system that you live in actually operates. To observe without judgment and without intense reactivity is a skill that can be developed. It does not come naturally for most people. It requires one to be willing to understand the emotional system that one is a part of well enough to *inhibit the feeling system*. Clearly, there is no way to figure out how to deal with one's relationships without being able to observe them. Only then can one begin to conceptualize how his or her social system functions. Learning to "think systems" has to start with the discipline of observing more neutrally how both you and the people around you function. Understanding your life, your family, and how you function in relationships requires effort. Our automatic ways of being can be hard to see and may resist our efforts to become more aware. Our little self or ego often has little tolerance for being observed or called into question.

Since many people are without access to a family system coach and have to learn through reading, one of the purposes of this book is to help you learn enough about yourself and your family to begin to be your own systems coach. Once you see your own family system and your part in it, you can begin to find, and perhaps create anew, your personal direction.

Have you ever been caught in the torrent of family habits, wishing for a Mindful Compass to sail in your own direction? The points on the Mindful Compass are: (1) **Action** (2) **Resistance** (3) **Knowledge** and (4) **The ability to stand alone.**

Let us consider the points on the Mindful compass and the reasons that make it worth the time to calibrate your personal compass. We know all of us have an automatic compass designed to enable us to act without thought. However, since stormy seas await us, we may need a more mindful and personally designed compass for those times when deep reflection and clear thinking are needed. A compass helps us focus and thoughtfully sail through the challenges in understanding complex systems. It takes knowledge to develop a personal vision of what we want to accomplish and to better deal with the social pressures we will encounter. We may find ourselves living in a sea of uncertainty and polarization, not knowing what is a fact or just gossip. Often we may be blind to the sea of emotionality around us. Fear blinds us, paralyzing us, so that we are unable to face our reality. Fear of an unknown or an overwhelming future can be like a virus, infecting us with anxiety and mistrust. Family systems ideas provide a way to strengthen our emotional immune system against this invasion. Knowledge of family emotional process enables us to have a broader view of our life, and the deep emotional sea we swim in. This vantage point enables us to consider a different way to be more effective as aware and thoughtful human beings, rather than reacting and playing a bit part in an old emotionally driven play.

Once we are mindful, it can be fun or just an everyday exercise to figure out and define our boundaries and our principles, while understanding the natural forces around us. The emotional forces will, without awareness, impinge on our ability to be thoughtful or to identify and understand our options and choices. Systems knowledge can help us to make better-informed decisions and shows us various ways to increase our resilience and ability to be appropriately responsible. There are many relationship challenges that can confound us as we began to implement some of our goals in both in our families and at work.

A Mindful Compass can be very handy to clearly see the possible difficulty others have with us or with our goals. It is useful to be mindful and, therefore, less sensitive to the pushes and pulls in our relationship systems. Of course questions remain. How can we see these relationship forces? How can we interact in ways that rally those around us to focus on achieving our clear goals without impinging on others? How does it happen that we can anxiously run over or completely ignore the people we love, respect or need to cooperate with?

Consider that more mature leaders can stand alone, resisting the pressure to judge others and to find simple, quick answers or to take reactive and immediate action. The ability to wait and to consider possibilities, or to unwind emotional reactions, creates more space for participation in long-term problem solving.

Being keenly aware, while being emotionally objective (so you can see the system work its magic), is not an easy skill to learn. We tend to blame people and in so doing, miss the system. However, knowledgeable leaders have often practiced the skill of saying "no" to a demand for a quick fix. They have seen relationship complexity emerge in the family or work environment. They have seen that they can interrupt the automatic tendency to go along with the quick fix focus, and know it works to consider the system, and to face the deeper issues in a more rational way.

Bowen would say your family was a system where you could afford to make mistakes. Trial and error enables leaders to understand how to say "no" and how to participate in the family relationship system in new ways that can enhance relationship knowledge. No one emerges from a social system without making mistakes, but a mature outlook allows leaders to welcome mistakes as teachers.

Mature leaders are able to focus on finding a thoughtful match between the cries to "fix things now" and the ability to see and solve relationship problems. These leaders take the time to deeply understand emotional process in relationships. They see that logic is operating at one level and primitive emotions at another. These primitive emotions are part of our evolutionary heritage and help form our perceptions so that it is difficult to distinguish between facts and emotions.[9] A leader's vision and decision-making processes are linked to an internal compass that guides him or her to the resolution of a problem, the implementation of a goal, or the successful creation of new idea. We all have some sort of internal compass that we use whenever a decision must be made. The question is how does our compass work? Is our compass on *automatic* or *mindful*?

Taking the time to develop a Mindful Compass means we also discover what our Automatic Compass is and how it functions. Depending on the circumstances, we need both types of compasses. Both the automatic and the mindful compasses will enhance our leadership skills. The automatic compass comes with us at birth. Emotional programming occurs as we roam about our family and in our very social relationships throughout life.

Our automatic compass is composed of all we inherit and all we experience that does not require us to be mindful and reflective. It guides us in automatic ways. It is based on instincts for survival. No one has to teach us how to use it. Through experience it becomes fine-tuned. Fear, along with our needs, hopes and dreams, collide with many of our basic animal instincts. Our guidance systems are all intertwined, and may even be fused, leading to our confusion. Part of our leadership compass lets us know that we need to become aware of our deeper instincts and feelings so they can become more integrated with fact based reality. The level of integration we currently have is apparent in the way we relate to others. Bottom line—it is up to each individual to become the informed regulator of his or her automatic compass.

By considering how we interacted in our first social system, our family, we will see how our automatic compass has been calibrated. If we can identify where the automatic compass leads us to be a bit too sensitive or promotes compensatory behaviors that are not useful, we are better off. If these behaviors continue, then we can use this information to rethink the orientation of our compass. This trial and error reflective process allows us to understand ourselves (and our families) in new ways and to change how we automatically think and act going forward.

A very broad distinction can be made between the part of oneself that one is aware of and consciously trying to improve, and the part of one's self which automatically and without reflection responds to the world. I call the first Self with a capital "S," and the second self, with a lower case 's.'

"Bowen's theory of the family as a unit of natural selection involves a measure he calls "differentiation of self." The extent to which each of us responds to new social situations relatively independent of our early family experiences is measurable".[10]   *Laurie Lassiter*

The Four Mindful Compass Points, sometimes referred to as the ARKS of life –

1. **The ability to take ACTION and to define a vision,**

2. **The RESISTANCE to change in Self and in any system,**

3. **The ability to use KNOWLEDGE to connect meaningfully with others, and**

4. **The ability to STAND ALONE and to be more separate.**

The ability to take "action" based on one's mindful vision takes time and energy. One must find one's deeper Self, see Self more neutrally and objectively as a participant in an ongoing relationship system, which is adapting over long periods of time. Reflect on and be sure of one's guiding principles. Then one is, then, far more capable of being able to risk defining a position for Self to others.

Developing your own Mindful Compass is a way to think about and understand the influence of the relationship systems of which you are a part and whether your actions are mature or immature as you move through life. In so doing, you will be less likely to be blindsided by the responses (reactions) you get from others as you pursue your own vision and goals. You may identify, in revisiting the history of your relationships, a few experiences that may be unduly influencing your actions today. At the very least, you will have considered what kinds of past events may be influencing your future.

Marriage is an example of how one choice can impact the quality of one's life, because deciding to marry someone is usually based more on feelings than on a rational analysis of oneself and one's potential partner. Mature choices imply that one can integrate feelings about a possible partner with a rational assessment of that person. It is very easy to act on feelings and ignore the rational part. How do feelings influence us?

Let's say you want to have a relationship with a man who does not have the same qualities as your father. Your father disappointed you by drinking too much and your mother seemed helpless. You had to take care of both your parents. So you might feel that you can avoid someone like your father by picking a non-drinker, the opposite kind of partner for yourself. But our emotional make-up is not quite so simple. Your feelings or deeper emotions may not "beep a warning" to avoid a man, who distances into work. You need your thinking system to see that drinking and distancing are related. Your "gut" may lead you to a man, who does not drink, but is similar.

Your feelings may not guide you to ask the hard questions. How did my father come to use alcohol? (Keep in mind that alcohol is one way for individuals to "manage" the challenges they face in a relationship system. Another way to manage the "same" challenges is to become distant or cut off from relationships that are difficult.) Being clear as to how someone you are dating is able to relate to his or her mother and father and his or her extended family has significant implications for the future.

You might ask yourself some of the following questions with regard to any significant others in your life. Questions can allow people to become more aware of family patterns. Greater awareness can promote more freedom to move away from engaging in anxiety-binding mechanisms like blame and shame. The unaware states promote frustration and make people vulnerable to being reactive and/or falling back into old automatic patterns. It takes

awareness to see such patterns and begin to change behaviors. Your answers to these questions may give you some clues about your vulnerabilities that you may not be aware of. Does distance or the threat of distance, between you and your significant other create a resistance to talking about issues? Do either of you pretend all is fine when at least one of you knows it isn't? How do either of you relate to friends? Can you and your significant other speak with each other openly? How much of the time do either you or your partner feel unable to talk to either of your parents? Sensitivity to the relationships in the past is reflected in the now and keeps us from having real relationships in the moment. We appear to live in fear of the past reasserting itself and become defensive or shut down or argumentative rather than take time to ask, "What is really going on here?"

If you can ask these questions and understand the part you play in being "caught" in an emotional system, then you may be able to rationally decide to speak up to your current partner or to your parents, and to at least describe the situation you are in and how you would like to work on your part of a too distant, or perhaps a shut-down, relationship dynamic. If no questions are asked then no real action takes place. Instead, you can follow your feelings, and marry a more distant person, which would most likely play out like the old story of the parental relationship in your family. This kind of vulnerability—of not being able to take action and speak up for oneself—has often been programmed in due to one's past experiences and current sensitivity. Once you begin to notice the influence of others on your ability to speak up, you will see it everywhere—at home, with friends, and at work.

Think about how past relationships in your life may have left you vulnerable to go along and avoid relationship issues; to function as Bowen put it, as a "pseudo self." If you would rather be mindful, then you can move forward into a clearer and more realistic vision for yourself, understanding that the ability to communicate with another person may be more of a priority for you than simply picking someone who doesn't drink.

Just remember, people communicate all the time, verbally, non-verbally, constructively, non-constructively, but communicating with the intention of focusing on what Self sees or thinks or feels is a truly unique way of communicating with others. *A Self-focus is not about getting your way or changing another. Instead, this kind of communication is about taking ACTION to be one's best, most authentic Self, and giving others that same respect to figure things out for themselves.*

It can be dangerous to have a vision of an unrealistic future forged in an automatic emotional process out of your awareness. The automatic often guides us to make decisions that feel comfortable for the moment but blind us to the past and the possible future.

Bowen spoke of "observational blindness," the inability to see how relationships in the past influence our relationship decisions in the moment. The overall goal of the Mindful Compass is to provide an opportunity for people to "see" the system they are a part of and to take actions based on an understanding of both the rational and the emotional components of a system.

We don't have to take time to clarify or define a vision based on principles for Self very often. But when the world turns upside down and times are confusing, such as after a death in the family, the onset of a major illness, the loss of a job or the start of a new one, then we are likely to be impacted and pressured by events that are beyond our control.

There are many automatic and unconscious psychological and social forces that are out of our awareness which can and do influence us. We can be more aware of them. Any event that stresses us may require us to rethink our vision for the future and how important relationships will be altered. When circumstances change, it is a good investment of time and energy to ask oneself, "Should I keep going in this direction or should I rethink, check the compass and prepare myself for the shift in relationships?" At times like these it pays to be mindful and less automatic.

I developed the four-point *Mindful Compass* to give you a road map to do just that. It is a mental model, a tool to give you various ways to see the complexity of the emotional and rational processes involved in the decision-making we all face in relationship systems.

The purpose of developing your own Mindful Compass is to enable you to better understand how social groups function, how they influence you and how you influence them. This understanding can help you resist your automatic or even reactive programming, while you develop strategies to manage self more effectively during any kind of change.

CHAPTER III
ACTION FOR SELF AND RESISTANCE AS NATURAL PHENOMENA

The Mindful Compass Point One: *The ability to take ACTION and to define a vision.*

People are under the sway of influences, many of which are hard to identify. Just because we say "I" want to do something, it does not indicate that an effort has been made to separate out the automatic self from the more Mindful Self. As you consider meaningful life altering decisions or turning points in your life, do they reflect choices you have made based on your own life vision, goals, and principles or are they "overly influenced" by the pressure put on you by others who are or were important to you?

Most people are psychologically blind to the kinds of pressure they are under, and this "blindness" sometimes leads to embracing goals to please others rather than being true to one's deeper Self. How does one deal with or even recognize the boundary between oneself and others? How does one appreciate the cost and benefit of discovering and being for oneself?

Distinguishing between the kinds of actions you have taken and what influenced them is a first step in identifying your vulnerabilities in social situations. The goal is to clarify to what extent your relationship systems supported, pressured or confused you as you defined and pursued your dreams and ambitions.

Connecting the dots of your decisions to the influence of your own principles or of the pressure of others gives you information about how important relationships in your life influence you. This knowledge builds mindfulness as you go forward in pursuit of your passions and dreams.

Some people think that their goals and the relationship pressures on them have nothing to do with each other. They say, "This is the way I envision the future and 'this' is what I am going to do to make it happen, no matter what others think or say." However, most of us want feedback (and probably the approval and encouragement of important others) for our actions, so we are in a lifetime tug and pull between identifying and pursuing our own goals and principles, and responding to the input and influence of others.

For example, someone might say, "I want to show my Dad that I am smarter than he is." This might be an instinctive reaction to compete with one's father. This person, however, could say to him or herself, "How can I compete or how can I harness these more instinctive forces and take ACTION for Self and not just react automatically? And of course, bottom line, how can I have fun moving more towards being and acting more for Self with my Dad?"

Someone else might say, "I'm in the middle of getting a divorce and that has to have an impact on my ability to make good decisions in the divorce process itself. Other parts of my life will be impacted. I need to be more for Self to steady my life at this time."

Understanding how you respond under stress can give you information about the relationship system you grew up in and your vulnerabilities to your family and other relationship systems of which you're a part. Consider these questions for yourself:

How can I identify, based on my history, what I tend to do automatically and instinctively when I'm under stress? Do I get too distant from others who are important to me? Do I get sick? Do I do too much for others (over function) when they're not "doing well"? Do I fight with others when I'm stressed? Do I run away from people that upset me?

Principles that can help support action for a more mature Self when one is under stress:

1.   Maintain as open relationships as possible

2.   Communicate what I observe

3. Communicate from an "I" position

4. Avoid statements, such as "you should" or "must do" this or that or blaming others.

One of the greatest challenges is to coach people without getting in their way. Bowen would say things like, "You can give high functioning families bad advice and they can make it turn out all right, but if you give low functioning families good advice it will become a mess." When I coach people, I try very hard not to become a parental or authority figure. I try to understand people and what they are up against in trying to move forward.

One of the best ways to do this is to tell stories that serve as the big picture for those trying to grasp a concept or to see. Often, examples of events from my own life or that of others, or off the wall comments will loosen people up and they will begin to figure out what to do to solve complex problems.

In riding alongside families rather than being the "expert" and telling others what they should do, you convey to people what these are ideas, some of which might be useful. No expectations of instant salvation. These are examples that come from observing emotional process and they may or may not be useful to them. I say to folks, "Use them as you like, or throw them in the trash." Unless an idea works with your brain and your family it is a useless thing.

Being a Self and having an "I" Position

People may be shocked when you say things to them that are not automatic and reactive statements but represent some kind of alternative emotional viewpoint. Having a position for Self can interrupt the way others see the world. Having a different viewpoint, based on Self's knowledge and experience, often interrupts the ongoing emotional process of the "way we should all think." By having one's own thoughts and cherishing differences, there may be greater respect between people.

People get into habitual ways of thinking and feeling. They can no longer think or reflect on what they are doing or saying. They are anxious and even defensive. They often want an answer that will change the other(s). When I am coaching people I have to discipline myself to be different and even interrupt others by saying unusual things. For example, if a person is feeling competitive with his or her father, I might say, "If this were my Dad, which he obviously is not, I might say to him, out of the blue, one sunny day, 'I love competing with you and I just hope it brings out the best in both of us.'" And to the person getting a divorce, I might suggest they challenge their more mature Self by saying something like this to the spouse they're divorcing: "Part of getting divorced will show me how dependent I have been on you to make decisions. If you are not around I might have to just imagine what you would do and then make my own decisions." In both of these examples, the individual shifts his or her focus to action by Self (not what the other person should do or did do to you) and acknowledges the possible relationship obstacles he or she faces in taking ACTION for Self.

Once you have some broad and specific ideas about the extent to which your vision, goals and principles come from Self and/or from the influences of others, you will have gained some important information about the emotional system you live in. The cost and benefits for you to take a different ACTION stance in your social jungle will become clearer to you over time. This thinking-for-yourself process can contribute to your clarity about what you believe, how you interact with others, and increase your potential for success as you define it.

Listed below are some topics and questions that can contribute to your personal wisdom as you use the "North" point on your Mindful Compass to take action in any social system.

Origin and Principles. Where did my idea for action come from? Is it based on principle? One example of the way Bowen would check for the depth and importance of peoples' principles was to ask the question, "Am I willing to die for this belief?" In other words, how deep are your guiding principles? If you have, for example, a principle that says, "I will not hide important things about myself from others," where do you draw the line? In the post-graduate program we were asked to write belief papers and to guess as to the origins of our deeply help convictions. People can go through their entire lives without putting in the time to think carefully about their beliefs and where they come from.

Social Pressure. When others pressure me, do I respond by doing what they want to please them or get their recognition? We are driven into these emotional traps by our instinctive need for social status. The idea of fusion is that people are automatically drawn into relationships where their functioning is part of others' functioning. They tend to do too much for others, sacrificing self without any awareness of the social pressure on them to give up self for others.

Fusion is the degree to which one's self fuses or merges into another self in a close emotional relationship.

The fusion process is silent and quick. Variations of fusion occur in any social group as individuals become aware of others' perceptions differing from their own. (Later we will see how research on social situations demonstrates what a powerful force social approval is.) Those who are able to stand outside of "groupthink" may feel increasing stress, but they may also be able to think differently and add diverse views to any group.

If, in a social system, one can maintain one's "difference" without fear, this individual stance may enable the group to learn to welcome different points of view, increasing the group's problem-solving capacity and effectiveness in working together.

If one has the social intelligence to see better answers to problems than those the group has discovered, then that person has to be able to:

1. Decrease his or her fear response when criticized;

2. Stay oriented to his or her own perceptions; and

3. Communicate, as best as he or she can, his or her different way of seeing or going. We can be pressured and can pressure others, but it pays to know the difference.

History. Time is your friend when it comes to reflecting on the past. It is useful to ask these questions: How long have I considered this action? Have I tried this before? Has anyone in my family tried this or the opposite of it? What are the advantages and disadvantages of this action?

Feedback. The important point here is to predict and prepare for the various responses and outcomes to your proposed actions that come from Self and are likely to affect others. How do other people within the system respond to your ideas? Have you floated a trial balloon? Have people told you what is wrong with what you plan to do? Are people afraid to give you feedback about your ideas? Do you ask many other people what they think about your ideas or just a select few? A select few are more inclined to say what you want to hear.

Asking many people is likely to result in more diverse opinions. Keep track and measure your own reactions to other people's responses and input. You can never know if your decision to take an action is "right." One hint is that if you have re-directed the anxiety in the system towards yourself rather than towards others, you're probably on the right track. Now you can admit to others you are a fumbler. You have good intentions but sometimes you just don't get it "right." Any Action for Self should take into account how to communicate and/or give feedback to others. Here are some principles to consider.

Nine Principles to Guide Action in Communicating

1. Take a deep breath and remember – I am a part of any problem that I can see, and will try to clarify my part in the problem.

2. Observe – how one person is influencing another and be careful about blaming others and/or telling another adult what to do.

3. Be loose in tense or serious relationships – It is OK for me to offer ideas, especially silly ones, but not OK to THINK I know what is best for others.

4. Take a neutral stance – Ask questions and maintain my curiosity about a situation.

5. Make "I" statements – This is the action I will take once I understand the principle for the action and the possible responses.

6. Communicate – Be clear in as simple a way as possible. I will try not to

bug people or repeat a message more than twice a week. If I do I will put a dollar in a jar to treat the person to ice cream sometime in the future. I will be patient and wait to try again and restate a message that received a negative or reactive response. I will use humor whenever possible and consider that there are things I did not understand.

7. Stay connected – If people react negatively to my effort to communicate, just give the person some form of positive feedback for at least trying to listen to my different viewpoint.

8. Work via person-to-person relationships – Clarify if the information exchanged is to be private and only between us.

9. Gossip and hearsay – People often bring in information or ideas about what others have said or done. Be sure to clarify what is useful and what is highly emotional.

If I am told gossip, as in, "So and so said such and such," I will say to the person with the "news" that I'm okay with hearing the gossip but would like to know if the gossip is backed up by facts. I might even explain that I believe that the listener has a responsibility to know if there are facts or if this "news" is just feeding the "blame game."

If the "news" seems to be delivered to hurt, I would use a paradox to say: "I guess it's your job to spread this "junk" as thick as you can so others will know gossip when they hear it." This can be experienced as a harsh interruption of the person's communication. But one is looking at the impact gossip has on a relationship system. Hearsay or gossip is one of the hardest things to refute and can destroy relationships. Therefore, gossip may require strong medicine to interrupt.

I will be careful to disentangle and to distinguish the way I communicate with others and seek to make more direct statements and/or use interrupting or paradoxical statements when people are blaming or gossiping.

I will be open to continuing the conversations by managing my reactivity and being clear about what I see as my responsibility and what I can and cannot do to respond to an issue.

41

By defining yourself to others carefully, you will become more knowledgeable about the automatic ways that people communicate.

By maintaining a focus on learning how to make your part in conversations more thoughtful, you will become a better-defined person, who can demonstrate deep commitment to understanding others.

There is no escape from the need to communicate to implement any plans and/or goals, but there are a few ways to prepare for the challenges, as we will see in this next compass point. The effort you exert to be more aware and thoughtful in communicating with others gives you solid grounding as you seek to become more of a Self with those you work with or care about.

The Mindful Compass Point Two: *The RESISTANCE to changes in Self and in any system*

Resistance is the kickback you inevitably encounter as you take steps that challenge the status quo in the social system you inhabit. You might think that resistance is a purely human thing but resistance to change can be found in most social organisms.

The earlier understanding of the drivers of change in social organisms has shifted from the focus on random mutation in genes (which are totally out of an organism's control) to epigenetics. This is the study of changes in gene expression caused by mechanisms other than changes in the underlying DNA. Changing external environments are facts.

Things will always be changing. However, can you see the changes and the adaption that is required or that is just happening to you? An awareness of the environment by the organism can influence whether genes turn on or off. Today, we have more and more scientific research pointing towards an understanding of just how gene expression functions. It is no longer just a random event that creates change in the genome. Environmental factors, broadly speaking, influence how organisms change. Little changes can add up to big changes in the way we adapt to changing circumstances and this can eventually impact our genes.

Therefore, a farsighted, courageous leader takes the time to understand the automatic nature of the system and prepares for the resistance as though it were an evolutionary gift. Resistance can both sting and wake you up. It is not always easy to see in the moment, but it can have long-term benefits for the system as a whole. That is, an individual may alter his or her system only one tiny bit by an effort to change Self, but that effort may enable the next generation to build on those adaptations.

Change and Resistance

Many people resist change because it is difficult and costs us life energy. Change is movement towards the unknown and it carries risk. When the effort to change doesn't come from within and another individual is demanding that we change, we can actively or passively resist those changes, even if we see that there's something in it for us to make the change. There are certain systems, like the armed services, that demand obedience, and people know before signing up that this is an expectation. The consequences for resisting what's required are clear. However, in families and other social systems, the "rules" about resistance are usually more subtle.

A change in one individual creates reactions and resistance in others and can result in an increase in fusion and confusion. Therefore, it is important to consider which thoughts and behaviors of ours are more automatic or thoughtful. Through this process, we can begin to see how we are functioning in relationship to others as our more mindful Self emerges.

The effort to change one's automatic self is very hard to do. It requires us to observe self and others with little judgment and this takes considerable preparation functioning in relationship to others as our more mindful Self emerges.

First and last, don't take the resistance personally. Even though it's natural that social systems change, that is not a reason that people can, should or will change without "resistance." You may have seen that you yourself resist change. This pull back from the new is part of the way systems operate. It is our job not to feel upset, unloved or attacked when those we love resist some great idea we have or something we would like to do. Breathe deeply and let go of the personal upset.

See the system, as it is, impersonally resisting change.

Even when you have made a substantial effort to alter your part in the system, the system can resist your efforts for a long time. Many people don't see the connection of the impact of change on the psychology and physiology of individuals in the social jungle. Some believe that "your problems" are not their problems and that wherever you do has no impact on them.

These can be rich, powerful, poor, or just stubborn people. They may live in the equivalent of a heavily fortified prison or in a steel bubble. They defend and protect themselves from a relationships view of life. Perhaps they're fearful that opposition will come and their worldview may crumble, and this makes them all the more hardened against new ideas.

Other people may be pinned down by symptoms that emerge in them as they struggle to maintain the status quo. For many people, belief systems about how relationships function stand unexamined, and change is warded off for years or even a lifetime.

What do you do if you can see that many people are unaware of the social forces surrounding them and are resistant to new ideas or your particular goals? Can you recognize these individuals and respect them?

Defining a Self and resistance in the middle of family changes

Perhaps you have watched or been one of those people, like me, that had a temper tantrum and tried to beat some sense into the resistant, blind ones. As you react to their reaction, everything becomes muddled. What a silly and frustrating position it is to find your reactive self saying, "Please change. I know it will be good for you, and I will feel so much better if you do. Then I can get on with my real life?" The automatic and dependent self tends to see everything that's wrong with "them" and to expend tremendous effort to try to fix or convince "them" with pleas and threats.

At times any of us can become so focused on our own goals that our actions will have a negative impact on the people we're attached to. People can get up a head of steam and run over others in order to make a plan or even a wish come true. But once you become a "systems thinker" you begin to notice and then get over the belief that you should or must fix and change others. A system thinker has a fallback position. Focus on changing yourself and figuring out how to effectively manage yourself when resistance emerges in others, who are important to you.

Change is required to adapt to nodal events like a marriage, a death, a new baby, or even a job change. Such changes can also force us to take new actions to cope with changing circumstances and can also create waves of reactivity in an emotional system.

When changes occur, people begin to put different levels of pressure on one another to deal with those changes. Some change is easy to accept and people are ready. Others stir up reactivity and resistance. Perhaps the last child is graduating from college and the oldest is getting married to someone that many in the family do not like.

Then, to add to the increasing pressure, the family leader decides he will start a new business. Tension rises as resources and energy are put into new directions and the marriage to an "other" becomes the focus of the family's emotional backlash. If the anxiety is high enough, one person in the family (the vulnerable one, perhaps the wife) may begin to cope by drinking or by getting physically ill or even by withdrawing from the group.

The group can blame the person who drinks or becomes ill or withdraws, and not see that all these "actions" are all part of the increasing anxiety or resistance to change in the family. The resistance to change and the blame that often comes with it can combine to make it difficult for people to communicate and solve problems.

What can one person do? Perhaps the family leader can see that all these events are putting pressure on people. Maybe the father, in this case, can see that his wife is drinking in response to the various changes that are occurring and that she is not sure of her own direction. Few see a symptom in an individual as a signal that the person has absorbed too much system anxiety and cannot cope with the changes underway in the system. The people with the symptoms really do not need more pounding or fixing.

Someone, who understands the complex nature of resistance, sees the symptom in the other far differently that the symptomatic person sees it. No matter the symptom or the form that resistance takes, the job of the leader is to ask him or herself, "What can I do to be clear about what is going on? What is my part in the problem?"

This ability to view the family symptoms more broadly keeps the family leader from becoming "other-focused" or blaming others for the problems in the system. Focusing on the "symptomatic one" in a negative way only makes matters worse. Old behaviors may become more extreme under pressure. The family leader can react and try to help out the spouse. But upon reflection and seeing the over functioning reaction in himself, the leader might say, "I have been too distant and then I rush in to help out and I end up making things worse."

If the husband can tone down his over functioning and speak to the way he and his spouse function, then his spouse may be able to see the situation more clearly. The over functioning person has to be willing to let the symptomatic person figure out how to manage self. The family leader has to figure out both—how to manage Self and how to really communicate with the other.

A family leader, who can see the relationship issues more broadly, is more likely to talk about the changes in the system as a whole and to ask thoughtful questions about how people are adapting. Leaders are aware of the tendency to distance and they can see this impulse to distance and override it and come back into one-on-one contact with individuals in the system.

Or take another example. Perhaps you say to your spouse, "I have thought it over and talked to you and many others. I've weighed the costs and benefits and have decided that I am going to take that new job." You know this will prompt some degree of upset or perhaps even anger and recrimination from your spouse. However, if you can stay calm and cool and not back down or give in, then your angry spouse may settle down.

Those who are caught up reacting to changes in the social system are unaware of the possibility of calibrating their Mindful Compass—they are on automatic pilot. The one who is ready to change, the thoughtful leader, is going to focus on Self and stay connected to important others to allow the system to change. The leader's systems knowledge helps immunize him or her to some extent to the reactivity in self and others.

None of this is easy. Everyone is resistant to changing our automatic self. But with an effort based on seeing and thinking systems, people will be more aware and find better ways to cope with the inevitable resistance and to become far more useful to others in being more separate and better defined.

One thing to keep in mind is that one person's forward progress can create a reaction in others and those reacting individuals can develop symptoms of their own due to their over involvement with or their perceived need for the other to "be the way he or she was." One can ask, are these people who have difficulty coping with changes in those they are close to or those they need, simply caught up in system's response to change? Can it be that the resistance to change is a personal resistance based on a fear of change?

It is an observable fact that there is an automatic resistance to forward movement to preserve some kind of automatic self. But once the situation is brought into awareness, people can find a better way to think about being caught up in an automatic resistance to change. There is nothing personal in the way a system moves anxiety around from person to person to deal with the perceived threat of change.

Thinking and seeing systems allows us to consider that symptoms in individuals are not fixed. They serve a function, absorbing anxiety, which can be observed in the behavior of the whole relationship system and all that is going on in it. This is a significant change from the automatic way that most people view symptoms as being in one individual and not a reflection of the state of the system as a whole and that system's ability to manage anxiety.

Change creates an opening for one's more mature Self to be able to observe and to interrupt reactive and automatic ways of managing anxiety. Each individual in a system that is undergoing challenge has the opportunity to become less automatic and reactive and thereby be more of a Self.

Encouraging Maturity. Growth often requires change and nowhere is this more evident than in raising children. Either the parent or the child can resist a change required by the aging of the child and eventually the aging of the parent. Whether the child goes to school, or if the conflict or intensity is about the time for the child to do homework, or time for them to learn how to drive, cook or even brush their teeth, a parent may be reactive and want to protect the child. The child can also be reactive and may wish to continue to be babied. These are both examples of reactive behaviors that are driven more by anxiety than by the reality of the situation. Either parent of the child can be resistance to the fact that growth in a child demands a change in the parent's (and in the child's) behavior.

When a childish demand is unmet, a teenager may collapse into the mother's arms and refuse to go to school. What positions do the mother and/or father have that reflects personal responsibility? The refusal of a teenager to adapt to the reality of his or her age and stage and take responsibility for Self, leads to the effort of parents to set up a way of dealing with the child that does not give into demands and offers consequences. How people go about setting up boundaries and conditions for growth is varied as the scale of differentiation notes. Taking action always depends on one's ability to see the system and to relate well to people without giving in to demands.

Bowen used the term "regression" to describe the time when people return to an early (and less mature) way of relating. These are the times when parents do not take a position that would enable the child to grow. Instead, they gave in to the demands of the child until the child is weakened in his or her ability to take responsibility for Self.

It is often difficult to know if a child's cries for help are real or not. Sometimes parents are faced with serious and chronic illness in a child or another family member. These kinds of serious symptoms can force families to change without being sure of how much to do for the ill individual and how much to wait and see what that person can do for self. The ill person adapts to his or her dependency or helplessness and the family has to adapt to doing more for that person. The death of someone in the system also requires adapting to events and facing changes that one is not always prepared to face.

Adapting to reality, whatever it is, requires each of us to let go of past ways of being to discover a more adaptive future. At the same time, each of us must keep in mind what we would like to do and how we would like to be at our best under stress. Changes are part of life itself and changes are coming our way. Eventually we will have to find some way to adapt.

Unpredictable Shocks. Not everything is predictable. All living systems are subject to unpredictable shocks. It can be someone getting pregnant, an unexpected death or divorce or a war or a national financial meltdown. Recovery from a shock, as quickly as possible, often requires acceptance of the change and then hope for the time to figure out the best position for Self to take. For most people, a shock will initially bring out the automatic reactive self rather than the thoughtful Self. But most people recover from shock and return to their prior level of happiness given time.[11]

Taking a Principled Stand to Manage the Resistance

There are a few times in most people's lives when an individual is willing to stand up and take an action that goes against the wishes, dreams, desires or rules of important others, against those one loves and cares about. For example, if I take a stand with my child and he or she gets mad at me, then I take a hit, psychologically and emotionally. I may want to knuckle under and do whatever my child wants, but in the long run going along with my child and doing things, which are against my grain or principles, sow the seeds of distrust and further alienation and greater immaturity in both my child and me. Awareness of this possibility can allow people to see that it's worth it to say "No" on principle.

On the surface, it is hard to see how standing up for one's beliefs and principles is forward progress because of the uproar it can create when people get mad and oppose you. But try to remember that sometimes it takes a fight, the airing of differences, to clear the air. People may be reacting and going along with something without thinking, such as giving into the demands of a child. If you refuse to go along and take the chance to air differences, that action alone can allow people to listen more carefully, to be better defined, and perhaps even understand and respect one another. Sometimes the best you can do is to just allow the differences between people to exist and hover in the air. Change that is significant can take years, or perhaps even a generation or two.

Although paradoxical, forward progress that comes with a fight or with resistance can still be seen as progress. While one step forward can cost us, and we might have to take at least a half of a step backwards, this is still better than entering into a regression with our near and dear.

There's no use getting angry with people who resist forward momentum. Bowen would say things like, "Why not just go over to a field of corn and yell at it to grow, then if it doesn't do so, pull it up by the ears!" The bottom line is that there are ways to work with resistance without taking it too seriously. Even if a stalemate exists for years, having principles and respecting others' different points-of-view can make for greater maturity.

In fact, resistance to change is to be sought. Struggling to see what is going in relationships, especially after an upset, and then be able to clarify any misunderstandings and/or differences, can force you to become more reflective and less of an automatic responder.

It does take time to develop the ability to think one's way out of impasses and to develop new strategies to cope with changes. But the over-arching goal during times of relationship challenges is to find ways to define Self while being able to co-exist and cooperate with others based on principles. In doing so, people find they acquire a more realistic view of life as it is and a calmer more thoughtful relationship system in which individuals are better able to bounce back from adversity with less reactivity.

Ultimately, resistance forces us to consider the whole system, the history of reactivity, the space where change might be able to take place, the ability to communicate strategically and finally to acknowledge the costs and benefits of change.

CHAPTER IV
SYSTEMS KNOWLEDGE AND STANDING ALONE

The Mindful Compass Point Three: *The ability to use KNOWLEDGE to connect meaningfully with others*

Knowledge continues to grow at an exponential rate. How does this impact us? We can know a great deal about psychology or any other subject because the Internet and Google have made information available to all those with access to a computer. But just how much do we need to know to manage ourselves successfully in the social jungle, in the complex social systems we find ourselves imbedded in? It is useful to reflect on one's own life course, learn from that experience and become more informed about systems in general and how natural systems function.

While few will take courses in Bowen Family Systems or in "thinking systems," a course in any of the life sciences can provide people with a more objective overview of life and even of human behavior. This kind of factual knowledge can counterbalance our very personal and mostly subjective knowledge about ourselves and others.

Due to the structure of our brain we overvalue subjective knowledge from those closest to us, and tend to ignore or fail to integrate objective and factual knowledge. Without objective and factual knowledge, however, it becomes more difficult to summon up the courage to take difficult stands and to take action, especially when we know we will get flack for doing so.

Knowledge of how other living systems function can help us understand the broader life forces that all living creatures are subject to. What can we learn from other species about aggression, monogamy, homosexuality or territoriality? What can we learn from ants, the stars, the tides, from bacteria, and even from snails?

The challenge of continually integrating new knowledge with old beliefs and habits is hard work. It requires us to break with the "old." This is especially difficult since the reptilian part of our brain likes the old ways and is resistant to the new. Even if we could attach a computer to our brain to sort out and highlight the importance of facts versus the devils of gossip, our own brains might oppose the accumulation of more fact-based knowledge. The part of us that loves the emotional and subjective cringes at facts. But without deeply examining our knowledge base, and how what we are doing might impact the future, we will remain vulnerable to the deeper passions and fears that automatically override our thinking brain.

Much of this book focuses on behavior in our most important relationships that is both difficult to see and to understand how it impacts our ability to make decisions. We believe a lot of things we don't know we believe. We may be unaware of our own racial, gender or age-related stereotypes. If people call you "old," research has demonstrated that you may not perform as well as if people say you are "strong." We are affected and influenced by subtle things that we are usually unaware of.

By five years of age, says Margo Monteith, Ph.D., many children have definite and entrenched stereotypes about blacks, women, and other social groups. "Children don't have a choice about accepting or rejecting these conceptions, since they're acquired well before they have the cognitive abilities or experiences to form their own beliefs." And no matter how progressive the parents, they must compete with all the forces that would promote and perpetuate these stereotypes: peer pressure, mass media, and the actual balance of power in society. In fact, prejudice may be as much a result as a cause of this imbalance. We create stereotypes—African-Americans are lazy, women are emotional—to explain why things are the way they are.[12]

Becoming more objective about who we are and how our brains operate requires us to keep gathering knowledge that challenges our old but dearly held beliefs. Just being curious allows us to build bridges between various branches of knowledge that we would never gather by sticking to a narrow road. Our mental models are enhanced and enriched by new information that often competes with long held but outdated views. It appears that we have to pay the cost of breaking down old ways of thinking to make openings for the new.

Personal Knowledge and Family History

If you are curious and motivated to learn, it will be automatic for you to gather knowledge of your family history, your root system. It is here that you will find personal clues as to how your ancestors traveled through the social jungle. Our far-distant ancestors tend to leave us more fact-based clues—a graveyard with a tombstone, a will in the historical library, a story written by your great grandmother, a short list in the family bible with the number of children born and when they died. Could it be that our ancestors will have left more factual clues than we will?

Today, many people are cremated and there are fewer gravestones to visit. Our lives are documented on various social media and biographical clues are in the public domain. Hopefully, our tracks will be worth following but it will still be left to curious family members or historians to search that data.

Gordon Bell, in his book *Total Recall*, suggests that we owe future generations a more complete access to our personal lives. This is a bold statement in the age of privacy. What do you think? Do people benefit from stories about their ancestors? Many generations in the future will have access to versions of our personal discoveries and times of growth and our attempts to adapt. Perhaps they will even know what values and principles guided us.

Any complete family history will show the stumbling blocks faced by your forebears and the role of luck and randomness in their lives. Our family stories will sometimes be clear and sometimes confused and disoriented. In any life there are successes and failures, saints and sinners. Each individual story is surrounded by others' stories, life dances, and taunts. And all these interactions impact how we, and even our immune systems, function.

Perhaps one of your ancestors was a lot like you. Will you go back three or ten generations to find him or her? When you do look at your family history, will it enable you to be more objective about how people in your family function? For example, I have a far-distant relative who was the eleventh person to sign onto the Mayflower as the captain's indentured servant. A slave, but an adventurous guy, during a storm at sea he didn't wait for the "all clear." Paying little heed to rules or conditions, he ventured forth onto the deck of the ship for some fresh air. The ship was tossing and John was promptly blown overboard. But denying fate, he managed to hold onto a rope and despite the storm was able to kick the side of the ship long and hard enough to rouse his companions below. They pulled him in. He went on to have the most children of any of those on the Mayflower. I shared this story with probably fifteen thousand families who are also descendants from John and Tilly Howland's ten children. To some, this story of the ancestors gives hope that despite our difficulties, our friends might pull us on back on board.

The evidence of generations of adaptability might allow us to take a deep breath before reacting to being "thrown overboard" by an upset or criticism or even a black swan event. It can be useful to discover the amazing tales of survival found in each of our histories.

Once we can see the past as part of our lives, the old sensitivities about "doing it wrong" can be put into perspective and hopefully we can reflect on these similar patterns and not react as much. For example, you might have had a parent, who was mean, or a very critical grandmother, or a too-distant father, or a sibling who abused drugs. What if you find these patterns repeating in new relationships you have? How can you tone down the feeling response or least live with it? Do you have enough knowledge to understand more about your past and to "separate" from it or will you continue to play the same old roles in the family drama?

Knowledge gives you the opportunity to put people and events into perspective even at a cellular level. Deep knowledge is what it takes to say "no" to continued participation in interactions that no longer make sense. One of the clearest examples of changing one's role in a family drama is how spouses of alcoholics are able, with knowledge of family history, to stop enabling, rescuing and blaming. They begin to figure out how to have an open dialogue that does not place undo demands on others. Instead, they learn to create space for Self (and perhaps for other individuals) to define what they will and will not do. Knowledge of the past provides examples of what did and didn't work when people were under relationship pressure. With that knowledge people are better able to develop strategies to be mindful and less automatic in responding to generational problems. Through such knowledge and strategic thinking, individuals gain flexibility and begin to change automatic behavioral patterns.

Questions to ask to gain knowledge in any social system:

- How much do I know about the history of my work or family group?

- How much do I know about my family roots?

- Is there factual knowledge to counterbalance the gossip?

- What more do I need to know?

- Am I operating with a "what is the cause" mentality? If so how can I learn more about nonlinear, dynamic systems, where little changes can make big differences?

- How can I see trends and possible tipping points within the system?

- How can I decrease my family-based sensitivities, especially in the social system I am trying to lead?

- Which relationships enable me to maintain my objectivity and which ones are emotional challenges for me?

Over time, the history of any system exerts a powerful force promoting sensitivity to various types of memories. These emotional memories make it easier or harder for individuals to sustain current relationships. Like Pavlov's dogs, with the proper cues we can be thrust into a stimulus-response world where every decision bears the shadow of our past. The antidote to this state of affairs is to see and understand one's personal history along with the history of relationships in the families of others who are important to us.

This same formula applies to the workplace. Just like families, organizations have potential sensitivities and obstacles for individuals. Knowledge of your own past as well as the past history of the system in which you are working helps ensure that you will not so easily be thrown overboard, but if you are, let us hope that courageous family and friends will pull you back on board.

The Mindful Compass Point Four: *The ability to STAND ALONE and to be more separate*

This point represents your ability to be emotionally separate while maintaining your connections with others. This is a difficult feat by any measure, but the ability to stand alone is necessary for anyone who has to think independently and find new solutions to old problems.

How can you enhance your ability to stand alone, to think and ponder and create workable new ways or to make necessary changes in your relationship patterns and in the systems you inhabit? What are your answers to the questions below about what you've seen in your family?

*   Do people take sides or are they willing to listen to different viewpoints?

*   Do people find courage by listening to family stories?

*   Do people learn to take criticism and to keep on his or her path?

In disturbed families or organizations, there is little room for differences and the pressure to agree is tremendous. In more mature families, there is a great deal of respect for different viewpoints. Consider the paradox that being separate and connected allows for more openness between people. Working to separate Self from others is a brand new idea developed by Bowen. It paradoxically allows people to say more about what's on their own minds, creating a small disturbance but eventually allowing for greater closeness as each person's differences are heard, acknowledged and respected. Put another way, instead of relationships creating scrambled eggs, you have two nicely poached eggs with the yolk intact. Your feelings say, "I want to be close to others" or "I want to be a scrambled egg," and your thinking says "In order to be close to you I have to respect and understand who you are," or "I want to keep my yolk intact but be by your side".

People who are at the lower end of the scale of emotional maturity enter into a feeling world where they believe that if an individual or group is not like them (a scrambled egg) and doesn't agree with them, then that individual or group (egg) should be avoided or worse yet, eliminated. In the worst situations, a regression takes place in which one person becomes a baby and is totally dependent on the mother (or the world) to provide all of his or her needs at the right time and in the right way. People can regress into such childhood states and become too dependent on the system rather than work towards the emergence of their own deeper Self. When this happens in a family system, the beauty of Bowen's theory is that only one person has to alter Self in order for the system to change. It is hard to comprehend how these regressions occur but Bowen Theory gives us a way to think about it and a way to take action.

Areas to be aware of as you point your compass towards the "East" to stand-alone:

1. Physiological Awareness. Develop a basic awareness of your body's responses to various "challenges." Pay attention to your heart rate, changes in your breathing rate and your sweat and vascular response (cold hands).

2. Feeling Awareness. Note how others affect your feelings when you are around them. For example, you might go to a dinner in a good mood and sit next to someone who is angry. You may find yourself getting angry about the anger of the person next to you. In general, if in an encounter you become defensive or argumentative or want to run out of the room, that is evidence that you're in the middle of a "feeling storm" or an "emotional contagion." It's time for a thinking break.

3. Thinking Awareness. Practice controlling your mind set. Watch, as a director might, the many movies your mind produces. Some thinking is jagged and leads you nowhere except into compulsive rethinking of this or that event. The movie is a re-run with little appeal. Repetitive thoughts are a way to bind anxiety and are not very useful. They can become obsessive and are like the chain on an upside-down bicycle, whose wheels spin round and round and go nowhere. New thoughts often occur when you are relaxed, after waking up, in a dream, in the shower, or driving your car. You mind is in the now and is also free to be creative.

4. Mind/Body Integration. Various kinds of mind/body training can help you increase your listening skills. Save yourself. Be very careful about trying to save others. Smile and laugh as often as possible. Even if you are pretending, it will change your biochemistry. The mind can be habitual, so if you interrupt a mind state by just taking your pulse or trying to warm your hands or watch your breath, any of these activities will restore the focus to your body. This helps you break the perseverating habits that may be indicators of stress reactions. A focus on your body can help you feel more in control and enable your mind to settle down.

5. The Discipline of Being More Separate. The mantra here is, "Never totally agree; create some breathing space as you connect." Being careful of automatic agreement is an annoying discipline. But if you are in the habit of being nice, agreeable and helpful, to others and saying yes to all who ask, then separating a Self might be the perfect exercise.

In this example, someone you like—a friend or a boss or spouse—might have to really work on you to agree to something. For example, after telling you some juicy piece of gossip, saying "So and so is... (fill in the blank)," and then looking at you for agreement, what does it take for you to get out of the triangle (to not show agreement with the gossiper), to stand alone and yet stay connected to that gossiper?

Here are a few ideas that have worked for me, but I admit they do annoy people. "Yes, I know you want me to tell you so and so is as you see them, however I have never seen them as a problem. If I did, I might say, 'I might be a bumbler but thought you might appreciate knowing what's been said about you this week.'" Here you are saying "no" to ganging up on someone. Also, you are giving the gossiper an idea about how to handle a more direct communication as to what they have observed about another person's behavior. For those of you who are willing to try to separate a Self and to make the effort to stand-alone and not be righteous, what is the outcome?

The outcome of trying to stand alone is that you are more of a self and this makes room for others to be their best self. If we give into pressure and are guided by needing, gossip, blaming, etc., we become part of the undifferentiated ego mass. Or, we lose our yolk and become scrambled eggs. We are decreasing anxiety and its spread in a system. We are stepping up to decrease the con-fusion that exists between anxious people.

The Mindful Compass allows us greater emotional freedom. By considering the four points – ARKS - you will be more aware of how to unplug from the programming of the stimulus-response world.

The ability to be mindful of automatic programming allows us to engage thoughtfully with our friends and family, or even complete strangers. The evidence is convincing that our lives are better for the discoveries of what it takes to be more of a Self in the social jungle. Other species give us insight into just how relationships impact us.

I learned a great deal from the research of Stephen Suomi, PhD. His research explains how socialization impacts psychological development. While at NIH he observed, among many impacts, how calmer relationships decreased the impact of social isolation in Rhesus monkeys. Dr. Suomi's work with non-human primates hints to the application of these ideas across species. Stephen J. Suomi is chief of the Laboratory of Comparative Ethology at the National Institute of Child Health and Human Development (NICHD) in Bethesda, Maryland.

(l to r) Michael Kerr, Stephen Suomi and Murray Bowen.

CHAPTER V
THE USEFULNESS OF DEVELOPING YOUR MINDFUL COMPASS

Awareness of Emotional Programming

We inherit many instinctual behavior responses. Mate selection and care for the young encourage us to cooperate and at times forgo our interests. However, we can also be provoked by an ancient fear response to attack our own when threatened. Often the social system asks the individual to function more for the group than for self. There are many social pressures. To thoughtfully respond requires a disciplined effort. The Mindful Compass describes a way to be aware of your "automatic self" in relationship to others, and then to have the ability to choose how to relate to and communicate with others.

To define a more mindful Self in a relationship system requires strength of conviction, an understanding of the way systems are organized, a sense of humor, and an ability to become more objective and strategic. It also requires that one endure emotional challenges and deeply understand the reasoning for taking on issues in one's family or work place.

If you are interested in doing a research project on your ability to change self, then you can choose to begin by creating a baseline. It is necessary to know where you begin and where you would like to go. How well connected you are to people in your family? How many people in your three-generation family do you have a personal relationship with and how many of these relationships are superficial? Over time, you will see that you are able to relate more directly to a greater number of people, as you understand your Self and the system.

People may not like being more separate but they do like having a more open and direct relationship with others. The most amazing thing about this effort is that families, in which one person is willing to undertake becoming more separate, have fewer symptoms and/or manage their symptoms better. When one person is willing to take on more challenges by defining Self and being more separate, the family organism has a more effective way of channeling anxiety. The space between people and the strength of the thoughtful connections allows for resiliency to develop in each.

Without this discipline the automatic takes over, people become overly involved in the functioning of one another or they flee and cut off. Bowen noted this sensitivity in how people automatically become overly involved with and sensitive to others, and called this "fusion." Fusion describes overlapping relationships. I have referred to the automatic taking over as producing scrambled eggs, or "con-fusion."

In order to counter this tendency to "fuse" with others, increasing the number of relationships you're engaged in takes pressure off each individual relationship. Consider that one's dependency needs and automatic reactions are more intense in the small nuclear family. Once you get to know others outside the family you have a more diverse tribal life. If you have twelve important relationships and six of them go bad, you still have six people to relate to until the other more challenging relationships calm down and you can reengage.

Having twelve important relationships also gives you more people with which to practice being your best Self. In this way you can strengthen your "emotional backbone" and practice being more of a well-defined Self. This entails not just having your own thoughts and ideas but also becoming more aware and less reactive when you have differences with others. For example, when you visit your aunt and uncle, are you usually less sensitive to "far out" ideas or prejudices than when you listen to the "far out" ideas of your Mom and Dad? Can you discuss things with your aunt and uncle without as much risk? Can you challenge them? Can you say to them something like, "Did you really say, x, y or z? I think about it differently."

Then tell your Mom that it was a real workout maintaining your ideas with Aunt but you learned a lot. Your mom might question you about details and you can tell her details are not that important but she can find out what happened from her sister if she wants.

Little exercises or challenges like this can be useful to open up the system and get people interested in getting to know his or her family members. And sure, there can be resistance or kickbacks as you alter the tenor of your relationship with others. But you're getting a good work out in your emotional gym, strengthening your backbone and increasing your resilience and flexibility at the same time.

The overall goal is to find a way to understand the emotional process between people and to be a more separate and defined Self with greater ability to be authentic in one-on-one relationships. In this way one sees the nature of the relationship system, and does not find one's life caught in a spiraling whirlpool, with life energy becoming more directed by the emotional nature of relationships. Being a more defined Self comes with time and knowledge as to how emotional systems function.

Overall, we are all faced with many of the same challenges. We need people; we need to be able to depend on them. Yet, at the same time, it is hard to put all of our eggs in one person's basket and take too many risks with the one who holds that basket. Therefore we become constrained and sometimes controlled by others who may not even intend to create this kind of an environment.

Your Mindful Compass can be useful in figuring out both how to see your personal life in context and to see how your day-to-day challenges are related to the evolutionary nature of the social jungle we inhabit. It is easy to become preoccupied with and over focused on the banter and anxiety in personal relationships. Therefore, a broad overview of human behavior helps us not take things too personally, be less reactive, and allow the time necessary to consider carefully our individual responses to life's impersonal challenges.

Altering One's "Role" in an Emotional System

Emotionally programmed to respond to others as we are, requires us to make a disciplined effort to become aware of that programming. The Mindful

Compass describes a way to be aware of your "Self" in relationship to others. People begin to know more about the difference between the little or "automatic self" and the "Self" that comes from self-definition. This holds true for all of us. There are always areas that can use shoring up, areas where we have just let things slide or we are just not as sure as we might be about where we stand. People discover more about who they are as they work on clarifying areas that need better definition. Questions occur such as: What will I do about my relationships with my extended family? My children? My friends? How am I doing at work in defining where I stand? How am I doing in my community? There are many areas that only become clear to us when we have to define ourselves to others.

To define a Self in a relationship system requires strength of conviction, an understanding of the way systems are organized, a sense of humor, and an ability to become more objective and strategic. It also requires that one endure emotional challenges and to deeply understand the reasoning for taking on issues in one's family or work place. A baseline is to know enough about the system you are part of to enhance your ability to be a more self-defined individual in the system. You might think of this effort as being both more separate from the group and more capable of being cooperative and functioning well in it.

People often do not like being more separate but they do like having a more open and direct relationship with others. The most amazing thing about this effort is that families in which one person is willing to undertake becoming more separate, have fewer symptoms or can manage them better. When one person is willing to take on more challenges by defining Self and being more separate, the family organism has a more effective way of channeling anxiety. The space between people and the strength of the thoughtful connections allows for resiliency to develop in each. Without this discipline the automatic takes over, people become overly involved in the functioning of one another or they flee and cut off. Bowen noted this sensitivity in and how people automatically become overly involved and sensitive. He called this "fusion" to describe the function of overlapping relationships. I have referred to his process as "confusion". But for all the humor, we also recall that the basic fusion process is emotional and takes us back to our lineage with cellular life.

In this way, one is keeping Self more separate and less under the control of the urge to fuse (the togetherness force). It may seem silly and it may surprise you how upset people get over little differences, but for building an emotional backbone there is nothing that gets you greater traction as to being a standalone self than being very careful in how you separate out over the little things. When and if you do it then you should be ready for the reactivity. As noted earlier, all forward motion is met with a little bit of opposition. You will be encouraged to go along with family members, and to join in and agree and tell everyone just what they want to hear. This is what you and I have been mostly programmed to do.

Some would say the emotional system has civilized us. Other would say we are so dependent on love and approval we cannot think or act differently in relationships to those we care about, because if we do then we will upset the apple cart. Little exercises like this can be useful and there can be resistance or kick back as you alter the tenor of your relationship with others. The overall goal is to find a way to be more Self with each person. This requires breaking down the barriers of polite habits and developing more authentic one-to-one relationships. It may be experienced as jarring if people are more focused on the separate ways we are feeling and thinking. The separation between people leads to greater respect and, as I have seen, more healing. It takes work to know where one stands and how one is different from others and then to communicate the separate nature of one's way of being with and caring for others.

Questions for Self as you go about altering how you function in relationships:

- Who are the people I am most dependent on for love and approval?

- Can I be more open with others without defending myself?

- Can I go visit people in my extended family without upsetting someone?

- Can I accept the way people are without reacting and gossiping about them?

- What does it take to be present without reacting to differences?

How will it help me, or the system as a whole, to get to know more about the people in my extended family?

Dr. Bowen would talk about how he stumbled on getting to know people in his extended family as way to get to know his father better. Both his parents were vaguely interested in the lives of their parents and grandparents but did not know much about them. In an effort to find ways to be more personal in relationship to his parents, he made a trip down south to find the facts of how his father's family had lived. He met a helpful historian in one of the small towns and gathered up new facts about the family history. Then he noted what a difference this information made in how people thought and talked about their family members. As he told these stories to the psychiatric residents, some of them began to relate better to those in their extended family and he noted how this seemed to alter the intensity in their marriages. It sounds like magic but the idea of knowing one's roots is very old.

As with all change there would be a smattering of complaints from the residents' spouses as people went off to figure out how to relate to the older members of their family and gather more facts of the family history. Yet, we know that one of the things to keep in mind is that change itself upsets people, and that is not the end of the world.

People can be deeply threatened by changes in relationships. If you can accept this then you can relax, enhancing your ability to focus and define yourself. If you are defining yourself to people in your Mother's family, perhaps they might be upset with you, but your Father's family might be more accepting and calm at the time. Enlarge your reach and you may be defining yourself to half a dozen social groups; your friends, your religious affiliations, civic groups, even exercise groups which you formed at the local YMCA. All social groups can present you with challenges. If all groups or individuals appreciate you, and there is no need to define a difference, then what are you learning? Are you being a people pleaser and just going along without regard for being your best Self? The overall point is that we need challenges at least half the time, since sometimes, appreciation, love and approval can lull us into apathy.

As a rule of thumb I suggest making an effort to be part of at least twelve important groups. (For example, twelve different groups might include your mother's family, your father's family, your grandparents, cousins, work systems, friendship systems, volunteer organizations, etc.) In this way, if six social systems are positive about you and six are difficult, you are somewhat protected from stress and can still continue to learn and be challenged. Balance and harmony are only achieved through a sprinkling of chaos.

Since many of your leadership skills took root when you were experiencing your first social system, your family, much of your internal strength was built when you were young and not really paying attention. Therefore, to help you see the connections between your early experiences and your leadership skills today, and to help you build on your natural ability to be a leader, I developed thirty-three questions. They can be useful in thinking about your family or in understanding others and their social system.

I gave these questions to each of the ten people whose interviews appear in the last chapter of this book, prior to the interview. The questions help me understand a bit more about a person and help individuals understand themselves a bit better as well. Many of these questions include people and subjects that people may not have considered while reflecting on and telling their own story. A big part of this is that we humans are programmed to ignore or to be blind to the relationship pressure and configuration of our family system. Often, we just take relationships for granted, and breathe them in like the air, which we also take for granted. Only under certain conditions do we have to truly think about relationships or the air we breathe.

Read the questions, think about them, and find your favorites to reflect upon. The questions are meant to stimulate your thinking about the structure and functioning of the emotional system you grew up in. There are no right answers. If the questions provoke you to write or tell a great story highlighting how you emerged as a leader, what strengths you have, and how you acquired them, and who has been important to you and how you learned from them, then they are good questions.

QUESTIONS: Values and events over the generations

1. Was there anyone in your family that you had (or have) an open relationship with? (An open relationship is one in which a person can

say what he or she thinks while the other listens. Then the other person is able to reciprocate by clarifying his or her views without undue stress. Open relationships promote independent thinking.)

2. How old were you when you chose principles/values to guide you?

3. How did these values fit with or differ from those in your family of origin?

4. How were you able to handle criticism as a young person, and now as an adult?

5. What are the qualities of the important relationships that you believe promote learning?

6. What events in your early years taught you about leading?

7. Did your sibling position result in an automatic leadership position in your family?

8. Did either parent's work inspire leadership values?

9. What are the qualities you admire in your mom, dad, grandparents, aunts, and/or uncles?

10. What leadership qualities would family members have seen in you when you were younger, or now as an adult?

11. When did you first think you had achieved something worthwhile as a leader in your family or community?

12. How did your grandparents and extended family relate to your parents?

13. How old were you when you were first able to articulate your values to your parents, siblings or friends?

14. How old were you when you knew you had a passion for your work?

15. How do you think about influencing co-workers, students or the broader

public?

16. What were (and are) the economic and social forces that affected your generation's family or professional life?

17. How accurate are you at predicting future events?

18. What are your criteria for identifying leadership qualities in others?

19. Do you have a formula for working with others?

20. How old were you when you developed a satisfactory way to understand others?

21. How do you decide when to be authentic vs. strategic?

22. What methods do you use to stay in contact with others following a dispute?

23. How do you maintain a positive attitude when others mishear you or even sabotage your efforts to create a better way to go?

24. Are there standout events in your early family life that taught you about leading?

25. Did you learn lessons from how your grandparents managed their relationship with your parents?

26. What would your parents and/or siblings say were/are your leadership qualities?

27. When did you first believe you could make a difference as a leader?

28. What is your favorite leadership story about you or someone else?

29. What are the ingredients of teamwork that you learned in your family of origin?

30. What are the values you learned in your family that you carry over into

your work?

31. When people pressure you to go along with them, how do you deal with the pressure?

32. What is the biggest problem you have worked on or solved?

33. What do you think will be the biggest problem for you to solve in the future?

The Discipline of Listening and Observing Others

These questions are designed to provide clarity about how much you really know about the relationship pressures on you and others in your family. Once you are comfortable understanding your family system then you might be able to ask such questions of others.

Laws today limit our ability in business settings to ask these kinds of questions about family life. However, you will find it useful to keep these kinds of questions in mind to have a systems perspective as you work with people. You can use the questions as a reminder for yourself that people are continually influenced by early experiences.

If there are times when you think it might be useful for people to know about your understanding of social systems, one of the best ways to communicate it is through your own story of emerging as a leader in your family. People learn best from examples that are personal. Stories about your experiences in becoming a leader are easy to hear and others can learn from them. Questions, such as the ones above, are very useful for people in trying to understand how systems influence individual growth.

Understanding Automatic Relationships in the Social Jungle

The relationships around us tend to organize in specific, emotionally based or primitive configurations. As noted, our automatic compass guides us to react in more instinctive-like ways with those we encounter in our social world. Since survival is the "be all" in the jungle, many of our ancient programs have tuned us to automatically put negative pressure on others and to take the pressure off of us. We can call people, who do "this or that" to us names, but name calling does not help us cope or understand. None of us can make a conscious choice as to what part of the jungle we are born in. No matter our functional position in our families or in society, we are all sensitive to relationships and how people treat us. As children, there is little we can do about our functional position. As we become adults, we begin to look at how we fit with others and what their expectations are for us and what it is we would like to do with our lives.

Gradually people find it is useful to have an understanding of social pressure. One way of gaining this understanding is to consider the relationship configurations we will encounter in the social jungle and then consider what we might do to increase our awareness and our ability to function more independently.

What Can We Learn from Reactivity?

When people pressure us to be for them or to do things their way, we can just go along and not notice that our immune system took a hit. Social pressure, in which one person or one animal begins to dominate others, creates stress. Our brain registers our place in the social hierarchy. Research shows us that even removing parts of the brain responsible for aggression does not alter dominance patterns. If a monkey is challenged after this surgery, he will respond to the threat and take a lower position in the hierarchy. If the monkey is not challenged, he will resume his former place.[13]

Just as with monkeys, people can automatically orient and react to social pressure, almost like an instinct, without much intellectual awareness. Experiences are sensed and stored unconsciously and new experiences are compared with the old. For example, we tend to be obedient to authority (boss, spouse, parents, and teachers) as our past experiences dictate and then to rebel, when too much pressure is exerted, because the cost of going along with others is too high.

If our parents were failures, we tend to go in a different direction than they did. Research indicates that when parents disappoint, older siblings, for instance, have more of a drive to bring new ideas into the world.[14] If our parents were heroes, we may experience too much pressure to achieve as they did, and we may not have enough natural talent to move up to their standards. In these cases, people can react and give up. If we can understand at a cellular level our own physiological reactions to social pressure, then we may be able to slow down the threat response often seen in elevated heart rates and other parameters. Seeing social pressure as a natural process in all living systems and our reaction to the others as the part of our programming allows us to understand that change starts with us. The ability to see one's position in the social system and to alter our responses to others based on changing Self gives us tremendous freedom.

Understanding the automatic nature of how relationships function can keep us from entering into reactive processes. Or, if we find we are reacting, understanding the nature of these experiences allows us to get out of these reactive states without taking them too seriously or too personally. The goal is to be able to alter our participation in the system. If we can manage ourselves in the rising tide of emotionality, then we can take positions that keep us from being swept away by these primitive, emotional forces.

It takes an intellectual effort to see that there are automatic positions into which we can be forced as a result of how our family system is configured. Researchers have classified how we are attached to one another but they have a hard time predicting exactly how one might grow up in relationship to problematic parenting. Our temperament is steady throughout life in terms of whether we are high and low reactors, but the small differences in how we regulate our arousal, for example, can make a big difference in one's life course. [15]

With realistic information we can learn to integrate the emotional and the intellectual sides concerning our opinions and ideas about our family life. Questioning others and ourselves we allow ourselves to feel, think and not to judge. All of this is a bit easier when we are more independent adults. When as children we are told how to feel or think and our ideas are not validated, our relationships can negatively impact us. Even children can see how a system is organized and have a voice as to the ongoing situation.

If as a child a person was not respected, it takes a longer time to grow self up in relationship to parents or to parental figures. Reacting and running away never helped anyone achieve a level of emotional maturity. Running away is a popular pastime that often leads only to multiple marriages and job losses. Until people can see what is going on, they are unable to change self. However, people can do something to alter their role in the worst of family emotional systems. Even a small change to take action to be more of a separate Self from the old automatic habits of being can have an effect.

Once a system is severely disturbed following a death or a divorce, there is often more emotional reactivity and less predictability as to the how the system is spinning and what the impact will be on people in the family. Under increasing stress, reactivity is often driving people's action. A great deal of what people can do depends on the system—the family history, the functioning of parents, grandparents, children and others in the close up family, the level of connection with the larger relationship system, and of course financial and emotional stability.

Embracing Emotional Reactivity: Decreasing Fear in the Social Jungle

If one sets out mindfully to interrupt a pattern of distance or over-focus on children, one becomes a "disruptor." As long as a potential disruptor is somewhat important to the system, the system will be motivated to retain the person despite the fact that the people in the system will react negatively. If those who reacted negatively to the disruptor fail in their efforts to get this person to change back, eventually new ways of relating will appear almost seamlessly. Eventually the troubles, the differences in the system will settle down. People will have integrated some better way of thinking about the issues that allows the relationships to continue. They will have found some way to adapt and adjust in order to continue the relationship.

The disruptor has no idea what the change in the others will be and may not feel comfortable with the eventual changes in the relationship system. The disruptor does not "win" in the conventional sense. The disrupter can pay a price for being his or her best Self in the system. They may have to admit they are wrong or they are a "bumbler." Therefore, the focus has to be on being one's best Self and giving the others freedom to do the same.

Changing self in a relationship system gone bad, mad, or that has sustained symptoms or cut off over generations requires a sustained effort to alter how one functions in it. There are many lessons in the effort to focus on self and not be controlling of others. It takes an emotional backbone and the ability to go without love and approval if one is to speak up and move towards a more realistic look at the health of the relationship system.

To demonstrate the challenge, let's say you are simply going to comment on the state of the relationships as they are playing out without judgment as far as possible. You might say, "I notice there is some distance in the air." Or "I am not sure if our son appreciates all the help he is getting." The person you made the comment to might react and get mad that you said something about things that one is not to talk about. If you are prepared for the resistance to being more of a Self, then it will not be too challenging. If anyone can speak and then not be defensive or reacting, they passed the first test.

It takes courage not to follow and obey a "You are wrong, change back" message. Innocent people, who are stuck in a system, must resist the change they do not comprehend. After all, detecting change can provoke an alerting response that can give a fear message to others. Often, they just want you be the nice way you were before. But if you see a reason for changing Self or for defining a different direction and you decide to keep going, the good news is that in most systems, the effort to change will alter the system. Bowen would say that sometimes no one wants to change and in that case there may be two or three people that die before the system can recalibrate to a higher level of functioning. Perhaps defining your Self to others is a total challenge to the ongoing dynamics and it might take years for the system to settle down. Therefore, one has to be sure it is really worth the cost of trying to change one's automatic self to be a more mindful Self.

One of the main keys to being able to alter Self in relationships is to analyze how alliances are functioning in the relationship system. Although it appears that one is working to be a Self with one other person, in reality, one is always working to be a Self in triangles. Alliances are the foundation of the inner workings of social systems.

CHAPTER VI
UNDERSTANDING TRIANGLES
IN THE SOCIAL JUNGLE

Murray Bowen – Drawing The Triangles

Side-taking, Polarizing and Neutrality

Triangles (two against one) are the basic building blocks of relationships and form the backbone of alliance formation. They offer an understanding of how relationships form automatic configurations to handle anxiety and tension. Few are aware of the automatic way that the three-person relationship functions. It is just so natural to be close to one and bad vibe another. Two people are close and a third comes along and then sides are taken. Most kids know how to divide and conquer parents. They get one to be on their side and use them to sway the other. Basically, a three-person system can handle tension longer that a two-person system, which tends to degrade rapidly under tension. (Note the high divorce rate, when people have only one another to blame.)

In addition, when anxiety is high, more people can be "triangled" into a tense situation. Have you ever noticed that when tension is higher there is more gossip, be it at the dinner table or the water cooler? In these cases a two-against-one situation can occur and the relationship system can bind up anxiety by identifying someone who can be blamed. That is the point of the gossip.

On the positive side, one neutral party in a three-person relationship can enable people to think and even act more thoughtfully. Yes, if one person is neutral and does not take sides then triangles can enable problem solving. The spread of tension in an emotional system can result in the forming of negative or positive relationships. Interlocking triangles form and they can function to polarize situations or help solve problems. In both cases, the anxiety or tension in the system is being managed.

It takes time to see and learn how triangles function. Side-taking is one clue as to how the anxiety in a system has been transferred from two people to a third outsider. As people focus on what is wrong with someone, they are transferring anxiety onto that individual. If one person is excluded or ganged up on in a system, the negatively focused individual's physical and emotional health is at greater risk. You can call this scapegoating, but each part of the system is participating. There are no innocents here, but all can be blind to the process of distributing anxiety. Blindness to social pressure exists both in those who carry more of the anxiety of the system and those who focus on others negatively. Paradoxically, negative focus on another enables an individual to function at higher levels—"I'm up because you're down."

Triangles are automatic and everywhere. They may not require words— sideway glances can do just fine to alter people's status. This two-against-one alignment can be seen if one person or one animal looks at another for cooperation, and the two then disregard or snarl at the third.

During periods of calm the triangles are simply expressing preferences and managing tension in an adaptive way for those involved. As the tension mounts—the lack of food, the hope for a new job—the vulnerable people or animals are at greater risk. Awareness can alter this automatic system response to increasing tension and allow people more choices in managing the direction of anxious thoughts or actions.

We see that in some cultures, nations and families there is an awareness of the downside of picking on others. Laws are passed, rules are changed, and adjustments are made to avoid exclusion and/or bullying. The rights of the minorities are at times protected from this triangling process. There are also many nations and social groups which reinforce discrimination and many religions or cults where the differences between the in-group and the out-group result in some being extruded.

Families also make rules to exclude those who are different. They tell us in subtle or direct ways to not date or make friends with those who are different in terms of politics, religion, sexual orientation, etc. It is hard for people to see how this kind of natural reaction to differences can make for trouble. The two-against-one tendency is a natural instinct based in our evolutionary past resulting in dividing families and society into "for or against" camps.

It is a little easier to see it when we have elections and the two candidates are up on stage triangling with the American public, as best they can, to show that the other is no good and thereby win a vote or two. This process is clear.

One assumption is that triangling persists because it is the natural way anxiety is expressed and comfort is found for at least two individuals, even though that twosome's comfort occurs at the expense of the third. Perhaps saving two at the cost of one makes some kind of evolutionary sense. Triangles also aid in forming new groups to oppose the status quo.

One of the best uses of knowledge about triangles can be seen in therapy with couples or in mediation. Here you have two sides and mounting tension. If a disciplined third party can refrain from taking sides and simply try to consider how to solve a very real problem, then the third person's ability to maintain neutrality can dampen down the escalation of anxiety and its sisters, blame and shame.

When a leader can see that there is a better way for anxiety to be distributed for improved problem solving, the aware leader may interrupt or disrupt the triangle pattern by inserting more Self into the relationship system. Some leaders can do this within the work system and not at home. Abraham Lincoln, for example, was one of these kinds of leaders. He made it possible for people, who were in the opposition, to be heard. He thought carefully about giving greater respect to the "out group" or those who are "done in" to benefit the larger group.

Lincoln was able to use his voice and influence to decrease polarization by respecting others and enable the possibility for people from various viewpoints to work together to benefit and preserve the union. This did not make him a perfect man with regard to his knowledge of emotional systems. The anxiety at home around the deaths of his children had a tremendous impact on his marriage and his ability to relate well to his wife. Yet, he could figure out how to take a stand and relate to all kinds of people, creating the opportunity for tremendous change in the larger society. The ability to be a self and relate well to the people in the system is part of what is natural about managing self in triangles.

Increasing Anxiety and the Shifting in Triangles

Since triangles are so basic to managing "comfort," it is useful to consider triangles as a fundamental fallback position to the way any increase in anxiety is handled. This viewpoint allows you to predict changes in relationship configurations. As you observe the formation of triangles and note the increase in side-taking, ask yourself, what is going on here? Are new ideas or demands for higher functioning being introduced? Are there new people who are having trouble fitting into an already formed group?

What are the pressures and what is your best understanding of the system? Is it accurate that people in a system often seem to automatically oppose new relationships, unless of course they are the one bringing in the new people or idea? If so, what does the leader do to bring this pressure to people's attention to enable progress through awareness?

You can see this in a family when changes occur. The older siblings do not always welcome a new baby. "You are spending time with whom?" New ideas can also be treated like babies or aliens. "Where did you come up with that crazy idea?" Sometimes people explain this by saying it breaks up the norm and now we have a "new normal." It is not always clear what a new behavior does, but it appears that when times are calm people prefer the old status quo and they pressure group members to return to the way things were.

Bowen would say that to some extent we all rise up on the back of the schizophrenic. That is, we all have the tendency to pick on others and to not relate well to others who are "different." There remains the temptation to identify the circumstances that make our life miserable as "in" the environment or "in" other people, and to see the others as "not us" and as "wrong or dangerous." Triangles express our automatic way of reacting to others. If we can use this information, then we can strive to see our part in relationship problems. A view of triangles enables us like an early warning system to be able to alter our part in relationship problems by becoming more objective and neutral while relating to various upsets in the relationship system.

What is the Problem with Two-Person Closeness?

Freud had a great deal to say about anxiety related to two people becoming close. By listening carefully to free association, Freud was able to hear fragments of fear-based memories. Did these fear-based actions really happen or was it pure imagination? Freud did not discriminate between imagination and reality. He was interested in allowing the repressed memories of those willing to free associate into the light of day. The goal was to listen carefully and to not react to the interpersonal traps his patients offered. By managing self in the "transference-counter transference," he was able to free people from acting towards him as fearful memories might direct them to do. Freud connected these memories of fearful interactions back to the Greek stories where fear in relationships led to all kinds of instinctive-based problems.

Bowen went beyond the transference relationship, finding a way to stay outside the system and let people work out the problems in their family. Instead of taking relationship problems back to the Greeks, Bowen took the problems in the neurosis and the psychosis back to basic biology.

The word fusion was used to describe the way that people in a family are stuck together and "share" an ego. This fusion resulted in a family in which people were more stuck together in their beliefs and actions. He called the results of this fusion between people the "undifferentiated family ego mass." Bowen regretted using the word "ego" as he was concerned that it allowed people to misinterpret and see some connection between psychoanalysis and natural systems thinking that might not exist.

In biology, fusion refers to the early relationship between cells. Billions of years ago, cells with a single nucleus fused to form a multi-nuclear cell. The early cells, prokaryotic cells, are independent. The guess is that long ago in certain hot spots, deep on the ocean floor, the temperature was hot enough to force the fusion of two cells into one. One cell then functions as the nucleus and the other as the outer structure.

This idea of this process of two or more individuals clumping together and then functioning as one was then used to describe relationships between people. Triangles were seen as the regulatory mechanisms where species were forced to adapt to a changing environment. Emotional pressure has been described in other species, such as slime mold, where the more reactive cells become the stalk and give support to the less reactive cells, which form the reproductive body.

To use an analogy, families were seen as clumps of cells. In more anxious and reactive families, some individuals lose the ability to function as independent entities. This clumping or fusion between the members of the family, allows the colony or the family itself to survive.

At the human level, we would like to know how fused or confused we are as people. That remains the question. When you have too much fusion-based closeness between people, no one is really being his or her most independent and genuine Self. A lot of pretending can go on in an attempt to achieve closeness. People get close and one almost automatically becomes the dominant one. The other person can be more adaptive or passive or just unsure of self as the fusion process takes hold of one's ability to be more self-reliant. One person can adapt more than the other to make things work. That person, who is the most fused into the relationships, is subject to being more squeezed in the decision-making process.

You can also think about the relationship dynamic as the martial seesaw. When people come together and form a union, they are even on the seesaw, but over time some kind of reciprocal relationships emerges. Someone adapts too much and that person begins to sacrifice "self" to fit with the other. The seesaw shifts. Then one person becomes more stuck in the down position. An uneasy truce may arise. The discomfort in these more adapting two-person relationships is real for the person in the down position. But sometimes people can be forced into a one up position by simple pressures. Can you drive the car for me? Can you get the groceries? People begin to respond more to the demands than to consider "what is important for me to do now?" Too much doing for others and one can feel anxious and out of sorts. As the tension in doing for the other or avoiding the other rises, people look for someone or something to make them feel more comfortable.

One answer is found in activating the triangle. The third person arrives in the nick of time. We can blame our troubles on the mother-in-law, the boss or the child. But can we see that the anxiety related to closeness, to being able to speak as to what is going on is lost or diminished? People become more fearful of engaging one another and the tendency is for these kinds of tense two-person relationships to eventually fall apart. As noted above, as tension arises and one of the two will bring in (or triangle in) a third person, and off we go to a new status quo or to a new symptom, if the next relationship configuration is not functional.

If you doubt the challenge of having a two-person relationship that does not triangle in a third person, try the following experiment: ask another person to spend 15 minutes only talking about self while you carefully listen, and respond, without talking about anyone or anything else. Then you do the same. It is difficult to maintain, even in a brief conversation, a direct and open one-to-one relationship with another. It is average for all of us to avoid the directness and to start to talk about a third person.

We can see it is natural for two people to get close at the expense of a third. Because the third person is usually the more impinged one, he or she can be motivated to change and not react if the anxiety is not too great and if the person who is being focused on has an impersonal and objective understanding of how triangles function.

In periods of low anxiety the outside position is comfortable. You do not mind if others are close if they are not criticizing or extruding you. However, when the anxiety goes up, being on the outside and being the focus of criticism can do people in. They can become symptomatic, feel like getting drunk or get angry or depressed. These are common symptoms due to one being focused on in a negative way by others.

If the outside person understands triangles they have an opportunity to alter the situation at work or at home. As a side point, this observing position of seeing how relationships function helps people interested in becoming family therapists. These people have often have siblings who have been the focus of negative parental attention and who become the symptom bearer for the family. This was true for my situation and for many others. If you see symptoms as a function of relationships getting uptight and intense, it is hard to see problems as being in an individual. Emotional symptoms are a function of fusion and confusion as to who is responsible for what, and the inability to manage anxiety.

Once anyone has an intellectual appreciation for the way triangles work they can then make plans to rise above the automatic response to take sides. If you are not controlled by the triangle to take sides or to flee, but are able to say in contact in a more lighthearted manner, it will eventually become a different system.

With experience, people do learn to stay outside of the side-taking and blaming and have more confidence to stay connected, even when being focused on negatively. This is not to say that at times we all need to take a rest, sit on the bench and come back into the relationship later. As people are better able to observe the conditions leading to controlling/dominating others or rebelling/running away, they are more able to see it as an impersonal reaction and not get so involved in fixing people. All of these relationship maneuvers are driven by anxiety as a result of the reactivity due to people being *blind* to the way a system controls people. Systems are about the business of distributing anxiety unevenly through a variety of interpersonal mechanisms, such as criticizing, side-taking, scapegoating, dismissing, paralyzing or stalemating. When things start to go "wrong," the first step is to overcome blindness by observing self in the system and wondering just what is really going on here?

Getting out of Triangles

As noted earlier, one way to get out of the triangle is to embrace the idea of describing the natural configuration to the participants. Yes, this can create "new information." We have made the case that most people are blind to relationships process. Therefore, by describing what we see, things might change. Of course you have to do it in way that the emotional system might "hear." You can make a "reversed" comment on how two might enjoy fighting. Or use a "crazy" metaphor like "Maybe you should put the troublemaker up on a shelf or in a cage.". There are many ways that two people manage one another and if you see it, others might. They can then decide what to do, but by describing it you are slightly freer from it. This is far from asking people to change to make you happy or them healthy, it's just about how one "sees" and comments in an offhand way about what is going on. Instead of asking people to "please change for me," you can encourage them to do more of what they are doing. If you have been part of a system that operates to control others (triangles) it can be useful to get outside by acting in a funny or paradoxical way. However, these kinds of psychological maneuvers are for advanced observers only. First, one has to deeply understand the emotional connection between people and how it is being played out.

These kinds of relationship configurations are not logical or subject to rational thought. If you have the courage to alter the way you relate, and a focus on remaining outside the control of the system, then when you speak to others, as to your different viewpoint, you are also ready for the resistance. For example, if you think your son is too close to his Dad, you can suggest they spend more time together. These kinds of reversals may seem silly and yet they often require the other to think differently once you alter your automatic position. Of course, when you stop being controlled by the system, all that you do or say to get outside the system will be initially seen as a way to manipulate others. It is really just a way to say what you see and to get outside of reacting to the process. But doing reversals or other maneuvers to get outside can be challenging and emotionally confusing to your near and dear. So be careful, build an emotional backbone and see what happens.

Consider this: They may be pushing you out, but you can enjoy that momentary freedom and see what happens when they get more and more aware of how they are "stuck together." This move to push others together and get Self out can shift the transfer of anxiety and throw the twosome for a loop. I observe this over and over again. I am not sure why it works this way but perhaps people do not want to be pushed around, even by their own guidance system. Once they notice the nature of the programming, they begin to wiggle out of the automatic.

The social jungle seems to be full of triangles. Alliances are here, there and everywhere. Adam and Eve, the "first parents," had two children who functioned differently. We can guess one parent may have protected one child and the other parent disagreed about that protective stance. One parent tries to convince the other to stop protecting or bothering or hovering, but that good advice is lost. In fact, good advice seems to have the opposite effect. Out of Cain and Abel's sibling rivalry, fertile ground was created for violence.

The Outside of the Triangle

In the social jungle, the person who gets angry in this case, Adam (because of Eve's overprotection of a child), is the one caught reacting to the two-against-one alliance. To alter the angry feeling in self, Adam has to be able to observe how people are—not just react to them. For Adam (or any of us), being able to slow down to see how relationships function as a pushing and pulling puppet show is the first goal. Even if you know enough to observe how triangles work, it is so hard to begin to alter one's feeling state and take an action for self, even if it's just breathing deeply, to get outside the "push" to be close and the "pull" to get mad at the other.

84

As long as being on the outside is "bad" or painful, and one feels helpless to alter the situation, the primitive, fearful feeling system will run the show. By seeing the situation for what it is, a triangle, one can embrace being on the outside and begin to move into a more free and fun state. Breathing can be fun. Pushing the two together can be fun. But simply reacting as you are programmed to do, puts you into the worst of all possible worlds.

Acting neutral until you truly become more neutral, offers a first step towards releasing yourself from the dictates of an anxious emotional system. Clearly, being a Self requires us to avoid reacting to relationships cues. It takes practice to be less serious and confused about others' shenanigans. We cannot fix them but we can alter our responses. Striving for neutrality is a first but not necessarily a cost-free way to change Self.

There is nothing harder than to alter an automatic feeling response to our near and dear. This kind of flexibility requires the pushed-out person (or the person who flees or is stuck and unable to think or act), to recover from the reactivity and see the system and his/her part in it. It also requires the strength to be more on the outside of the system and to stand alone until you are no longer "controlled" by the reactivity in the system.

The automatic responses are to feel mad and sad and to blame others. Keeping self outside the emotional programming and pushing the others together is known as detriangling, and it is hard to do because it does not feel natural. But it does create relationship space for something new to happen.

Detriangling is complicated and difficult, but it is a good example of how one person can alter an automatic configuration. Anyone who can see a triangle as an emotional system and who has the wherewithal to stand up to these natural but potentially harmful alliances can reorganize the family anxiety.

Humor is a good way to deal with alliances without assigning "blame." If you can be funny while you push the twosome together, then you are outside the system. This helps you avoid getting caught up in the reactivity of the triangle. It requires an understanding of how triangle mechanisms work, so that you see these alliances as objectively and impersonally as possible.

These alliances, based in triangles, have occurred in nature for millions, perhaps billions of years in all kinds of life forms. In the human, alliances are formed when people feel that someone is on their side, often because there is a common goal or enemy. But for individuals, there are costs and benefits to aligning with a group to achieve something. Choosing a side can be costly since there are "others" who may no longer trust you, and now you have lost your more neutral position.

Parents say "I am not taking sides," but the child knows they have. One parent can say, "If I pick your side it will make things worse for you and better for your sibling." The child knows this is true. They can hear this description of the situation and see things just a bit differently. They may not calm down, they may still threaten, but they are beginning to hear and, therefore, to see that you are responding differently.

How Do Triangles Function at Work?

Alliances are formed out of triangles. Once formed, triangles are hard to alter. This happens whenever two people agree that others are the problem. Anxiety is bound and relationships are set as a protection against increasing anxiety. It happens so innocently. We often find the ones we agree with at the water cooler or in a meeting. Then we have lunch and find that working together is great fun. Many organizations encourage this building of trust in structured exercises, but what do they tell you about how trust can erode as anxiety increases and the two begin to complain about a third person?

Triangles work in organizations just like they do in families. People take sides when they get unsure or anxious. A once-open boss can shut down new ideas and find him or herself only trusting one other person and becoming negative about all those who do not agree with him or her. Under command-and-control authoritative leadership, people take sides based on a paycheck. Some individuals do not have much choice other than to go along with the authority.

When there is no projection of blame or negativity towards others, new alliances can form and new ideas are welcome. The benefit of joining with others is that you have a group who will carry forward an agreeable agenda in a cooperative way. It is far better to move forward with each person being as aware as possible of the negative power of complaining and gossiping to the flow of anxiety in a system. This does not imply that people should not complain, but rather that complaints are indicators that one is stuck in a triangled relationship. If complaining helps one to figure out how to de-triangle and get out of the one-down position, then complaining turns into strategic thinking.

Triangles are an automatic way to bind anxiety at the cost of the outside person's functioning. Triangles, when used automatically to bind anxiety, are used to control and affix the problems onto one person. These are negative triangles, because they do not solve long-term, reality-based problems.

If one can alter his or her part in a triangle, then functioning should improve. After all, the way in which the anxiety was bound up was keeping people from being more responsible for self and cooperating with others. If anxiety goes down, then people are freer to cooperate and they can function more for Self at higher levels.

CHAPTER VII
REDUCING CON-FUSION AT HOME AND WORK AS YOU GET TO KNOW YOUR EXTENDED FAMILY

Solving Problems: Using Neutrality in Relating to the Group

When people are able to deal with anxiety and solve real problems, there is less pretending to agree or less stuck togetherness. Deeper and more realistic cooperation is possible when there is no force applied to go along with others. If people can learn to see systems, they are freer to define a Self and to comment on the process as they see it. All this leads to greater personal responsibility for each person to manage Self.

A thoughtful leader, who experiences resistance to a goal, will not blame anyone for problems. If problems occur, he or she can take things up with that person. Leaders or a person who has a well-defined Self is able to take his or her time moving forward and will keep the "other side" engaged by talking with as many individuals as possible to overcome complaints or resistance to change. Those who are able to stay in good contact with the others who disagree will see a gradual decrease in tensions. If one person is able to relate more neutrally to others instead of taking sides, there may be new psychological room to respect different viewpoints. This allows for more divergent and creative thoughts and actions to emerge.

Detriangling simply sets a tone in which the leader can talk about side-taking and not engage in it. There are, of course, many situations where the leader has no interest in engaging and creates higher functioning for self by blaming others and not engaging in problem-solving activities. It is easy to see how triangles lead to polarization and blame as individuals in a system struggle to understand problems and to preserve personal functioning. However, leaders who see what needs to be done do not flinch in the face of the struggle to overcome polarization in family or work situations. When there are fewer polarized relationships, people are freer to act for Self and not spend as much time reacting to others.

My goal is to give you some tools so that you can develop your Mindful Compass. Perhaps you will figure out a new twist on alerting yourself to the challenges in an emotional field. Perhaps your compass will become part of the new trend towards wearable technology and will beep when you enter a highly reactive emotional field. Then you can decide who to push together and who to join with and when to stand-alone. Currently, the Mindful Compass is a silent companion or mental model. It lets you know that there are tools to help you get a better picture of the alliances at work in any tense situation. The Mindful Compass can also help you consider what might possibly change. Try drawing an informal chart of who takes sides with whom around various topics. This chart might take the shape of a triangle, with two sides (two people or two groups of people) against one side. In the diagram below, A and B are close in the triangle and C is on the outside. This is a function of automatic functioning due to increasing anxiety in or around the social system.

A B are together, close, united or fused and C is on the outside.

Ideally, C has the ability to relate to each one; thereby, diminishing the intensity of the triangle, the scapegoating and automatic mechanisms due to high anxiety.

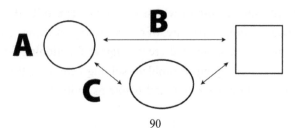

Adding this knowledge to what you already know about the people involved can add depth to your assessment of what is really going on. Definitely try to maintain your sense of humor. If you get serious and start to blame people for how they are "participating" in a triangle or increasing emotionality in a polarized system, you will find your leadership ability dropping off the edge of the cliff. People want to know one thing—what you are going to do?

Triangles are primitive and ever present. To get outside the emotional system, one has to manage powerful, internal feeling states and take meaningful positions in relationship to others. Triangles show us how anxiety runs through relationships thereby altering their shape and altering our ability to function. There are many ways we can deal with triangles once we can see them. The goal is to become emotionally more neutral and mindful as we venture forth into the social jungle to see it for what it is.

Who am I and who are you? Where do I begin and end? Sometimes it is hard to know the answers. We have so many overlapping needs and desires for the other to be as we need them to be, and as they need us to be. Yes, our egos overlap. We borrow emotional energy and even self from one another. Bowen used the term *undifferentiated family ego* mass to describe the nature of the problem. He and others have given us many methods and techniques to know Self and to be better able to define more of a Self in any emotional group. Understanding the system or the ego mass is important. One way of making the effort to be clear about how you see things is to describe the situation to yourself and make the effort to be as neutral as you can in describing the pressure in the system. Consider that most are blind to the pressure and will not see it the way you do, but just do it as practice in the effort to be more of an individual Self.

Being Objective in a Pressure Cooker. Being objective is very hard to do and it is very powerful if you can do it well. The positive result is the outside person can take mediation to a new level. The traps for the outside person are emotional in nature. One such trap is wanting others to see it your way. Another is your own confusion in being caught wanting or needing positive responses from others (like being told that you are so kind, thoughtful and right) and instead you are met with the cold truth—they do not see it your way.

We react to being "rejected." After all, it would be so nice to be seen as a positive person and to have the love and approval from others. However, if you are trying to be more objective and neutral and relate to all, then you are going against the instinctive nature of the group.

There is an automatic or instinctive-like response to problems—the automatic effort to fix problems by making people change. It is hard to put on the brakes and not pressure others to change as a way to make peace. But this is to deny reality. People have problems and they can often work things out using information and some kind of non-intrusive support. In order for us to gain clarity, we need to focus on what is our part of the problem and what can we do about that, and to then leave the person with his or her issue, having confidence that with time he or she will figure things out.

The confusion around what is my responsibility or my part of the problem leads to the erosion of self when the automatic response (to protect the togetherness) kicks in to high gear. Becoming over or under involved in others' problems is so automatic. In family stories you can hear about this process as it unfolds in the lending of money, the rescuing, the protecting, the name-calling and the cut offs.

The sensitivity to over and under involvement has taken many generations to appear. In a way, they are no one's fault, since people cannot fully understand the problems they are creating when they ask others to change. It is the problem of people looking for comfort and not being able to see the consequences of this kind of pressure on others. In the extreme, people can blackmail others to be more the way they "should" be. There is a common belief in families that cut off from the problematic people is good. They cannot see how running away from problems like this will produce greater weakness in future generations.

Techniques or methods to alter the automatic process, like describing the problem more objectively, using reversals and paradoxes, can loosen up the system eventually. They are NOT about you necessarily defining a more principled Self. They are about seeing the emotional process for what it is, and despite pressure, being able to be more of a "differentiated" Self, one who is not eroded in the social group. There are many reasons to make a move to get out of the reactive box, as the Ping-Pong world of reactivity can leave people in a one-down position, severely damage their personal relationships, and even decrease their immune system functioning.

Using Humor in Developing Your "Self." Humor is great for reducing anxiety within most any group. It can also be used to avoid problems or to put a safe distance between problems and self. Used well, humor can allow us to relate to people who are being negative. It can also soften the sting of a negative comment and erase the need to react directly to such comments. Then if the situation is too complex and humor fails, there are some psychological tricks that can help. If the system is "seriously" reactive, that is, everything is taken "very seriously," well then the brave can try psychological reversals or paradoxes. Reversals and paradoxes require considerable thinking and practice to be effective.

Reversals are very strong medicine. They go against all you have been taught and have learned to do for eons. However, when you are getting tired of telling people, over and over again, the same answer to the same issue or problem, why not throw in the towel and give them a "backward" answer (also called a reversal) and let them figure it out? Of course, doing something outrageous like this is only for the advanced person who has the deep knowledge that telling vulnerable people what to do backfires. The more you say, "Just say no to drugs.", the more money is spent on drugs. Such an answer would encourage stubborn people to do more of what they're doing.

Here is a successful but unpopular reversal. I coached a loving and over-functioning, protective wife to offer 100-proof "booze" to her husband, who she thought drank too much. I encouraged her to reverse her protective and angry stance, and to tell him this "good booze" is a faster way for him to get high and, just in case, to provide a bucket for him to throw up in so he will have everything he needs.

Paradoxes are useful when people in your business or family are looking for certainty and straightforward answers that are unworkable. You have tried your best, been helpful and found that people refuse your good help. If you don't want to get too deadly serious, then what else can you do? Perhaps at some point the best you can do is to tell them a Zen-like story containing a paradox that they in their own good time must solve. For example, take a highly sensitive family in which people are refusing to talk to one another or allow access to children following a divorce. The person who is caught up in this and being denied access to the children "should" feel really mad and might consider filing a lawsuit. Parents and grandparents can end up in court when one is doing something the other opposes. In such a case, the person seeking access (in this example a grandparent) could write to the parties involved and say something that shows the shape of the bind. There are many ways to decrease the power of a bind by describing it: "Your spouse wants to protect you and so you must protect your spouse. If my grandchild suffers by not having contact with the extended family, oh well, at least they are protecting the parents. Small price to pay."

The thesis is that if one can see just how these automatic mechanisms work, to bind the anxiety or fear in a family, then that person has a different worldview. No one is doing things to hurt another. They just cannot see the disadvantage of these mechanisms for the long haul. It is automatic when anxiety increases to look for comfort and to bind anxiety with distance, conflict giving in, (and perhaps having physical and or mental illness) and or projecting problems onto the weak. You do risk having the anxiety pointed at you by thinking out of the box and putting in comments to disturb the emotional system. Therefore, I often ask if it is worth it to be a suffering leader and let people point at you rather than others? You are not telling others what to do; you are pointing towards a different way of seeing and being in an anxious group.

If you, as a leader, can begin to act differently, then you can observe what kind of new behaviors emerge from others. How do you keep track of your part in the system? Are others reacting as you thought? Can you stay steady if they get upset? How long does it take for the system to settle down? Have you stepped outside the system far enough to provoke yourself and others into thinking differently?

The Web of Life and the Extended Family. Bowen pointed out that by getting to know the people in your family in a non-judgmental way you can increase both your knowledge and your connections. If you thought of your family as a tree, then a growing root system is useful to keep you grounded. In addition, going back in search of your family history can give you more experience in acting differently with others. Listening to your more distant family members as you study your family history extends your relationship network and provides you with invaluable information. You can even learn to separate out the gossip from more factual information. This effort allows us to be more aware and less fused and confused by the people around us. By getting to know both the stories and the people in our extended family we will be experiencing being a more separate Self. Knowledgeable about your family's past and where you come from allows you to be less sensitive to a host of issues and to become more of a Self.

Here is an example of a discovery an individual made, altering his fear of failure. Believing that, "If I go into business on my own I will fail,", he discovered that his great, great grandfather failed in the leather business in the mid-eighteen hundreds. That knowledge enabled him to begin to be more realistic about his own opportunity now versus his great grandfather's challenges back then. Yes, the shadow of the past does move forward over the generations in silent ways. People may not recall a family story, but can react as though the story is in their brain. It is as though early experiences leave a shadow memory that influences a fear response. These sensitivities can be passed on through generations as if the fear from the past is a current reality. By growing our relationship knowledge and ability to understand emotional process we can be more realistic. Without such an effort most of us will have little idea what it is that we inherit and live out emotionally.

Bowen would say that if we went back four generations, we would find someone who was very similar to us. Yet we have a hard time connecting the past with our lives today. We do not know much about the reasons we are reacting to one another. But it is clear that knowing about the past can help people not to repeat the past and to be less reactive to events or emotionally tinged issues. There are saints and sinners in every family. Learning about these others can help us to be less judgmental.

Knowing the people and seeing the facts around the stories about one's family has the following important impacts on people: 1) It keeps us curious as to the facts of family history and aware of the difference between facts and people's feelings; 2) It gives us practice at learning how to relate to all kinds of people; 3) It promotes seeing how your family members imagine all kinds of things about you from what others have told them; 4) It motivates us to be our best self with others; 5) It allows us to know people for who they are, not as the people who we have heard about, helping us to separate facts from gossip; 6) It gives us a deep respect for the struggles of our ancestors; 7) It promotes the acceptance of both the importance of one's life and the insignificance of life; and 8) It allows us to imagine various ways that the past can impact the future.

Thinking carefully is a leader's job. Research suggests that it takes close to 10,000 hours of thinking-based "practice" to understand simple rule-based systems like chess, for example.[16] Families are far more complicated than a game of chess. It takes a long time to recognize the formation of various patterns and what you might do to make more of an impact. Think about how long it takes to deeply understand our extended families, since the families' rules have never been written down or in many cases clarified. For those willing to take the higher road to a stronger, better defined Self, the history of relationships tells what one is up against, and just where one might be able to find chances to grow Self in altering old relationship patterns.

Being a Self will, at some point, require bucking established trends and patterns. Take the case where you decide that you are going to get to know people in your mom's family. Your mother's older sister is having a wedding for her daughter but you are not invited. The two families have not communicated since the grandmother's death. There were "words" over the visitation of the grandmother when she was hospitalized, and even more words over the will. The two families have not been together for five years. What will it take to get invited to the wedding? What does it cost you not to try and to accept the status quo? Becoming more aware of the old triangles, not buying into the polarization and figuring out a way to talk to both your mom and your aunt without taking sides is not going to be easy. But once you let them know you see things differently, that in itself may very well provide a clear road to go to the wedding. If you come to see that families with more cut off have more symptoms, then it may very well be worth the effort.

Usually one has to see the long-term advantage of the effort to be more of a

Self. This kind of an effort is not done to make oneself happy, as initially it often upsets those you dearly love and value. If your mom gets mad at you then you can admit you're not the smartest when it comes to saying the right thing the right way, or that you might even be a bumbler at trying to relate well to the broader family. The goal is not to react or defend Self. If you do not fall into the reactive trap it gives others more of an opportunity to think, instead of reacting back.

All things being equal, small changes make for big differences. If your aunt will speak to you and your Mother can hang out with your Dad, then you are a bit freer. If the heat in the family kitchen becomes too great, one can always retreat, at least for a time, and just find another valuable social system, like friends, who do not care what you are trying to do in your family. Friends can accept your struggles without feeling threatened by the change in family alliances. They may question you as to what can be so important about your family or wonder why you care that much about going to a wedding? If you try and explain to them the importance of family roots or relationship knowledge, and what it's like to be more nimble in the web of life, they might just laugh.

No one wins every battle. Change takes a long time. It takes a long time for people to think differently and take a position that reflects one's more mature Self rather than automatically being negative or going along with others. If you have a viewpoint based in principles and knowledge, then differing with the emotional status quo and taking action to relate to the cut off people in your family can be worth the time and energy. Once you understand that increasing the ability to relate to various kinds of people decreases the vulnerability to symptoms, then the importance of building your emotional backbone begins to make sense.

Few who have taken a stand based on principle in the relationship system want to do it again. It is difficult to be a Self and alone in your convictions. Yet, when you see how the system is simply reactive, and manipulating everyone out of fear itself, then going against the automatic makes more sense. If you take a stand and get isolated, then, just relax and try to enjoy being in other, more comfortable systems, until this one can loosen up. Being able to stick with your convictions and not back down enables you to build up your ability to resist being guided by fear. Responding to threat automatically may be a useful guide in the social jungle of old when a lion or tiger might attack, but in the relationship jungle, fear leads to an anxious and even paralyzed system. Problems are frozen in time and issues are unable to be resolved. Once you can see how the ice age of our memories has an upper hand in guiding the relationships system into fear-based actions, it becomes easier to move forward to resolve old problems that were often created before you were born.

I can still recall when my great aunt said to me, "I do not like you because your grandmother called my daughter fat." I said to her, "I was not there, but I thought my mother was the fat one?" If you take the bait and react, it gets more serious and you are on the low, emotional reactive road. High road or low, it can be exhilarating to discover and use your unique talents to be more your Self than to fit with the emotionally powerful others. It helps to keep in mind that you are not that special. Just like those individuals generations ago and into the future, we are all faced with the challenge of becoming emotionally stronger, building our observational and leadership skills, learning from our relationships, from stories, and from mistakes.

Awareness - Consider the Past and Choose the Future. Whatever our dreams, ambitions or goals, they come to life only within a social system. To operate successfully, to achieve specific objectives, we need the ability to spot the critical connections between individuals and to understand what this indicates about how the relationships system itself is organized. We need to be able to observe and evaluate the group's potential to understand our ideas, and at least make educated guesses about the kinds of resistance we are likely to encounter in order to achieve our goals. This increased awareness of relationship dynamics is our golden road to providing realistic leadership within any system, be it in our family or at work.

The four points on the Mindful Compass keep us aware of the process of defining a Self in relationship to important others. As we mature, we are more able to know and define where our principles came from. We can use them to stand steady in the face of relationship disturbances. A mature person has to be able to separate Self from others and to stand alone without needing, commanding or rejecting others. This cannot be done unless one can see the signals being sent in the social system. Understanding your own and others' social systems allows you to find your own way. Emotional systems are knowable but not self-evident. It requires discipline to see how we have been programmed and how our automatic compass functions. It takes time to recalibrate and develop a more mindful compass.

Here is the way one person described his process: "It's like I just stopped following the clues others were giving me about how to behave. I finally stepped off Shakespeare's stage." People sometimes laugh and say they were written into the wrong family play. Most of us have an ability to be objective and neutral in learning about how natural systems function. It is possible to realize there is nothing that can be done about the family any of us were born into but most can rewrite his or her part of the family script and play a different role. This requires one to be less automatic and more creative and open minded when promoting very different ways of being one's best Self in any social system.

If "thinking systems" and managing Self appeals to you as a way through the tangle of social quagmires, then understanding and developing the four points or ARKS (Action, Resistance, Knowledge and Standing Alone), on your unique Mindful Compass, will allow you to function more effectively in the morass of social systems that you, as a leader, inhabit.

CHAPTER VIII
RELATIONSHIP AWARENESS
AND THE EVOLVING BRAIN

"Not until looking back did I realize how Lancelot Law Whyte's writing had influenced my formulation of *increasing awareness as the major thrust of evolution*."[17]

Michael Kerr, Murray Bowen, John B. (Jack) Calhoun

Social Systems and Relationship Dynamics

Awareness allows us to think about the past and to some extent, shape our future. Whatever our dreams, ambitions or goals, they come to life only within a relationship-oriented, very busy, social system. We humans pay more attention to social cues than do ants and bees. Therefore, to operate successfully, to achieve specific objectives, we need the ability to spot the critical connections between individuals and to understand what they indicate about how the relationship system itself is organized.

We need to be able to observe and evaluate the group's potential to understand our ideas, and at least make educated guesses about the kinds of resistance we are likely to encounter in order to achieve our goals. Few people, if any, can shoot from the hip with an action plan. With awareness of the dynamics of the social system, how it pushes and prods us, we can practice defining what we will and will not do and then communicating to the system itself.

Once we grasp the essential insight that the system is ancient and has evolved to react to differences (nothing personal here), most of us can learn to reflect and carefully plan how to alter our position in ongoing relationship interactions. Increasing awareness of relationship dynamics is a golden road, enhancing our leadership skills, in both family and business systems.

Families are the original social system for us worker-bee humans. Whether we see it or not, we are still influenced by the rules of our particular social group. It is hard to erase the early experiences and the sensitivity that goes with such relationships. However, our families are not the only influences we need to understand. We also are quietly, but considerably, influenced by our evolutionary heritage, about which many of us are blind.

The key to increasing our own maturity is to become aware of our family's or workplace's "rules." These are not unlike the rules of the colonies of other species, because they too determine how our mind/brain/body is programmed and modulates our automatic compass. In some ways, we humans are similar to worker bees that automatically respond to specific stimuli and then go about our tasks very contented with our place in the system.

New knowledge can enable us to alter our early programming and sensitivity and to be better able to manage ourselves in groups. As I have noted in other chapters, we begin by carefully observing relationship dynamics. We can keep track of how our social system is wired and how we are programmed to react to any small difference in what our fellow members are doing. The ability to sense changes in the environment and to react automatically is part of our evolutionary heritage and lives in our brains. Our brains are partially formed by genetics, giving us many similar emotional responses like those that regulate other species (fear, flight, freeze, conflict, distance, and giving in).

Our brains are similar to the brains of other mammals living in social groups. Our genetic heritage and the mechanisms of perception and fear are similar to other mammals. Additionally, all mammals are impacted by life experiences that begin during childhood.

Experiences have undue influence on the specific triggers for anxiety and the way we perceive the environment, explains Joseph LeDoux. [18] As he notes, one of the major jobs of our brain is to detect danger and to keep a memory of it available to then compare to our current experiences.

Fear Overloads the Brain, Triggering Repetitive Thoughts and Actions

Unfortunately, the memory of various fear responses can overload the brain, triggering us to think certain thoughts and to form preferred memories. Activating hormones, these fear states penetrate deeply into the brain's circuitry, perpetuating arousal, which can then lead people to live in highly anxious states. These highly aroused states are not correlated with the reality of the current situation.

If our automatic compass stays on high alert, it costs us in terms of our physical and mental well being. In order to live healthier lives, we then have to figure out how to inhibit these fear-based circuits. There are many ways to do this, from the very popular and easy to take prescription drugs, to the harder to do exercise and various forms of meditation or neurofeedback. Whatever way one finds to calm self down, and think carefully about one's challenges, the better for your body and your brain. The goal is to find ways to build resiliency in this over programmed mind/body.

In my coaching practice, people usually come in with the goal of solving some crisis. Often they are frustrated, trying to fix someone else. They lay out the challenges and the reactivity to others. People are often amazed to see how the mutigenerational patterns from the past are impinging on life today. They often get fairly quickly how patterns of reactivity and strength have developed over the generations.

We talk over possibilities of refocusing on what they might do to alter their part of the relationships quandary. They are challenged to think of the family as a social jungle where its members are often operating automatically. In the cognitive bullpen of coaching, anything is possible to consider.

After discussing their circumstances, I hook people up to neurofeedback equipment. The goal is to allow people to integrate what has been talked about and to allow time for the brain itself to find a less aroused state. On the computer screen they can see how the electrical activity in the brain becomes feedback, allowing the brain to learn from its own state. (See http://www.Zengar.com) This mind/body integration of experiences, plus the opportunity to think differently about navigating through the social jungle, all contribute to people being able to take responsibility and alter the way they interact with others. Val Brown, PhD is the genius behind the software and his lifelong effort is to learn from one's brain.

The effort to be different in relationships tends to make people anxious in the short run. Performance anxiety appears as we try out new responses to our very old and often very frustrating predicaments. None of this is personal. It is just that any individual organism or social system "likes" the status quo.

People will put pressure on the members of the group who begin to act differently to resume the correct behavior and fit in with the group. People in groups easily collude to keep things the same.

Often, just two or three people act in unison because they share memories of right and wrong. "All pink pigs are dangerous." This statement then becomes "truth" throughout our social system. These kinds of beliefs and memories can reach far back in time and load (or overload) the system's members with greater sensitivity to one another.[19]

We can see how deeply ingrained the memories of the past can be and how it can influence or even foreshadow the future. We are wired "to act" whenever we perceive even a slight threat due to the brain's wiring.

Reacting fast to the perception of fearful stimuli is what we have in common with other animals. All this reactivity to threat has paid off in all other species and it has for us as well. We have to know who is trying to get us and we have to respond adequately or the struggle for life is over.

Therefore our automatic compass is regulated by the brain's amygdalae (which are found on both sides of the brain), processing our perceptions of fear. You can see in the drawing below how close the hippocampus and the amygdale are. Yet, the amygdale is so much faster than the hippocampus at processing external stimulus.

Flight, flight or freeze reactions occur immediately. The perceptions then go to the hippocampus. This part of the brain compares the fearful perception with memories, often shedding light on the difference, say between a stick and a snake.

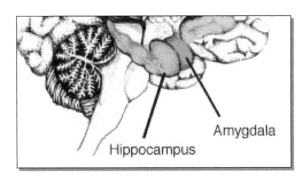

Drawing from "Functional Anatomy of Neural Circuits Regulating Fear and Extinction," Texas A&M Professor of Psychology, Stephen Maren (http://tamutimes.tamu.edu/tag/stephen-maren/)

These amygdalae are the first stop in our brains where we react to fuzzy perceptions of the outside world. The hippocampus can act like a brake, keeping us from over reacting to our perception of patterns that may or may not be a threat.

In this way, the hippocampus keeps the amygdale from hijacking our emotional self. The amygdala is part of the emotional center of the brain's limbic system. It is responsible for regulating fear, aggression, pleasure, and decision-making. [20]

This is not to imply that the structure of the brain controls all of our functioning. Let us consider other research that looks at the power of social systems to influence behavior despite the loss of the amygdale.

Karl Pribram points out in experiments with monkeys that even when the amygdalae were removed, the animals' behavior was still regulated by the way the social group interacted. If the animal, which had his amygdale removed, was greeted as the leader, he would resume his role. But if he were to be met by a more aggressive animal, he would take a lower status. Brain structure does not totally rule behavior. [21]

Research also shows that the brain is influenced by the size of the social group we live in. "We know that primates, who live in larger social groups, have a larger amygdala, even when controlling for overall brain size and body size," says Lisa Feldman Barrett, PhD, of the Massachusetts General Hospital (MGH) Psychiatric Neuroimaging Research Program and a Distinguished Professor of Psychology at Northeastern University, who led the study. "We considered a single primate species, humans, and found that the amygdala volume positively correlated with the size and complexity of social networks in adult humans...the results of the study were consistent with the 'social brain hypothesis,' which suggests that the human amygdala might have evolved partially to deal with an increasingly complex social life."[22]

How the hippocampus recalls past challenges (memories), foreshadows the future. If there is no memory or social group to dampen the automatic triggering as to a perceived threat, the amygdale can go into action. The brain's amygdale does not need to think, it simply responds. And the truth is that we do not always have time to think about our reactions.

Our perceptions or responses are pre-set and we are pre-rigged with many subtle ways of affecting one another's bodies and minds in the "moment." Generally, social interactions are regulated through the amygdale, which work closely with high-level executive structures to regulate emotional processes. So even though many of our perceptions or responses are pre-set and we are pre-rigged to react, our awareness of these mechanisms in our social groups and within ourselves, enables us to inhibit various cues that trigger runaway states of fear.

Recognizing Manipulative Situations. Our responses to others and to situations can be strategic or manipulative. There is a great deal of social science research on how people can be manipulated to think, feel or even buy products. Robert B Cialdini, PhD., in the preface to his book, *Influence: Science and Practice,* notes "In the last 30 years, we have identified, tested and deployed core principles of influence proven to create positive change across organizations and industries. In fact, they are the subtle, yet powerful 'gears' capable of transforming virtually any interaction." The six "principles" are: influence, reciprocation, consistency, social proof (e.g., canned laughter), liking, authority, and scarcity."

There are subtle ways of influencing us to "go along" which we do not recognize as a potential threat. It is easy for us to see a snake as a threat. If we confuse the snake with a stick we can recover from this confusion and calm down. However, if we do not even see a threat (i.e., the six principles Cialdini referenced) then we will be overly influenced by these subtle manipulations.

We are vulnerable beings. Just provide the correct trigger and we are more likely to buy products we do not need or want and be influenced to act automatically in response to a planned stimulus designed to regulate our behavior.

Yet, we are less vulnerable to manipulation within our various social systems and relationships if we understand how we are wired, and then develop a map of where we want to go and use a compass that helps us navigate away from automatic behavioral responses to become more thoughtful and aware.

Because our brains "like" to conserve energy, we have a tendency to operate for long periods of time on automatic pilot or in states of relationship blindness. Our automatic compass has advantages and disadvantages. But how do we stay aware of the state we are in? Each of us is different in terms of our vulnerability to not be aware and to be on automatic and get side swiped. It's best to consider when you tend to go on automatic. When are you mindful or "awake and aware?" When do you have your blinders on, leaving your automatic compass "in charge?" For example, I can notice I am often on automatic when I am listing to people in authority tell me what to do. Having this awareness, I can slowly become more mindful and to some extent alter the automatic response to go along with authority.

Fake it Until You Make It. Of course, to alter one's part in a system is easier said than done. I recall hearing this maxim from Murray Bowen many times, "To gain a basic knowledge of relationship dynamics requires careful observance of self and others, it can take years to be sure of self, *and sometimes you have to fake it till you make it*." Bowen stressed that changing one's role requires a neutral, objective understanding of how social systems operate and of just how sensitive and virtually "wired together" we humans are as both a species and as members of small, social groups.

Our sensitivities, while contributing to our automatic "reactivity," also enable us to learn a tremendous amount from just a few facts. We can impose order on our experiences and gain knowledge of more than just our own experiences. We can construct mental models and communicate this knowledge to future generations. We tell meaningful stories, learning from our lives and the lives of others, to reaffirm and set in motion relationship specific values and beliefs.

Finally, it is possible that through the study of various disciplines we can see how systems operate in the natural world and learn to see the natural processes influencing our lives.

Decisions, Learning and Checklists

It takes time to understand how your automatic compass functions. One way to learn from your own experience is by keeping a journal and then writing or telling your story. (We will hear more about this in Chapter X.) Often people take up journaling in their teenage years. This is the time most young adults are beginning to separate from parents and form friendships on their own.

Taking the time to reflect on who said what, how that made you feel, and what you might do about it, has a long history of being useful for people. Journaling is building awareness. In addition, when you write you do not *have* to get feedback from others. You can be a bit freer to express your confusion, to see where you may have been unduly influenced and/or where you have been stressed and impulsive and made poor decisions.

Writing may help you to be a better observer of relationships. It may help in understanding nature's ways: the importance of the multigenerational family, the influence of our parents, siblings and friends. Journaling is a discipline that can help you become more objective and neutral.

If you apply journaling to your work situation, there too, you can become mindful of sensitivities and repeating patterns. In addition, there are many creative ideas and connections that will be made as you relate to others. The discipline of keeping note of such ideas affords you the opportunity to review what you've learned.

Writing helps us look at situations in a more detached way and keeps us from having too many free-floating thoughts that may not be useful. Taking pen in hand can help to clarify your view of life and it is relatively risk free. A useful way of becoming more mindful and less automatic is to keep a daily decision journal of the *reasons you make decisions*. Or you might develop a checklist for the future that is especially useful when you are under the stress and pressure of the moment.

Pilots and surgeons make excellent use of checklists to avoid automatic non-thinking and inappropriate actions when things go wrong. Atul Gawande, in his book, cites many compelling examples of how checklists help both individuals and teams organize for eventualities and/or work on complex tasks.[23] Being "awake" assumes you know when you are on automatic pilot. Some people focus on being in the now and turning down the stream of thoughts that run through their minds. I think it is deeper than just being present. It requires an ability to understand emotional systems, your part in them, and to then figuring out how to be strategic in order to be one's best Self in the future.

Consider the Mindful Compass as you develop a checklist to help you deal with emotional complexity. Your Mindful Compass combines the wisdom derived from your experiences with a manifesto to continually increase your knowledge. It promotes a way to develop a deep understanding of Self and the pressures you face in the social system.

Ongoing knowledge grows by leaps and bounds. We are never sure how much knowledge can influence the reactive brain. Without discipline, knowledge is probably very superficial and just will not penetrate the brain circuits. After all we are habitual creatures. We prefer comfort to change. However there are pathways to enhance survival too. The human brain is rigged to automatically function for you to survive and prosper during challenging times, but it's also rigged to allow you to develop a toolbox to change Self when required.

John B. (Jack) Calhoun explained how he noticed that animals, who had failed to have positive interactions, would retire to a spot and lie there with eyes open. They appeared to be resting, as though they were calmly considering other alternatives. If the lowly rat can learn to relax and learn from experiences, then there is indeed hope for the human.

We know that under stress or conditions of uncertainty we can go on automatic pilot. However, we can also create an alternative response to dampen our automatic stress response.

It is very possible for anyone to become more disciplined and thereby create new pathways in the brain. This does take practice. (Some research suggests it take three weeks to establish new habits.)

In social systems, establishing a new habit also takes making a plan to deal with the habitual ways that people relate to you which may sustain the habit. People can be critical of your weight or of how you speak or they can react to your attempts to change. All of these social interactions can then make it more difficult to alter self, unless you alter the way you interact with others.

The emotional system is ancient, therefore the tendency to "fuse" with others (or to go along or to rebel) are both behaviors generated by the "togetherness" force, as Bowen called it.

Remember having our lives overly influenced by others is Mother Nature's idea. She loves social systems and the way they can survive over many generations despite the silliness, the greed, the revenge orientation, or just the pure selfishness of some individuals.

Mother Nature also left wiggle room for new adaptations. She just did not make it easy for the new to persevere. The automatic is for individuals in a social system to respond automatically to the cues aimed at controlling our behavior. It is up to aware individuals to risk and thereby to alter the automatic response and to eventually create a new social order.

Systems, Social Roles and Tribes

Our brains are rigged to ignore many of the fundamental facts of relationship dynamics. We are born mostly blind to some subtle relationships cues that control our responsiveness. After all, it was not that important to consider relationships when we lived in very small tribes. Long ago, we roamed the world in tribes consisting of twelve adults and eighteen youngsters. People were required to be alert for the things that threatened survival but functioning as a group was a positive back then.

Most of the energy was devoted to figuring out if the person was one of "us" or "them." Now, we have more than basic survival needs to shape alliances. In the course of building alliances over thousands of years, we have become so reactive to one another that divorce, cut off and autism are increasing. Our ability to participate in complex interactions seems to be decreasing. We text, we tweet and we no longer write handwritten letters that go on for pages.

Who has time to explain in a text or tweet our reasons for this or that? The presidential candidates are limited to three minutes. The Lincoln-Douglas debates are part of a historical era when we the people wanted to know how deeply people thought. We no longer even spend time writing our observations of the birds in the trees and the sounds of nature that so used to beguile us. All of these changes change the brain.

Although we no longer live in one tribe, many high functioning people do belong to twelve social systems. Jack Calhoun thought that belonging to

111

twelve tribes or social systems was essential to survival in the increasing density that seven to nine billion people on the planet might demand.

Under conditions of higher density we relate differently. It's not all bad. It's just different. It's too early to know just what will help us to maintain ourselves in the coming transitions.

Twitter helps us to communicate instantly with those who are half way around the globe. We may find it easier to have more "gratifying" (but superficial and less open) relationships with a faraway tribe member than with the ones close to us..

Now people can people can be more superficial than when they lived in tribes because there's no daily face-to-face interaction in which people can take a reading of the whole person and how they are doing in relationship to others in the tribe.

The risk of being rejected in all twelve systems or by all twelve people is low. There is usually a balance between those systems where we are held in high regard and those where we may find frustration. As long as the seesaw of frustrating and gratifying relationships remains about 50-50 we are learning and we feel deeply appreciated. A balance of frustration and gratification provides learning, challenges and an opportunity to relax and feel secure.

Brain Changes Over Time. Changing conditions have influenced the brain over long periods of time. Jerome Smaers, Ph.D. researched seventeen species over forty million years and noted, "Over evolutionary time, several key brain regions increased in size relative to other regions. Great apes (especially humans) saw a rise in white matter in the prefrontal cortex, which contributes to social cognition, moral judgments, introspection and goal-directed planning.

The white matter carries axons, the wires connecting different brain cells, suggesting that that the great apes' brains were evolving for greater neural connections. When great apes diverged from old-world monkeys about 20 million years ago, brain regions tied to motor planning also increased in relative size. That could have helped them orchestrate the complex movements needed to manipulate tools, possibly to get at different food sources."[24]

John M. Allman, a neuroscientist at the California Institute of Technology, is a well-recognized expert on primates, cognition, and evolutionary neuroscience. He has speculated that the pressure to cope with the larger relationship system may have been responsible for the human brain producing a larger forebrain where executive or decision-making functioning is found. There is a correlation between brain size and social groups and more decisions have to be made in complex social groups as to whom to trust and how to cooperate.

Allman focuses on three themes:

1. The primary role of brains is to deal with environmental variation; therefore sensory awareness is extremely important.

2. Every evolutionary advance in the nervous system is costly.

3. The development of the brain is dependent on the establishment of the human family as a social and reproductive unit.

You may not know that the human brain has become 20 percent smaller. Allman asks an intriguing question, "Why has the human brain become smaller in the past 20,000 to 35,000 years?" His answer, "The domestication of plants and animals as sources of food and clothing served as major buffers against environmental variability. Perhaps humans, through the invention of agriculture and other cultural means for reducing the hazards of existence, have domesticated themselves."[25]

Our social life has changed. We no longer need a large brain to manage the primitive environment; instead we need to manage relationships. Navigating complex relationship systems requires more knowledge and skill than our ancestors may have had to employ when there were only a few thousand people wandering the earth.

Our *cause-and-effect brains* are comfortable with stories giving us simple answers, shortcuts and solutions. These short cuts probably worked very well for our ancestors thousands of years ago. So we see the brain is oriented to find a quick solution and then conserve energy and relax. Therefore, it is so very hard to seek out or even accept complexity, as it requires us to go against the grain and work harder. The brain has an automatic command that says, "Please conserve energy and accept the simple, quick solution."

It's a fact that we don't live in a linear, cause-and-effect world where problems are simple and causes are easy to identify. Instead, we are being forced to make our brain function in this complex, multi-factor universe.

No wonder we can get stressed and burn out. The problems we confront today are increasingly complex. We are under the delusion of cause and effect thinking and we can't easily flip the switch in our brains to think systems.

There are many brain-training programs available now to help us see more than one variable at a time. It may seem paradoxical, but it just may be that by embracing the complexity of our social lives, via a deep awareness of social interactions, we can also increase our ability to gracefully handle complexity.

Social Systems and the Research of Jack Calhoun

John B. Calhoun (1917–1995) was a famous ethologist and experimental psychologist at the Nation Institute of Health. He developed a theory on crowding and the stress endured by the rodents he studied. This research caught the public imagination in the 1970s as people were highly invested in understanding the ability of the earth to sustain an exponentially growing human population.

Calhoun coined the term "behavioral sink" to describe aberrant behaviors in overcrowded population density situations and "beautiful ones" to describe passive individuals who withdrew from all social interaction. His work gained world recognition. Calhoun saw the fate of the population of mice as a metaphor for the potential fate of man. He characterized the social breakdown as a "second death," with reference to the "second death" mentioned in the Biblical book of Revelation 2:11 His study has been cited by writers such as Bill Perkins as a warning of the dangers of the living in an increasingly crowded and impersonal world.

Calhoun believed that his research provided clues to the future of mankind as well as ways to avoid a looming disaster. During the 1960s, he and Dr. Leonard Duhl formed an informal group, the Space Cadets, which met to discuss the social uses of space. The members of this group came from professions as diverse as architecture, city planning, physics, and psychiatry.

In Calhoun's own words:

"Our success in being human has so far derived from our honoring deviance more than tradition. Template changing always has gained a slight, though often tenuous, lead over template obeying. Now we must search diligently for those creative deviants from which, alone, will come the conceptualization of an evolutionary designing process. This can assure us an open-ended future toward whose realization we can participate."[26]

Among his many findings, Calhoun noted that if you taught animals to "cooperate" or to "dis-cooperate" in order to get water, they seem to become more aware of the interactions with others and had less pathology. This rat colony was then able to tolerate eight times the crowding, compared to untrained colonies.

These experiments were continued for several more decades and Calhoun continued to write on the implications for humans.

One of the implications was that animals, which were trained to become aware of others, were also more creative, in spite of increasing stress from random interactions. Another of the implications for the human was that biological reproduction would be replaced by creative acts so that the numbers of human on the planet would stabilize and then decrease.

In 2008, Dr. Edmund Ramsden, a medical historian noted, "Not all of Calhoun's rats had gone berserk. Those who managed to control space led relatively normal lives."
[http://nihrecord.nih.gov/newsletters/2008/07_25_2008/story1.htm]

Striking the right balance between privacy and community would reduce social pathology. It was the unwanted, unavoidable social interaction that drove even fairly social creatures mad.

What is it about social interactions that can drive animals and humans mad? Calhoun saw that if a "non-cooperative" trained animal accidentally got into the "cooperative" pen he would refuse to notice that the rules for obtaining water had changed. The rat still had the ability to notice others. He or she was not autistic, but a rule that was basic to survival—how to obtain water—changed in a way that the animal could not understand. Some have suggested that the rule about how to get water was similar to an ethical command.

Research has shown that in schizophrenia, there is no ability to adapt to changing rules. What the rat observed other animals do, made no impact on this rat, which had a different "rule" to follow in obtaining water.

No matter how many rats he saw marching two-by-two to get water, this animal refused to change. If another animal approached him to help him get water, he would bite them. There were endless fights as the "cooperative" rats tried to maintain the old rules in their group and the "non cooperative" rat tried to maintain his old rules, and neither could see that the difference in rules was making it impossible to cooperate.

In 1960, Heinz von Forester published a paper in Science, "Doomsday Friday, 13 November AD 2026," noting how the world was entering a unique and ultimately transformational crises in which humanity would either change for the better, (which he called, Dawnsday) or lose the ability to notice, cooperate, and or care about the environment and others, (which he called Doomsday.)

Both Calhoun and von Forester predicted the challenge around the stabilization of the population, the challenges moving from the current seven billion people to a possible stabilization of eight or nine billion. Calhoun was able to provoke a culture of increasing awareness for rodents, thus increasing their chances of survival. The question is, can we maintain the big picture of the human's impact on planet earth, and solve complex problems for our species?

As we understand more about how out triune brain (the reptilian, the mammalian and the neomammalian) functions, we will be better able to integrate knowledge of the past with a more ration view of problem solving, especially in our close up and personal relationships. Much depends on our ability to recognize, instinctive and automatic behaviors and to moderate the influence of reactivity mindfully.

Paul MacLean (pictured below) was a devoted researcher and first to identify an outline of the triune brain. His work reminds us we are a living part of evolution with the need to survive and the push for short-term solutions, which are often traps. He highlighted our ability to be playful and to care for others, as we wisely use language to knowingly make our way through the social jungle.

Murray Bowen with Paul MacLean

CHAPTER IX
THE RISE OF SYSTEMS THINKING IN THE SOCIAL SCIENCES

Complexity and the Social Sciences

Social systems and relationship dynamics cannot be understood by cause and effect thinking, as they are influenced by many variables. Complexity theory and chaos theory (dynamical systems that are highly sensitive to initial conditions and are non-deterministic) are theories that have been useful in understanding various kinds of systems that operate far from equilibrium. One day they may be useful in understanding the human. So far, we do not have a perfect enough understanding of social relationships, which tilt us this way and that, to measure social relationships in any predictable way.

We are buffeted by the winds of various influences and a changing environment. The weather changes, the basement floods, the bills arrive, the mother-in-law visits, the son wants nothing to do with the father, the boss has a migraine and is getting divorced and all of a sudden, you have complex problems that no simple solution can fix. Multiple variables make it tricky to find simple explanations and quick solutions. In addition, our brains often use memory to evaluate the reason that any of these events are important, dangerous or worth ignoring.

Michael Mauboussin is currently the head of the board for the Santa Fe Institute in New Mexico. (Note that he is my son-in-law.) He has written four books, the last one clarifying his interest in decision-making in complex areas like sports, business and investing. Each of us has an interest in understanding social research about how the human brain is set up to perceive the environment, and how that then influences decision-making.

We humans are prejudiced and can easily be blindsided by innocent or manipulative stories parading as facts. Mauboussin has been considering what one might do to overcome our short cuts and prejudices. We can see the process involved in decision-making but we are never able to predict exactly what might occur when it comes to living systems. In his latest book, Mauboussin notes, "You should be very skeptical of anyone who claims to be able to predict results whenever social influence is a factor."[27]

Murray Gell-Mann, a Nobel Prize winning physicist and the founder of and a Distinguished Fellow at the Santa Fe Institute, says that we all live in a bubbling sea of nonlinear systems dynamics. Here a child learns a language in a similar way to how bacteria learn to adapt and to build a resistance to drugs. [28]

Yet, there is tremendous resistance to seeing this brave new world. Despite our being aware of the need to control population size and to preserve biological and cultural diversity, there is clearly a challenge, he notes, to establishing a multidisciplinary research agenda in order to formulate a sustainable future for the human race and the earth itself. Cause and effect still predominates the research world. Sometimes it appears that life changes are being "caused" but, truth be told, they are unfolding. After the fact then, we tell stories to make it seem that we predicted and understood the unfolding, because that is how our brains work.

Chaos theory takes us beyond cause and effect to see how many factors are invoked in change. James Gleick traces the ideas of Mitchell Feigenbaum and his "Butterfly Effect."[29] Gleick explains that simple events, like the fluttering of a butterfly in some obscure garden, can create mighty and unpredictable effects in a living system, such as ours. In nonlinear systems, small effects become magnified in unimaginable ways. Therefore, our job is to keep our brain open to the new, the unusual and the complexity in all its various forms.

One way we can do this is to keep an open, questioning mind. There are many factors that can influence a situation. We are prone to see cause and effect and then close our mind to other variables.

There are situations that can be measured which are only slightly impacted by other variables. For example, we can measure the speed of a falling apple but not the path of, or how to prevent the destruction of a hurricane. If the apple falls during a hurricane it becomes more difficult to predict. There are so many more variables at play when it comes to looking at our own life or that of others. To understand the trajectory of our lives and what can alter a life course, we must await a multi-factorial research paradigm.

Seeing the Consequence of Short-Sighted Thinking

It is frustrating to be able to recognize trends but not predict them; to see possibilities and not certainties when it comes to predicting the future. Unfortunately, there is no certainty in predicting the specific direction of a living system. A good example of just how dangerous such predictions are is that we convert guesses into rules. Cause and effect thinking guided people's actions as Hurricane Katrina was pressing towards New Orleans.

Based on their past experiences, many people living on the Gulf Coast thought it would be possible to ride out that terrible storm. Some thought it might even be fun to stay and watch Mother Nature's show. Still others thought it would be easy to escape at the last minute if need be. Simple "if this, then that" solutions were dominant.

No jazz was playing in the background as, day after day, wrong-headed, short-term thinking led to a grim reality. Remember the problems with rules that are not flexible and do not fit the situation? Remember the clogged roads going out of the city while the other side of the road was empty? Recall the pictures of buses lined up to take people out of the city but no drivers for those buses. Remember those trailers that lacked proper paper work? People in New Orleans desperately needed places to stay. But the local system could not adapt to the solution offered by Federal officials. The trailers would spend endless months in Kansas waiting for permits to go to New Orleans—where trailers are not allowed! How long did it take to understand the realities of the event even as we watched much of the chaos unfold on television?

Hurricane Katrina is a good lesson in how living systems really operate, not necessarily how we wish they operated. It's not simple to predict the future.

The lesson for us all is that the past does not always predict the future and as it turned out, it was not so easy in the "Big Easy."

This is just one example of the catastrophic consequences of applying short-term, cause and effect thinking to an impending challenge. We all have some access to a "bubbling sea" of systems information, but our tendency towards cause and effect thinking influences (in this case negatively) our ability to anticipate and respond realistically to the potential challenges that are likely to occur.

Cause and effect thinking was a term often used by Bowen to show how people look for simple answers and are unaware of a systems view. Cause and effect thinkers say a hurricane is coming and so we will do what we have done in the past. Stress increases, so the tendency to search for a "cause" and a "fix" is automatic. Under these stressful conditions, one's focus narrows to simple answers that maintain the status quo, e.g., "Let's stick this one out. That hasn't been a problem in the past." People behave as though they completely understand what they're up against.

Even though Hurricane Katrina was far larger than any other hurricane to hit New Orleans in recent memory, no new ideas or well-thought-out contingency plans were considered by either government agencies and/or individuals living in the area. The mechanisms in the brain that are activated under stress led to an increasingly narrow focus and, at the same time, eliminated the ability to think and plan for the unexpected.

What would happen if people were aware that when they encounter a new type of threat the relationship between factors has to be considered anew? If bus drivers do not show up, then the plans we made to transport people will not work. Trailers are one solution to housing people who've lost their homes, but not if such housing is not permitted in the area. A failure in one part of the system does not lead to the catastrophe. Rather, it is the complexity of many factors and a constantly changing environment that requires leaders to provide the broader view. They can then help ensure that the social system knows that it is dealing with possible system-wide failure and find the energy (and mindfulness) to deal more effectively with the challenges it faces.

Cause and effect thinking is useful and works well in many short-term situations. For example, you think, "I cut myself. I need a bandage." In this case, the cause is known and the solution found. But when there are unusual events or big challenges, cause and effect thinking often ignores important variables and offers no way to alter the rigidity of the way the system operates at the individual and group levels.

The more complex a situation, the more difficult it is to grasp the nature of the challenge and come up with realistic and useful interventions that can make a constructive difference. Cause and effect thinking, which has been the dominant way of marching science forward, leaves us with unreliable data for solving problems that are a function of multiple variables interacting in surprising ways.

In our desire to reduce the "pain" of the challenge or the ambiguity about the "best" solution, we can easily overlook many variables that might allow us to see and influence or even solve the problem. If we could see how the whole system operates, just for a moment, we could get beyond short-term thinking, finger pointing and blame and perhaps see how one event or decision will have multiple effects, triggering many changes. We are more likely to come up with solid plans for dealing with challenges if we are better able to see the "whole picture."

There are many other examples of the results of short-term, cause and effect thinking. Take a look at your newspaper's financial section. Since 2006, we have watched human nature lead us over financial cliffs. Looking back, some of the decisions that led to the financial crisis were based on absurd predictions about the future, for example, that houses "will never lose value" or that the financial houses on Wall Street would never do anything that they didn't understand and jeopardize their financial stability.

How hard it is for us to learn from the past by using "logic" in the face of greed, herd behavior and overly simplistic thinking? It seems that with hindsight, people were guided by fanciful thinking with regard to Hurricane Katrina and the financial crisis. Some call it delusional thinking. However, it may be more accurate to see how ordinary it is for those guided by beliefs (such as a simple cause and effect world view) to ignore complexity in systems, which was at the root of these failures.

Philip Zimbardo – Can You Be a Sweet Pickle in a Vinegar Jar?

We are all vulnerable to the allure of short-term comfort at the expense of ignoring the longer term consequences of behavior. One of the most shocking pieces of research about delusion and the impact of the social system on our functioning is Philip Zimbardo's Stanford Prison experiment. To discover how Hitler convinced normal people to behave in cruel ways, twenty-four "normal" students were randomly assigned to be either guards or prisoners. The experiment, conducted for five days, resulted in the abuse and humiliation of prisoners by guards. Yet, even the researchers, who were involved in evaluating the program, could not "see" what was going on.

Philip Zimbardo confesses that he was blinded by his focus on the short term and his over involvement with his research. These are common blind spots for us humans.

Zimbardo said, in an interview, posted on a Stanford web site, "I wondered, along with my research associates Craig Haney, Curtis Banks and Carlo Prescott, what would happen if we aggregated all of these processes, making some subjects feel de-individuated, others dehumanized within an anonymous environment in the same experimental setting, and where we could carefully document the process over time. . ."

"Maslach, [then Zimbardo's girlfriend, now wife] walked into the mock prison on the evening of the fifth day. Having just received her doctorate from Stanford and starting an assistant professorship at Berkeley, she had agreed to do subject interviews the next day and had come down the night before to familiarize herself with the experiment. At first, she said, she found it 'dull and boring' . . . Later that evening, Maslach said, she suddenly got sick to her stomach while watching guards taking the prisoners with paper bags over their heads to the bathroom before their bedtime. Her fellow researchers teased her about it. After leaving the prison with Zimbardo, she said, he asked her what she thought of it. 'I think he expected some sort of great intellectual discussion about what was going on. Instead, I started to have this incredible emotional outburst. I started to scream, I started to yell 'I think it is terrible what you are doing to those boys!' I cried. 'We had a fight you wouldn't believe, and I was beginning to think, wait a minute, I don't know this guy. I really don't, and I am getting involved with him?'

Zimbardo was shocked by her reaction and upset, she said, but eventually that night, 'he acknowledged what I was saying and realized what had happened to him and to other people in the study. At that point he decided to call the experiment to a halt.' Says Zimbardo: 'She challenged us to examine the madness she observed, that we had created and had to take responsibility for.'"[30]

We are all vulnerable to being blinded by our investment in our own way of doing things. We are caught up in the moment and want something, so we may no longer be able to override our "instincts" to proceed, even though we know our actions may not be the moral, honorable or simply the right thing to do. Lying to your mother (which is sure to be discovered and punished in the long run), or cheating on your spouse (seriously not good for a long-term relationship) are just two examples of short-term "gain" with the potential cost of long-term loss.

There will always be a conflict between short- and long-term goals. But those who think for the long-term have a decidedly adaptive advantage if they plan to stay in the same set of relationships for a while. Mature leaders are able to see the big picture and to postpone gratification. They are not seduced by short-term rewards.

Are such leaders born with this maturity? There is research showing that young children, who can postpone gratification, can be identified. And, this social skill can be taught, benefiting children's ability to manage stress and frustration and to do better in life.

The so called "marshmallow test"[31] research has followed these children for more than twenty years. It demonstrates that children who could delay gratification found success in life as they matured and developed. It is clear that some individuals cultivate the ability to see the long-term outcome or the big picture and alter their automatic, short-term behavior to improve that outcome. I believe it's possible to learn and change.

The fundamental question is this, how do we prepare our brains to see differently—to see the big picture—so that we can function effectively despite the stress we encounter as to the ways that both our brains and society are oriented towards short-term results?

Relationship Blinders and the Development of "My" World View

All of us have mental models of how relationships work, formed by our experiences and beliefs. But how accurate are those models and how do they influence the way we "see" the world around us? Although difficult, it is possible to change our current, inaccurate mental models of how the world functions. We not only have the ability to do it, it is to our advantage to do so.

If we can recognize that our brains have serious problems with loyalty (fusion leading to confusion) and, as noted above, over-rewards us for short-term gain, then bringing into awareness your doubts and seriously questioning your preferred way of believing and operating can be a fabulous discipline and is sure to increase your maturity.

Most of us no longer believe the earth is flat. Because so many people once did, we know that we are continually at risk of accepting beliefs that limit our ability to solve problems. The human tendency is to accept the status quo, just as we did when we were young, without questioning, thinking carefully or analyzing facts. But most of us have been to the school of life and have been challenged to think critically.

Remember Katrina and the recent financial crisis. The pressure is virtually on each day to solve more and more complex problems. We have to adapt to this reality. To do that, we need to loosen up our brains. We need to take off the relationship blinders designed only to see the status quo because those blinders limit our ability to see the big picture.

It is very hard to see beyond cultural norms or the quiet authority of family (or even bosses at work). Mother Nature gave us these relationship blinders for a good reason. So before you commit to removing them, remember that "seeing" can be costly because these blinders can save us from expending too much energy.

Blinders allow us to be on automatic pilot for mundane tasks so that we don't spend our lives in endless states of hyper-alert, hyper-awareness, always on the lookout for danger, always trying to find solutions to the problems we see. But it is useful to take off the blinders once in a while to see the beauty of complexity, habits, subtle connections, and the dominant influence of relationship processes on how we function. Taking off our blinders does not have to be a full-time effort.

By recognizing the traps of hypervigilance or blindness, we are a bit freer to focus on what is useful and productive. If you find yourself blaming an individual for a problem, that is a sign that you have your blinders on. In reality, one person is almost never the "cause" of anything. Taking off your blinders can allow you to see the interaction of many different and seemingly unconnected parts of a system.

Where are the Set Points on My Automatic Compass?

To give yourself some preliminary perspective on how you operate as a leader in a social system, and what influences you, ask yourself a few questions:

1. To what extent are the positions I take based on emotional, feeling-based reactions to people and events in my social systems?

2. Do I have principles that I can stick with even when the people I love oppose me?

3. When people are upset with me, can I relate to all the different factions in my group without taking sides with any one individual or any one faction?

4. Can I describe the play that I am in and the role that I have been assigned?

5. Can I talk to people about the roles they seem to be playing in this social system?

Question three deserves a bit of explanation.

If you are like me, you have spent much more time taking various people's sides and listening to gossip than you have spent trying to be a separate individual analyzing the situation from outside the fray.

The fact is that most people are not overly fond of a person who does not seem, at least for a moment or two, to take their side.

Over the long term you may learn, as I did, that taking sides results in increasing emotional intensity in the group. It comes without the benefit of a solution and does not help you adapt well to greater complexity. But, it is easy to do and has a lot of short-term rewards like love and approval.

On the other hand, refusing to takes sides also increases the tension in a group and it leaves you out in the cold. However, standing alone makes you a far better observer, which in turn makes you a better problem solver.

When you stand alone you are not subject to the intense pulls that come with needing to accept others' viewpoints just to reduce the tension. Additionally, when you stand alone you have the added benefit of watching how the rest of the group adapts, because you are not overly involved in helping them make the right decisions. You are able to be more open and allow others to be more open. This is the biggest pay off, as it allows people to grow away from one another via tuning down fear- and dependence-based reactivity and opening up to greater respect and even compassion towards one another.

Most of us, who take sides, do so based on office gossip or what we hear in our family or social systems. Inevitably, this means that we side with the people we need the most, because we are loyal or perhaps fearful of upsetting them and they are the easiest to believe.

Going along with others seems to be part of nature's automatic programming for our very social species. We find quick ways to know who to be close to and who to avoid. But those of you who want to be mature leaders will look at this blind spot (you can call it social preference) and select observational and factual knowledge over automatic alignments (togetherness) in our systems.

Hopefully, it will not be that hard for you to become aware of the emotional gossip that runs through the system, and to find some way to stand alone, while still relating to one and all. Developing the knowledge about how your social systems are full of sensitive people allows you to see how people are naturally wired to align with one another.

People agree with friends and doubt the ones they have had a negative relationship with. Relationships have a hard time orientating to facts. Some say that anything my friend says is a fact.

Seeing how the unfolding of triangles leads to alliances based on feelings is a vital component of increasing your leadership skills. This awareness of managing self in triangles, when you run into blocks, is very basic to moving your ideas forward in any social group.

Questions to Ask Yourself When You Are in the Process of Making Decisions

1. What are the rewards for going in this or that direction?

2. Who will oppose me and for what reasons?

3. Where can I build alliances?

4. What are the incentives for making this change?

5. Have I carefully thought through the consequences, even if this decision entails minor risk?

What Does It Take To *See* Relationship Alliances?

Awareness of relationship processes allows us to develop the four points on our Mindful Compass. Before we begin to change ourselves, we have to challenge our way of thinking and behaving and find ways to keep track of relationship alliances, decisions and our overall way of seeing. After all, it is our current way of seeing and believing that influences how we act. As instinctive animals, our automatic compass is fine tuned to react to others. Understanding how the brain has been sensitized by experience allows us to unlock the holds and habits of the past. If we can do this, the old story of how we understand our lives is very likely to change.

We will ask better questions and explore broad areas of knowledge, increasing our potential to grow. Just as those who participated in preparing the city of New Orleans for Katrina, or those involved in decision-making around the financial crises are hopefully reexamining the facts and the way they made decisions, we too can learn by seeing how they were unable to think about the complex variables in the system. Hopefully, by taking more factors into consideration when making future decisions, the short-term thinking of the past will provide a lesson for the future.

Trying to find the *one* cause for problems may decline and be seen as a seductive, but a maladaptive response to complex problems. Some people are born with the ability to endure frustration and postpone gratification, but we can also learn these skills. The social systems we live in shape our roles and our destiny. Therefore, it is important that each individual learn how to manage the automatic self in social systems rather than be defined by the systems, as was the case with the participants in the Stanford prison experiment.

By enlarging our worldview to embrace multiple factors as beautiful and not so bewildering, we will be able to see ancient patterns as they arise in a social system, influencing the behavior of the social group. The best that can happen is that one or two individuals begin to see differently and define a better way to do things. Little by little, those who are more aware may take on leadership roles in the social system and the level of maturity will rise.

Courageous leaders face impersonal forces that assign people to play out various roles that are not useful in cooperating and work to solve real problems.

People are sensitive and can be easily swept up by the automatic way the system has been organized. By simply observing the system, individuals can increase their freedom to act and think more broadly about the way systems function.

Emotional systems are impersonal and with real effort we can be different in them. Systems thinking give us more choices. In this brave new world there is no one to blame, there are no simple solutions, but many ways to be observant and creative in our responses.

CHAPTER X
WRITING YOUR STORY: LEARNING AND REFLECTING

Changing Self in Relationships Systems: Decreasing Sensitivity, Increasing the Immune Response

As a leader, changing yourself to deal with problems or any challenges is the way to influence and lead others. Nowhere to look, no one to blame, just listening, understanding the complexity within the social jungle and using one's best Self throughout the various relationship systems. This is the royal road to wisdom.

To be able to lead from a more mindful position a leader must not be overly sensitive to and, therefore limited by, the shadows from the past. The bottom line is that to change yourself, you will want to increase your knowledge of yourself, your family and the other important social systems around you.

This is not necessarily an easy task since most of us are blindsided and held captive by social systems that have all kinds of rules and beliefs about how we are to behave. In addition, people are saddled with complex feelings— real and imaginary memories about old relationships. These feelings and memories make it difficult to relate without "agendas" in the here and now.

Those who tell a story about their life and are able to be more objective and reflective or even put a positive spin on events, tend to function better. James Pennebaker researched how journaling strengthened immune cells, (T-lymphocytes). Apparently writing about stressful events helps us to reduce the impact of stressors on our physical health. [32]

Common stressors are control issues within the nuclear family. For example, people are told by family members not to have anything to do with certain individuals in the extended family. They are encouraged to stay home and remain in the usual nuclear family relationship mix. Visits outside the nuclear family to aunts, uncles or even grandparents can be seen as threatening. There are loyalty issues that might "rock the boat." Many families set limits about contact with the larger family and devote themselves to the nuclear family. Taking time to get to know extended family members rather than going on a golfing vacation is considered odd.

If you are willing to undertake the task of building family relationships or even go further and explore your family roots, you are going against the norm. If your leadership planning takes you even further, to the step of writing up your experience, you may find criticism awaiting you. Your spouse can say, "Those people are jerks. What have they ever done for you?"

If you think it's important to deeply understand how social systems function and influence you, you might be willing to take on the effort of enlarging your relationship base and possibly altering your biases and perhaps even increasing your flexibility in many relationships. If you think this is important then you are operating on principle to take an action.

How you go about altering your stance towards family members or others can take many different pathways. The important thing is that you are acting on a rational, defined principle. As you create new levels of knowledge about family history and increase the number of people you relate to in your family, you will have more people to challenge or perhaps nurture you.

Both the family history and the depth of relationships will be carried into the future. These people will be with you for generations. Your ability to know them can impact future generations.

From Rumor to Facts: Knowledge of Your Family Can Shock You

Knowledge about our family roots is often disparaged, but the past can teach us about the possibilities and we can guess just how the future might be influenced by the past. Building family relationships is an adventure that may overturn some of your most cherished beliefs. For example, my family would speak of one branch of the family as "those poor Irish." You know, the ones who had been more or less done in by the "mean English." They were the ones who were brave enough to flee during the potato famine.

However, as I was digging into the family roots, I found that one of the families in this "poor Irish" family line was named Brabazon. A funny name for an Irishman one would say, and yes, I discovered that they were not really Irish. They had migrated in 1660 to capture Ireland for the English, under orders from Henry VIII, taking the land from the Irish.

Clearly, I was part of the so-called "mean English" family.

This family history both upset old prejudices and beliefs and led to my going to a family reunion in Ireland where I was able to meet many new family members, increasing my adaptability and decreasing my prejudices.

It is difficult to have the motivation to go back into the past unless you can see how knowing more about your family roots can help give you perspective, resiliency, and an ability to think more broadly. I call this a workout, where you are going to "the multigenerational emotional gym."

One can know that family relationships are the most challenging and the easiest to ignore, and choose to stay within the confines of the past ways of relating. Or, a few brave people can seek new knowledge and a richer, more varied relationship system. I encourage the brave to learn more about their own family.

It seems that people, who reach out to the extended family and take this effort seriously, have fewer marital and child-focused problems. People say the effort produces greater neutrality about how they think and feel about others.

If getting to know your extended family seems overwhelming, it is understandable. People have many objections and problems looking at personal relationships. Remember, we are not supposed to see relationships and their influence on us. As someone once told me, after I made this suggestion, "I am here to learn more about my role, as a husband and father. I am not here to learn how to upset the apple cart. It makes no sense that getting to know my extended family will ever influence my child, marriage, business problem, etc."

I responded with a metaphor. "A strong root system can stabilize a tree when the storms come. Cutting off the roots may never be noticed till the storms come."

This man told me, "I am not a tree." After this reaction he paused, and looked outside the window perhaps eyeing the trees. "Well," he said, "Perhaps I could begin by trying to understand my friends and gradually work up to consider just who were my great grandparents."

So I said "OK, you can start anywhere." He began by picking five friends who had played significant roles in his life and had influenced him to change in some way. His goal was to write up his memories and then give it to each of them to see how he could manage the reactions they had as to his viewpoint.

Does it sound like a lot of trouble to grow a root system and to alter one's natural proclivity to focus on what is wrong with the spouse and the kids? The goal here is to build awareness of relationships and the pressure we put on one another. Eventually, he might get interested in how this pressure exists in his multigenerational family.

No one has to start with the extended family. My coaching was to promote awareness and ask this man, who was suffering, to try writing about a relationship with anyone who is important to him and see what might be learned.

If people are willing to open up and talk to or show others, it's one way to build more of an emotional backbone. To some extent, it lets people know what you really think and asks you to accept and not react to others' ideas.

There are many reasons to do this exercise. One is to learn how to reflect on the ways that relationships have influenced you. Remember that the periods of fruitful growth (times when you were able to advance your goals or ideas) and those of necessary retreat (when you felt overwhelmed by the odds against you) are equally significant. Who were the people in your life who made a significant difference at those times?

Choose Five Important People to Write About

It is an adventure to write a brief summary of your relationships with the five people you choose. The stories might involve a difficult challenge, an opportunity, or simply your efforts to negotiate a particular role within a system. Every name will connect you to a story, something you heard or saw, something that someone said or did that affected you in a positive or negative way. It may have been a parent, a teacher, a friend or even an enemy, who (perhaps unwittingly) taught you to think or act differently. Little by little, as you tell yourself these stories, you will be describing the emotional forces that influenced you in the past and continue to influence you today.

You might write about a conflict in which you remember making a breakthrough change in the way you deal with people. Remember, it's not always what happened to you that is important, but how you respond that makes the difference. Whatever the experience, reflection and awareness are the keys to profiting from it.

If you find this task somewhat daunting, encourage yourself by remembering that once you have formulated your stories and have seen afresh how you reacted to others during times of challenge and growth, you will have a better idea of how you became who you are today.

You will see how those individuals, and your interactions with them, helped shape the way you react to events now. This newly heightened knowledge of yourself will enable you to make any needed changes as you begin to rely more on your personal and proven strengths of which you are now more aware.

Six Questions and an Example From My Life Story

The following is an example from my own life. I've built my story around five questions that helped me to focus on the importance of specific relationships in my life.

1. Was there confusion or conflict that led you into a relationship with someone who became important to you as a young adult?

My parents reunited after WWII. They coped with my father's post-traumatic stress by drinking. He had been on the intelligence staff of Curtis LeMay and had participated in the fire bombings of Japan's civilian population. One night my parents were both drunk, caused a disturbance in the neighborhood and were arrested. At the age of nine, my two younger brothers, ages seven and almost two, were sent with me to an orphanage for three days. We were rescued and eventually adopted by my well-off, responsible, but not-very-aware-of-psychological-issues maternal grandparents.

I think about what my parents were up against in their era. Who among us might have done better? The way they managed anxiety was very ordinary. There was comfort and safety with my grandparents. There was no talk of my parents. There was worry about our behavior and attempts to fix problems with the boys. I was, so far, the helpful older sister.

When I was fourteen, I was sent away to boarding school, Georgetown Visitation Preparatory School in Washington, D.C. At first, I had separation anxiety and was confused. I knew no one. I did not know what was expected of me or how I might survive in a completely different system than that of my family.

One morning, a nun, Sister Mary de Sales, came into my room. She said she had a dream that I was going to be the best athlete in the school. I asked her how she knew such a thing and she said she had seen me playing kickball the night before. I asked her what I had to do to become the best athlete. She told me to try out for the various varsity teams and win the tennis competition.

That was the beginning of my quest. I did not get best athlete award my first year there, but by the end of high school I had achieved the overall best record for any student athlete during the four years. Having an important person in the social system who could see that I had potential and was willing to support me and encourage me to work hard, reinforced what I loved to do.

2. How did this relationship help you to build on your strengths (and perhaps decrease your annoyance with your own foibles)?

Sister Mary de Sales actually played sports herself and would coach me in kickball. She helped me laugh at my shortcomings (especially spelling and grammar) and encouraged my strengths (athletics and humor) to persevere. We would have talks and she proved to be someone with whom I could communicate about a wide variety of things. She had a great deal of patience to explain things to me and best of all was not upset with me in the areas where I struggled.

If I had a problem, such as not being able to learn Spanish she would say, "You are smart and work hard. I know it is frustrating not to be good at everything but that is a small problem that summer school will solve." In addition, we were both terrible spellers. In my senior year, as president of the athletic association, we had to make signs advertising a marshmallow roast and, of course, they were all misspelled. My classmates and Sister Mary de Sales still laugh about our common foibles.

3. How did this person enable or encourage your desire to change for the better?

Sister Mary de Sales was the faculty representative to the athletics department on campus. She came to all the games and gave me realistic feedback on my performance. I saw what Sister Mary de Sales had done to help me and others function at our best. Because she was a prominent person on campus, my peers noticed her encouragement and belief in me. I felt responsible for doing and being my best because of her public belief in me. And because she was funny, that encouraged me to be funny. One year I was elected the class clown. Both of us laughed about that.

4. Were you able to incorporate your new behavior into a leadership position in your group?

As a teenager, having someone, who believed in me, motivated me to put in the extra effort to be better. The people in my class noticed the effort and liked my sense of humor. I was willing to help others like Sister Mary de Sales had helped me. I went early to practice and stayed late. By working hard, others in the group noticed what I was doing and how my playing improved. They respected the effort that I made to help others. In my sophomore year of high school, I was unanimously elected treasurer, which was unheard of, and then in my junior year was elected president of the athletic association.

5. Was there any negative kickback from the group or from the relationship system as a result of your new position?

Some of the kids teased me about being a teacher's pet. Overall, the risk of being teased vs. the motivational relationship with Sister Mary de Sales made me think being teacher's pet was a positive thing. This pathway was duplicated, almost step-by-step, when I met Dr. Bowen. My relationship with him was eerily similar to that of my relationship with Sister Mary de Sales.

Bowen played a different kind of "kickball," but the acknowledgement of my skills by this leader allowed me to have a better position in the social group. The triangles in the group after the death of Dr. Bowen produced a somewhat negative focus on me. Such things happen. Awareness of the impersonal force in triangles was useful in not getting so involved in the debates and trying to clarify my roles and responsibilities in the group. Being special to a leader can and often does produce challenges, but these problems are the small price of learning.

6. What has been the impact of this relationship on you as you have thought about it over the years?

Although my story about Sister Mary de Sales is told without a great deal of emotionality, this relationship made a huge difference in how I was able to settle down in school. It showed me the importance of doing well in the things I liked. These experiences reinforced a pathway for me to have confidence based in my ability to perform in groups and, most important, to feel comfortable in establishing trust with authority figures.

I saw the valuable impact that one person can have on another's life. Both Dr. Bowen and Sister Mary de Sales helped me see how becoming a leader in a social group takes a disciplined effort but has a great pay off. You could think about this interaction with her as a kind of a tipping point in my life. This relationship set me on a path, which was then reinforced by other relationships. My work as a family therapist is part of this same path, as it allows me to influence the lives of others just as Sister Mary de Sales and Dr. Bowen influenced mine.

If I had chosen a more difficult relationship to use as an example (maybe with my mother, father or brothers) that revealed greater adventures and disasters, the story would very likely have contained both more emotion and more meaning. Even the simplest, most straightforward stories take time for us to understand and to clarify the impact of relationships. It takes more time to figure out a positive way of thinking about our more emotionally charged adventures because they tend to be more contaminated, subjective, and defensive. Nonetheless, they too are important clues to understanding the unresolved nature of our attachment to the past.

The most important relationships are with our caretakers, since that is when we are most vulnerable. Other relationships can compensate for difficulties in our early years, as did Sister Mary de Sales' relationship with me. These more positive relationships can lend us strength to reflect on, understand, and even alter other more aggravating or confusing relationships.

What You Can Learn From Your Own Story: Using the Family Diagram

After you've written a short story about the five important relationships, try to figure out how to write your family story. Constructing a family diagram helps you gather evidence about how your family has operated over the past three generations. Initially, people look for the facts for each person. When and where people born and educated, what kind of work did they do, where did they live throughout their lives, when and to whom did they marry, how many children did they have, where did they die and what was the cause of death? In addition, you can note the intensity of how people relate to one another (the emotional process) and any symptoms (e.g., divorce and illness) in any of these relationships. Below is an example found on the Internet which is part of a government training manual. The family diagram is very useful, showing us at a glance the outline of the families of Franklin and Eleanor Roosevelt.

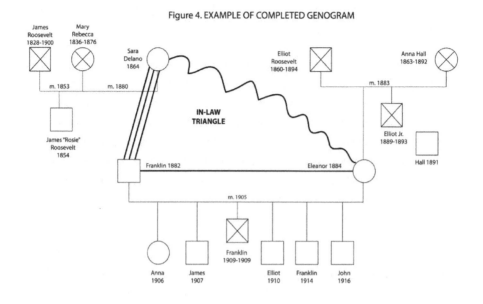

Figure 4. EXAMPLE OF COMPLETED GENOGRAM

http://www.dss.mo.gov/cd/info/cwmanual/section7/ch1_33/sec7ch25.htm

When people need to gather more family information from and about relatives, they often start to ask questions about family members who are the most distance from them. It seems to be less upsetting to begin by asking questions about one's grandparents or even older generations. Nowadays there are many online services such as Ancestry.com that can be useful in finding basic information about family members. However, there is something very different about asking questions about the family dynamics. One way people do it is to research the historical record and then compare and contrast the more fact-based data with the gossip you have heard about people. This is what Bowen did in tracing back several generations in his own family.

The Emotional Shock Wave

People have very subjective impressions of their ancestors that often vary greatly from the historical record. In addition, family events, such as weddings and funerals, offer a wonderful opportunity to learn more about your family. Though difficult, times of great stress, such as a death in the family, can be a learning opportunity, because it is during these times that people tend to be more open. In addition, family gatherings present an opportunity to observe the natural alliances, and the intensity of negative and/or positive gossip following the death of a patriarch or matriarch. The openness is there even if people follow a prescribed ritual for expressing grief. Some are more present and others are more dazed and "out of sorts." But if one person is prepared to be more present, it can influence and improve the quality of the connectedness throughout the whole system.

A deceased person leaves a hole in the system. It is as if one of the planets in the solar system jumped out of its orbit. Others' orbits are impacted. In the year or two before or after the loss of highly important family members, stress and anxiety increase in what Bowen referred to as the family reaction to death.[33] Family members make decisions that are just not as wise as those made when the system was more intact. For example, soon after a father dies one of his sons suddenly gets a slew of speeding tickets or has a "one-night stand" that results in the birth of a child with a woman to whom he's not married.

The anxiety around the loss is absorbed by a few who become more anxious, and that anxiety then has consequences in how well people can think over the reaction to loss. Due to our ancient defense system, many such dependent connections are denied. I often hear people trying to understand connections with denial, "That person was not important to me and I see no connection between the death and my subsequent struggles."

After a funeral, you see the emotional system come alive and begin to compensate and adjust to changes. All systems begin to "reorganize" after the loss of an important member. Stress can increase if people have not prepared well for the change. About 75 percent of people adjust well to the loss of old relationships and the need to adapt and to function differently.[34] The cost of adapting for the remaining 25 percent may be the reason we often see symptoms in families in the year or two following the loss of a major leader.

These symptoms reveal the circumstantial evidence of how people are connected to one another at deep levels. Dr. Bowen called the phenomena, the *emotional shock wave*. This is correlative evidence of the connectedness and dependency of all, as well as the capacity of the system to reorganize and maintain its integrity in the face of changing circumstances. We see greater strength in families when there is less bitterness or blame after a death and if people are able to stay in good contact. When this does not occur, often those, who are more distant and less capable of being self with others, take a bigger hit in absorbing the anxiety.

This is how natural systems function. Individuals in the system are simply trying to adapt to the increase in stress. Visible symptoms, such as illness, temper tantrums, and withdrawal, to name a few more, may emerge in the more vulnerable family members. This is a mechanism that operates in all social systems.

Under stress, a bifurcation occurs as individuals and the system as a whole absorb the anxiety. It takes a great deal of awareness to see the automatic nature of a social system, when, in the big picture, there is no one to blame—it is just people responding as well as they can to pressure. There is magic in not blaming and seeing the big, complex social system operate as it must. When your mind is more neutral, others, who relate to you, are freer to find a new, healthy way to relate.

There is no use trying to pretend, as one has to *truly* be more neutral. This kind of neutrality does take time to establish. When this is possible, new configurations of well-functioning relationships will arise.

After a death, people are often challenged to alter their functional position within the family group. If they can do this from within their deeper self, then greater leadership will emerge. Defining one's self to others is a way to take on the anxiety generated around a loss.

Corporations also have similar problems to families, as they are subject to reactive behavior around the clues that there is or is about to be shifts in the functioning of its members. When new leadership must take over, anxiety is generated and people have to adapt. Polarization and emotional intensity occur as often in corporations as in families or conversely, there can be more openness and less fear. One person (sometimes the leader) can set the tone for a more mature level of interactions, just as in a family. The relationships may be more or less intense, as one's future reputation and ability to maintain oneself is at stake.

If you are willing to reflect upon and write your story around a death or transitional event in your family or at work, you can learn a lot. This can be very useful in becoming more objective and in understanding the family as a system of emotional forces and pressures, as you watch how a system responds during and after a crisis. Below are a few ideas about what you might do with any story you write to get the most out of this kind of an exercise.

Family stories and the effort to be a steady Self

Once you have written your stories and started answering some questions for yourself, the next challenge is to consider presenting these vignettes to the people who were the players in these stories. Are you curious to know how these people might react to your memories? Do you think they remember the events as you do or will their memories be different? Possibly, the people involved in your stories will not remember the events just as you do and their feelings about events will differ from yours.

Our memory is illusive and often deceptive, but if left unexamined it guides us automatically.[35] Therefore, it is worth the effort to take the risk to act differently in relationships with what I like to call, "the family force field." (From the womb on we react to others positively or negatively, reinforcing multigenerational patterns without thought, thereby forming a relationship system that is hard to change.)

Perhaps you hesitate, and with good reason, to wade into your force field to say or to be different. It might be shocking to check in with those people you are close to and reveal your different view of life. It takes time for different perspectives to be heard. It takes time to seek others' ideas or to find the relationship "facts." This effort can put you in the middle of an emotional storm as people sort out divergent memories. If someone tells you that your uncle had an affair, they expect total agreement of this as fact. But you can state a different viewpoint. "Well, if he did and I did not see him doing it then it is just hearsay."

The person might now appreciate your attempt to be "different" or more of a Self. Remember, sometimes drawing a bit of short-term negative energy may recalibrate the system and eventually allow for more open relationships.

Despite the emotional cost, talking to the other people involved in your stories is the best way to see how factual your own memories are, and the very best way to practice managing self and to come out with a more open and comfortable way of relating. It gives you the opportunity to respect different memories or beliefs that people have about the past and to clarify your own position. In addition, this kind of exercise can give you valuable insight into just how much you have been or are being influenced by other people's viewpoints.

Bowen would tell how he would drive away from Menninger Clinic, and after an hour or two, would find he was far more neutral about the people highlighted in the staff gossip as the "impossible ones." Becoming more objective and neutral is not an easy assignment.

When you go in search of the facts and separate out different opinions from facts, you will be stepping out of character. You will be performing a role that's different than what is expected of you. This can upset in the others involved and provoke a strong response from them. When that happens, how do you respond?

If your goal is to grow, you don't want to respond by resuming your old role. Whatever responses you get to your story, your job is to remain as neutral and calm as possible. Initially, you are just observing the reactivity and remaining neutral.

The goal is to be emotionally separate and stand alone as you explore the dimensions of the social system you see "buzzing" around you. You are a kind of researcher, "a participant observer," if you will. If you have a relationship with someone that goes back in time, you already know that there are expected ways of relating.

Often a dominance order has been established. This is true in friendships as well as in family and work situations. If in the process of telling your story and experiencing the other person's reactions you can keep from reacting and re-creating the old relationship dynamic, you will know at a cellular level that you have created a healthy space between yourself and others, a space from which you can observe and think and plan ahead.

Dealing with the Reactions to Your Stories

Armed with knowledge about yourself and your family, the influence of the old automatic system's alignments, or what I like to call the force of the "love lock," diminishes. It is just automatic to get in step with others you know, love and appreciate, or perhaps even need. But it can be dangerous because it blinds you to what is really going on.

Are you a leader, who can maintain a detached, "unlocked," objective stance while gathering information (such as the information you've gathered in your own family) and interacting with others in a sometimes highly charged atmosphere? If so, you have an extremely valuable skill.

Leaders, who have trouble maintaining a separate self that is strong enough to deal with others' differing opinions, tend to create family and corporate "yes" cultures. Surrounded by "yes" people, these leaders lose all ability to deal with dissent, which in turn makes it almost impossible for them to take in new information.

This is one way in which leaders become isolated and find themselves in serious trouble. Just recall Enron, where leaders insulated themselves from information that diverged from the party line and ended up weakening the system and, ultimately, contributing to its demise.

Separating Facts from Fantasy

In the July 2, 2006 issue of *The New York Times,* Sharon L. Allen, Chairwoman of Deloitte & Touche, tells us how useful it was to find the strengths in her multigenerational family relationships.[36] Her great-grandmother was one of the first women in the Idaho State Legislature. Yet, no one expected Sharon Allen to become the Chairman of an $8 billion organization. What else did she learn from her family? She knew that her nightly walks with her Dad to check out the crops on the family farm had given her first-hand knowledge of 1) the value of attention to detail, 2) how

145

hard a person must work to make things turn out right, and 3) the importance of independence.

Her parents always stressed she could do anything she set her mind to. This is what gave her strength. The article is an entertaining personal story of a few of the factors that encouraged one woman to become aware of and use the strengths gained in her family relationships to be successful. Some family stories are more factual and encouraging while others are more emotional and polarizing and require people to overcome serious obstacles.

Can we find evidence-supporting facts in ours or others' stories? Or is the "information" really just emotional gossip and we should be suspect? Sharon Allen knew some facts about her family and saw a link between her life and the history of female leaders in her family. We don't know exactly what happened on her walks with her Dad, although her current life points to something positive. However, we can verify the facts of her great-grandmother's life as a political leader.

Our automatic response is neither to challenge the current family story nor to idealize our relationships with our near and dear, or believe all kinds of negative gossip. As you write your family stories, you may find that some of what you are hearing is more fantasy than fact. This discovery, however, is not necessarily a bad thing.

There is nothing better than taking off the psychological blinders and working towards seeing others as they really are. Seeing facts can help us do just that. Sometimes looking at facts and trying to see deeply how people lived their lives and the pressure they were under can help us understand and talk about our own predicaments.

Another advantage to listening to our own and others' stories is that the extreme challenges or even the soft spots in our lives can translate into resiliency and greater empathy for others. This is important because mature leaders have the dual challenge of being clear about who they are, while remaining open and less judgmental about their own and others' foibles.

There are only so many ways to peel an apple. When it comes to harvesting leadership wisdom, the apples that fall from the tree of knowledge are both informative and entertaining. Stories can help us see beyond our preconceived notions of what is, and how (or even whether) to change our life.

For thousands of years, we humans have used story telling as a model for moving beyond our preconceptions and shortsighted views. Our brains are designed to be receptive and to consider whole new worlds that stories bring our way. In addition, stories are created as we talk to people about their experiences or even when we interview people.

A few words of caution as you go about collecting stories. One of the things you may notice is that you become entangled with the storyteller. Research shows that when we listen to a story, our brain waves become correlated with the storyteller's brain waves. "The researchers found that when the two people communicate, neural activity over wide regions of their brains becomes almost synchronous, with the listener's brain activity patterns mirroring those sweeping through the speaker's brain, albeit with a short lag of about one second. If the listener, however, fails to comprehend what the speaker is trying to communicate, their brain patterns decouple."[37]

Consider yourself a researcher of your family story as you talk to people about how they experienced various events in the family. In this stance, you may find it easier to develop a slightly more separate space so that you don't become overly involved with the storyteller. By developing questions ahead of time, we can shake more of the apples from the apple tree since we are not limited by what comes to mind in the moment.

It is a discipline to be more separate from others while listening and carefully clarifying relationship issues. Stories are one of the ancient learning tools on our path to lead, follow, question, empathize, see beyond our blind spots, and construct new mental models. All of these enable us to create new perspective about our lives and how to deal with the challenges we face. Working on self in relationship to others is the key. But the key to knowing self may be hidden by our past history, about which we know next to nothing.

On another level, it is amazing to think that we can learn more about how families function and the rules of emotional systems just by listening to stories. It seems almost too easy. After all, our brains find stories appealing. We are entertained, but how do we know what it is that we are learning? There has been an effort to learn the science of storytelling through MRI studies.

Raymond Mar, a psychologist at York University in Canada, showed the activation in the brain wave patterns, which were created as 86 people listened to stories. The evidence showed how the brain constructs a map of others' intentions, activating the neurons in specific areas to produce a personal theory of mind.[38] Listening to stories and acting in our own story are similar processes. We learn as we listen. Our brain is firing away as though this story we are reading or hearing about is about us.

As we develop and write our own stories, we have new opportunities to create different relationships with the people we care deeply about. Our ability to be present and less reactive is tested. Learning to be objective and genuinely curious about our past can improve our ability to function in the present.

In learning about the facts of our three or four generational families, we can begin to grasp a different and better informed viewpoint about the past. This creates an opportunity to enlarge our vantage point as to our future.

Life is often about change, but we adapt based on the trajectory of the past. The past can foreshadow the future. Writing your family story gives each of us an opportunity to change our past and then, possibly, our future.

As we seek to understand our own social system, we can assume that there are similar mechanisms in other families. In discovering the nature of one small social system, we can improve our ability to listen to others, to understand where we have been and communicate where we want to go. If one person is clear, this can give room to others to shape their own life. This effort to see more clearly and to alter our relationships reshapes the way we see the past, live in the present, and plan our future.

CHAPTER XI
WHAT DOES IT TAKE TO BE A SELF IN ANY SYSTEM?

Togetherness and Individuality: All for One but What if One is Not for All

Just as no one ant can build an ant colony, no one person can create for him or herself all that is needed for survival. We are dependent on the work of others for our food, water, clothes, education and protection, among other things. By cooperating, we benefit. Therefore, the pressure to fit in and cooperate is enormous and can intrude on our equally deep urges to become our unique selves.

Murray Bowen, in collecting the facts of family functioning, observed how this tension between the two forces, to be for self (individuality) and to be for others (togetherness), resulted in what he called one's level of *differentiation of self.* Evolutionary theory and Bowen theory both consider how these two forces have formed the bedrock for life itself.

The emotional system consists of instincts. It is an automatic guidance system. Some of its ancient mechanisms no longer function well in our modern jungle. The tigers in the social jungle have been replaced by traffic jams. Our biology is over reactive to threats.

Without a Mindful Compass, individuals find it difficult to be calm or even to cooperate. Instead when we are on automatic pilot, our compass does not "see the system." We respond automatically to the reactive emotional system's feedback and dictates.

The basic signals from the emotional system can be observed in the same way we observe the movements of the planets. The greatest challenge for any observer is to get outside the system in order to see it. Instead of planets, we see our parents and siblings pressuring us to conform or reacting to our commitment to our own forward progress. Of course, it is hard to be neutral about our parents and others. And without neutrality it is hard to be an observer.

Understanding the two forces of togetherness and individuality may help explain some of our sensitivities, prejudices, and even what seems to be the capricious or nasty side of human nature. In order to see how relationship systems impact the individuals in them, Bowen described the patterns of the tugs, pushes and pulls (or the sensitivity and reactivity) within relationship systems that lead to some being able to develop more independence than others.

In 1967, Bowen published his description of his own efforts to redirect the anxiety in his family and to step outside the system itself. This effort required him to be less reactive to others and more aware of the tendency of relationships to form in predictable coalitions. Bowen observed how the family unit determines the actions of individuals. He saw that when people did not behave as they should, social pressure was put on them to act the way that was expected or even needed by the group (family).

Since we are often not aware of the nature of the system's influences (togetherness) on us, we take things personally and are reactive. Bowen understood the primitive nature of the emotional system. Given "the family force field," he understood the importance of preparing himself to stand aside from the pushes and pulls of the system. The ability to respond to the social system in a more thoughtful way Bowen called *differentiation of self.*

The emotional system, the family unit, has its own reason for exerting an influence on individuals. It needs the individuals to function and perhaps to absorb more anxiety than is "fair."

In early life we are more vulnerable to the "commands" of those around us. When we are young we can act automatically. If we are brought up in an anxious system more is required to manage ourselves. For many, the emotional system distributes anxiety unfairly to the weak and vulnerable and stunts emotional growth.

Mixed signals as to one's ability to be more independent compromises one's ability to see and think for self. Independence from while maintaining connections to the family system requires a disciplined effort.

Decreasing reactivity is central to any effort to grow beyond the needs of the system. By riding the waves of reactivity and seeing how systems operate as part of the primitive nature of emotionally driven relationships, one can sustain the effort to create more mature relationships.

Through the effort to see the family or the emotions as part of an impersonal system, we grow in awareness. We create more adaptable relationships, different from those we experienced in our early family life. It takes an effort to be different in the here and now.

The shadow of sensitivity, which orients our automatic compass, has been passed down to us through the millennium. Bowen postulated that a relationship system operates with same the emotional processes found in all social species. He pointed to the evidence that natural selection operates on both individuals and the social groups to which they belong.

Social Pressure and the Precious Few Ways We Can React

Under social pressure individuals have the following six behavioral options:

1. Distance – not relating to others: withdrawing emotionally or physically, and at the extreme using an emotional cut off to maintain the distance from the difficult others

2. Conflict – posturing anger to being seriously mad and or aggressive fighting, to keep from knowing the other

3. Triangles – seeing one person as a problem and using alliance with another to bully, gossip, and other actions to exclude one

4. Reciprocal relationships and forming hierarchies – "giving in" or giving up self to others, functioning in reaction to others where there appears little to no choice to change self

5. Project all your anxious worries onto the children or anyone. The most difficult one to see as we can convince ourselves we are caring and helping the helpless or poor other one

6. Differentiation of self – redirecting the flow of anxiety in the social group through the effort to be more mature as to how one functions as a more separate Self, based on principles, in relationships systems.

Bowen explained the primal nature of and the challenges we face in our ordinary efforts to fit in with the group and at the same time, to be our unique selves.

"The emotional system operates with predictable, knowable stimuli that govern the instinctual life behavior in all forms of life. The more a life is governed by the emotional system, the more it follows the course of all instinctual behavior, in spite of intellectualization to the contrary . . . a well-differentiated person is one whose intellect . . . [can] function separately from the emotional system...[39]

"A more differentiated person can participate freely in the emotional sphere without fear of becoming too fused with others.[40]

"It is the pseudo self that is involved in fusion and the many ways of giving, receiving, lending, borrowing trading and exchange of self... The borrowing and trading of selfs... ends up with one employee in the one-down... position, while the other gains self... The exchanges can be brief – for instance, criticism that makes one feel bad for a couple of days; or it can be a long-term process in which the adaptive spouse becomes so de-selfed, he or she is no longer able to make decisions and collapses in selfless dysfunction-- psychosis or chronic physical illness . . . the process of people losing and gaining self in an emotional network is so complex and the degree of shifts so great that it is impossible to estimate functional levels of differentiation except from following a life pattern over long periods.[41]

"Every emotional unit, whether it be the family or the total of society, exerts pressure on group members to conform to the ideals and principles of the group.[42]

"The overall goal is to help individual family members rise up out of the emotional togetherness that binds us all. The instinctual force towards differentiation is built into the organism, just as are the emotional forces that oppose it . . . The togetherness forces are so strong in maintaining the

status quo that any small step towards differentiation is met with vigorous disapproval of the group . . . Without help, the differentiating one will fall back into the togetherness to get emotional harmony for the moment.[43]

The Advantages of "Thinking Systems"

Many people with family or work problems continue to believe in this commonly accepted analysis, which has been part of medicine for decades—turn the problem over to professionals. The professionals will reassure us that one person is indeed seriously "troubled," symptomatic or deserving of blame and should be diagnosed, medicated, helped or fired.

Extruding troublesome individuals from organizations or medicating symptomatic family members are seen as the answers for most severe relationship issues in the workplace or in families.

Instead of focusing on a symptomatic individual, Bowen outlined a process to develop the capacity to neutrally observe and understand family, and by extension, work and even larger social systems. (It is clear that it takes an intellectual and disciplined effort to be able to be aware and outside the commands of the emotional system.

It is not yet clear how the brain handles and integrates the often competing 'voices' from the intellect and from the emotional system.)

The intellect can say, "I will make an effort to stand outside the commands for agreement or for submission and I will stay connected to these people or that person. Despite the fact that someone is upset with me I will not react and be upset." Good intention, but life can shock you. At some time, you might innocently be relating and suddenly something is said and you find yourself reacting—twitching with anger, sadness or some challenging emotional feelings. Despite our best intentions we are not always able to manage our feelings.

At another time, it might just be important to stay connected and let the deeper feelings be experienced. Emotions can connect us to what is real. I say this with caution, as it is also true that emotions can be used in very harmful ways, as can the repression of feelings.

People can be angry and not know it and yet act revengeful. People can be sad and deny it and then find they are giving in and rescuing people.

If we could see that people impact us and we impact them, then we might be able to allow time to sort out relationships and the gaining or losing of self in the bargaining.

Neutrality is a goal. It is a way to look more objectively at how anxiety is absorbed, often in one or a few individuals in the group.

A broader viewpoint allows us to see the reasons that we do not want to feel as the system is prompting us to feel. Clearly, we do not want to be manipulated by the group. It is like magic that when one is not participating in the families' ongoing conflicts, it often automatically reduces the intense focus on "fixing" the symptomatic one.

Work and social groups, while often less intense than family groups, contain the same reactivity and relationship patterns as families. The urge to dominate and the urge to please or get out of the way, (and many more functional patterns) all play out in relationships at work and at home.

The people Bowen coached could tell him how problems in one generation were transmitted to the next generation, and he would coach them, depending on their level of emotional maturity, to begin the process of being more observant and objective as to just understanding how the system worked and how they were participating in the system.

In watching Bowen work with people, I noted that he asked people how their functioning was being influenced by their position in the relationships. The overall question, as I watched, was what would people do to become a more "differentiated self?"

It seemed that the more Bowen learned from them about the nature of their interpersonal involvement, the more they learned from him. This seemed to be Bowen's research design—to check the facts of each family's functioning against his theoretical concepts about relationship systems and how people might find a way to alter their sensitivity in relationships to the emotional system.

It was Dr. Bowen's powerful observational skills that allowed him to see similar patterns of behavior in all families, from those with schizophrenia to the neurotic. In developing the "differentiation of self scale," Bowen noted that for those individuals with the most severe symptoms, their intellectual and emotional centers were fused, making it more and more challenging to make logical or principle-based decisions.

The more anxious people are the more the feeling system dominates, the more confusion they experience in relationship to others close to them. Those without the ability to know the difference between their thinking and their feelings are the ones who initially become symptomatic. However, as Bowen noted, people can also develop symptoms in an effort to pull up their functioning.

Is Your Family Preparing You to Think Systems?

Often, people who noticed how their symptomatic sibling had been focused on and worried about, are in the position of being able to "see" systems operate. They know somehow that there is more to the ups and downs of behavior than what is inside a person.

Others cannot "see" connections between the way people are focused on others, (negatively or positively) and how that person then behaves.

It is difficult for some to see that the expectations of parents are out of touch with the reality of the capacity of the child. They treat the child as if he/she could see when the child is blind. When the child cannot see the parents intensify the focus on the child to do more. We also see the opposite, that is, parents who do not demand anything of children and who are afraid of them.

Neither parent's reaction to the child is based in reality. Children can be held responsible according to their ability. What does it take to see that? The child has to be more than an extension of the parents self. The more fused and confused the parents are as to where they begin and end and where the child begins and ends, the more the relationship will be way beyond the usual frustration. It might pay to ask yourself – "Am I seeing this child accurately? What is my responsibility and what is his or hers?"

Those who become observers of the system may see how the pressure moves but can still be caught up in being too critical. They say the parents are too harsh or too lenient and then try to influence the way the parents relate and tell them what to do. This gets them nowhere.

Once exposed to Bowen theory in a book or in a coaching relationship, these are the people who can alter their focus on changing others. They are able to "see" the system and the automatic pressure on the vulnerable ones as part of a multigenerational history.

These individuals can become more objective through different methods, such as journaling or coaching. They can more easily understand the cost of giving into social pressure. They automatically seem to know when the cost of doing things for others is too high a price to pay. It just seems to make sense to them that social pressure is as powerful a force as genetics.

Walking Off of Shakespeare's Stage

There is something deeply empowering when an individual begins to think systems and is more neutral and able to relate about things that are going on in a less anxious way. People comment, "It is like I walked off of Shakespeare's stage." This is the experience of being freer to relate to those he or she cares about.

Others report deep gratitude at seeing those they care about being able to grow more independently. I have asked people, "What does it take to step off 'the stage?'" And they say things like, "All it takes is to remain above the fray, and to refuse to take any emotional bait."

It seems like once someone experiences being more separate while remaining connected, they are hooked and want to know more about how systems function. It is not that people want to run off and claim: "I am now a system thinker," and then claim to be defining a self here, there, and everywhere.

Systems knowledge is more like a secret weapon. If things get to be disturbing there is an answer—to focus on what "I" can do and then watch how relationships might be influenced by an action stance for Self.

Many people have said to me, "This stuff (emotional process) has been going on for generations." Systems thinking (or Bowen theory) provides a view of actions for Self that one could do in order to alter "the predictable" future and somehow now they have the courage to do it. Now they know it is their choice to go along or to figure out a different way!

One of the hallmarks of Bowen theory is that if the individual understands what is going on in the emotional system, and is not critical but is focused on altering the part he or she plays in problems, then this person is less reactive and more effective no matter what they do.

In addition, this individual is often in better contact with a broad variety of people in the extended family. What comes first, the ability to manage a variety of social relationships over time or the ability to manage self when people we care about are upset? When people know more about the family, systems ideas make more sense. People are willing to make an effort to strengthen the family roots knowing that more knowledge about the family is protective when the winds blow.

Systems thinking or building one's emotional backbone in relationships, is not for everyone. It is a useful method to calm people down so that they can, in a more objective manner, see how relationships system's function automatically. When we can see, in an impersonal way, how anxiety functions to wind people up and to create greater vulnerability in some, then it becomes easier to not blame and react when things go wrong.

If people have a way to think systems, they can see how increasing anxiety is more the problem than the shape of the symptoms that occur. Anxiety degrades relationships and then symptoms occur. Because of the way people relate to one another when they are under stress, a few develop symptoms for the group.

Anxious people are more likely to maintain a negative or over-positive unrealistic focus on others, and it's the vulnerable ones who then show symptoms. First comes the interpersonal worry and then comes the symptoms if and when the anxiety gets turned up high enough. This tells you that the effort to turn the anxiety down can make a tremendous difference in people lives.

Systems theory tell us that anxiety can be burned off by both mental and physical exercise, mindfulness training, neurofeedback and other efforts to manage self. When people are aware of the state of the system and know how to decrease anxiety in self, they have a better chance to relate realistically. Fewer individuals will have to absorb anxiety since there is less of it to go around.

Anxiety can be absorbed in the effort to manage self. For example, if one is stressed, he/she might collapse, go to bed, get mad at someone else, or get "reorganized." By "reorganizing" self, an individual can find a more mature way to deal with the increasing anxiety and take an action stance more for self than following the dictates of the emotional system. This is very appealing to people invested in thinking systems.

Yes, systems theory is a completely new way to think about human behavior. No one knows what the outcome will be for those who are able to think in system terms, relate well and define a more responsible self. Few things are harder but more worthwhile.

Who Among You is Willing to Change Self and Relate Differently?

It would seem that families have a life of their own. They transmit roles (functional slots), values and beliefs over the generations. You could think about families as little ant colonies. This might give you a broader viewpoint on how interactions impact behavior. When one member of the colony is willing to change self and the system can accept this change, then over time the change makes for greater tolerance of differences and less automatic and/or reactive behavior. When people are able to relate to one another differently, it can create upsets but it can also give people valuable information. What is the nature of the programming that holds family relationships together?

Over time, in coaching family members, Bowen saw that individuals could increase their emotional and cognitive functioning. While gathering information on their own family history, people began to tell more coherent stories about their life experiences. They became more aware, more observant and less reactive towards spouses and other family members.

The efforts to understand self in their relationship system often increased the opportunity to form new relationships with extended family members. By diagramming the three generational family relationship systems, people were able to have an impersonal view of how anxiety flowed and infected the whole group. In addition, the effort to be more aware and responsible translated into differences in how people performed at work.

Motivated individuals achieved a new level of functioning, and then, one by one, others in their families became less reactive and better defined. The main differences were that individuals were more understanding of family members and were able to interrupt the automatic cues pressuring them to react in the old ways. They could then engage in new kinds of relationships.

By studying families over many years, Bowen saw that a percentage of people do have the ability to see the family as a system and to do something about the part they play in maintaining the anxiety-driven status quo. Some individuals can describe beautifully the pull of the intense reactivity to others and are capable of almost immediately inhibiting their own reactive responses. Others take a long time to see that reactivity as an emotional yank from the system, which propels them into con-fusion, and makes them more sensitive and vulnerable.

It takes time to see how a system functions. During the early years of Bowen's work with families, he noted that only about 25 percent of psychiatric residents were able to see the importance of extended family work. It is not something you can sell. A coach has to be able to let people change at their own rate. Only a few were willing to work on their extended family relationships. Getting to know people in one's extended three- or four-generation family can seem like a waste of time or even nonsense to those in the middle of an intense marital crisis or in the intensity of an expansion of one's business.

Most people, in the face of rising external anxiety or intense opposition at work, will retreat, hoping to find comfort in their nuclear family. But this automatic reaction only increases the pressure on each family member to manage the increasing anxiety, with fewer and fewer places for the anxiety to go.

The overall goal for motivated individuals is to discipline self, and to not react to ongoing issues by taking sides or being pulled into the togetherness. The effort requires focus on observing patterns, resisting the lure of status quo thinking, and defining one's differences with others in as playful and flexible a way as possible. People in relationship with a good Bowen coach can slowly change their thinking from content thinking ("It is his fault!") to seeing the anxiety and figuring out how to respond thoughtfully.

People have more of a choice about how to function once they know something about the system in which they live. A systems view avoids blame and an automatic focus on the "other" and gives people choices in the management of anxiety. When one is able to think more objectively about the ongoing nature of the relationships system and one's part in it, new options appear. People can see some way to stay in an "I" position and allow others to have choices, too. If the symptoms are intense and the anxiety is high, it can take years for people to become surer of being a more contained and separate Self.

It is difficult to stay on this higher, less reactive ground, as it can be washed away during family storms. However, if people have put effort into developing their emotional backbone and sticking to their self-defined principles, they are more likely to avoid becoming caught up in the confusion with others. It is a relief to know there is a way to manage self rather than thrashing about in the confusion of blaming and focusing on others.

Increasing your knowledge of your relationship system by getting to know members of your extended family requires that you see the advantage of having more information about family emotional process and more opportunity to define and separate a self. If you can make an inch of headway in establishing more open communication and a wider network, all the better for you and your offspring.

CHAPTER XII
LEARNING FROM OTHER LIVING SYSTEMS

How Do Ants Know?

As mentioned earlier, you can think of the family as an ant colony. I mention this because it is possible that there are general laws organizing emotional systems. If so, we should see evidence for some kinds of emotional process in other forms of life that could inform us. No one can be an expert in all the areas of the natural sciences, so with gratitude, we turn to experts to learn more about how living things manage to live and work together.

Deborah Gordon, among others, has demonstrated that if you remove ants from one job, such as searching for food, the colony automatically compensates for this by decreasing the rate at which ants assume the tasks of removing garbage or defending the nest. The functioning of one ant is communicated and impacts others, but the individual ants need no "awareness" of this. The mechanisms for guiding the behaviors of ants in the colony are present and nothing has to be learned. Body scents and touching antennae are all the signals needed to provide functional role assignments. Without much of a brain, ants know what the others in the colony are up to.[44]

Of course, ants cannot say to one another, "I am making this decision to alter my functioning based on the numbers needed for the various jobs." Neither humans nor ants need much of a brain to pick up signals about the needs of the group or colony and what we then need to do.

Ants also build complex cities, go to war with other colonies and take slaves (which they care for rather than eat). They raise and keep other insects for food (just like humans raise cattle). They are the only other species, besides humans, that cultivate food. They may be most well known for cooperating and for teamwork with each individual becoming part of an organism called

161

an ant colony.[45]

Humans, like ants, do not act as one colony, yet are able to cooperate because they have an automatic sensing capability attuned to changes in the relationship system. Our highly emotional interactions are coded into memory, and perhaps, like the ants, we read and react to one another's functioning states in ways that are out of our awareness. We humans are more capable than ants of independent thinking and are aware of the cost of social control. Humans understand that the group does not always know the right way to go.

Sensitive and reactive individuals are more prone to respond to pressure from others by rebelling or adapting and conforming until the social pressure creates symptoms in vulnerable individuals. The most common family problem is parents' pressure on children to do well in school. The children rebel by staying out late, having parties, and using drugs.

Sometimes harder to see is a husband who comes home and "demands" that his wife listen to his problems and then she begins to drink. In the best of times, social pressure results in individuals in the group "cooperating" well enough to enhance survival. The children do well in school and the wife actually helps the husband deal with his problems.

We can also see how the impulse to help others occurs on a societal level. When there is a tremendous crisis, like the hurricane in Haiti or the nuclear plant meltdown in Japan, people do all kinds of amazing things for one another without question or the hope of being paid back for the effort. But as social pressures increase to solve impossible problems, the cost of "helping/cooperating" becomes higher than people can bear. They may seek distance, blame the government, or become symptomatic themselves, at which point the initial impulse to "cooperate" breaks down.

The cost for some individuals becomes too great. Individuals, who increase their awareness of the pushes and pulls of the relationship system, have a better chance to define in some reasoned way, the limits of what they can and cannot do. A deeply emotional impulse to help others often has no limits.

Ants, unlike humans, may not have the flexibility to turn down the urge to cooperate and go along with the group. Then again, ants and bees that form social colonies are not operating under the guidance of fear states generating cortisol (or hydrocortisone is the primary stress hormone) as they have no adrenal glands. Instead, ants and bees operate under a kind of democracy. "Bees operate with a quorum set high enough to guarantee that swarms make highly accurate decisions rather than just super speedy ones."[46]

They wait for the crowd to decide which direction to go and that turns out to be the best strategy when organisms need to choose accurately not rapidly. Ants and bees have little reason to develop individuality beyond role specific functions. What is amazing is that these little organisms have the same basic genetic heritage, and yet so many physical and physiological differences emerge in the colony.

Up the Evolutionary Ladder to Awareness and Fear States

Humans are sensitized by states of fear about which they are unaware. They bump into one another and exchange information about the state of the social group. These encounters between individual humans can change their chemistry but not necessarily their awareness. People say,

"My parents died when I was young but that did not bother me." Yet when you look at the brains of these people, you find the "chemistry of depression."[47]

The biochemical pathways tell us what the mind cannot. These people are unaware of the impact the social group has on them and cannot perceive the environment accurately. Drugs used to alter their brain chemistry give these individuals a greater chance to integrate the reality of their situation and to promote a better adaptation to the changed environment. Depression is a symptom that can inform people that their view of reality is skewed. Drugs may alleviate some of the suffering but do not necessarily increase cognitive functioning or awareness.

Our automatic compass is built on automatic signaling processes enabling us to fit in with the social group. This can result in making decisions, like ants and bees, that spring from the importance of the group, such as deciding

163

where to build the hive and where to find food. Individual ants do not have to decide what to do. They are dependent on the group's perception of the environment. Even with our complex brain, we are often unaware that stress can result in our being overly sensitive to and dependent upon social relationships. Perhaps we become more like ants under stress.

It is safe to say, however, that sometimes we all live in psychic darkness, with many emotional states unavailable to us for reflection or introspection. It is impossible to be totally aware of all our unconscious motivations. However, that is not the end of the story. We know we can form hypotheses and look for facts to support our viewpoint. To check out our hypotheses, we can talk with others about our ideas. This is often part of a therapeutic experience—to talk about our ideas and to be challenged by a good coach to see things differently and call into question the beliefs we hold onto most tightly.

The Brain Lights up Relationship Pathways

For many years, we had only clinical descriptions to explain how relationships influence people's functioning. Now we can see the impact of relationships reflected in brain chemistry. We can ask people to think about different scenarios—from winning at tennis or looking at someone we love, to a situation in which we feel afraid—while we examine their brain chemistry through machines like MRIs. This research verifies that different areas of the brain "light up" at the thought of different subjects.

Investigators have even tried to understand the "chemistry" of love.

A handful of researchers, armed with MRIs, have begun to sift out the chemical mix that makes up love. "Until recently, we regarded love as supernatural" says Helen Fisher, a professor of anthropology at Rutgers who is one of the world's leading researchers on brain chemistry and sexual relationships and half of the team of scientists poking through my cranium. "We were willing to study the brain chemistry of fear and depression and anger but not love. I love thee with serotonin produced by my Raphe Nuclei. I love thee with testosterone receptors deep in my hypothalamus. I love thee with dopamine that floods my primitive lizard brain."[48]

The brain is multilayered, evolutionarily designed, and connects us with other mammalian and reptilian species. Because of the "design" of the brain, it is very difficult to become aware of deep emotional states in one's own brain or self. We have in common with reptiles the most primitive instincts, such as mating, defense of territory, and giving in to the dominant ones. These behaviors reside at the top of the spine and in the center of the brain. These areas lack the neuronal connections to be in direct communication with the more cognitive part of the brain. Instead, the newer part of the brain, the neocortex or "slower" part of the brain, has to inhibit the older, faster parts of the brain (the limbic and reptilian complex) when necessary.

The three parts of the brain reflecting our evolutionary heritage (reptile, mammalian and the cortex) are inter-connected, but one is never sure which part is in charge of actions and reactions.[49]

A good example is the fear response. It can only be inhibited once our biochemistry is activated. Once the stress hormones are released into the bloodstream it takes time to deactivate the stress response. Fear in the reptilian brain complex does not say to the higher cognitive center, the neocortex, "So do you think it is reasonable that I react to that stick?"

Instead, we just react and then the memory of all things pertaining to sticks kicks in. The limbic system contains the memory of the past and is able to remind us that usually sticks are inert and so inert objects tend to be sticks, not dreaded snakes. It can take a long time for the different parts of the brain to send signals to inhibit the initial reactivity to the "stick/snake" and there are physiological consequences for the one who experiences the fear response.

The basic biological values of all mammalian brains were built upon the same basic plan, laid out in consciousness-creating affective circuits that are concentrated in subcortical regions, far below the neocortical "thinking cap" that is so highly developed in humans.[50]

Perhaps, as neuroscience advances we will discover general laws regulating the primary emotional states of humans, mammals and reptiles. For example, we know that species are linked to others species because of the biochemistry and structure of their brains.

This is the reason we can be relatively sure that if drugs work on mice they just might work on men. We also know that there are instinctual structures in very ancient parts of our brain. Their job is to provide us with some very old directions about the value of specific sets of behaviors like reproduction, defending territory, and the urge to be altruistic and to survive. As a complex evolutionary tool for living, our brain also has a cognitive capacity to interpret or explain the social world we inhabit.

We have been able to explore the biochemistry of both the "fear" and "care" pathways in the brain. Animal research shows that the biochemistry of care and feelings of safety produce opiates in the brain.[51] The chemicals that can inhibit fear or promote caring are disrupted when people are fearful. Those with disrupted relationships early in life show markers of disturbance and neuronal overgrowth in parts of the brain leading to the inability to self-regulate. People with these kinds of markers often repeat negative stories about their life experiences. These stories reinforce the overconnected pathways in the brain.[52]

These are the people who are vulnerable to drug use later in life. In various forms of cognitive therapy people make the effort to correct the deficits from increasing stress, a loss of caring relationships, etc., by having healthier relationships and telling more positive stories.

Most mammals and invertebrates, like ants, have no need for a sophisticated apparatus like the human brain to become aware of how their actions impact others. They are simply influenced by the interactions and the needs of the colony and their body chemistry reflects the cumulative and current state of relationships in the colony.

Darwin's Life as an Example of the Force to be an Individual

Charles Darwin's life is a fantastic example of one individual who had to figure out his way around the togetherness forces in his family and society. Early on, Darwin had to triangle in his uncle to get his father's permission to take the voyage on the *Beagle.*[53]

Darwin's "use" of his uncle is a good example of people naturally knowing about triangles and what it takes to become a more differentiated self. No one had written down the methods, but somehow Darwin knew and overcame the emotional forces to give up and go along with the group (his family group to name just one).

Charles Darwin was concerned about how his theory, which he finally articulated in his 1859 book, *The Origin of Species,* would be received by his peers and his family, especially his wife, Emma.[54] Emma Darwin was a religious individual. He was concerned about taking a very public position that was different from his wife's cherished and deeply held beliefs. Hesitating for more than twenty years to publish his work, Darwin gradually formed a loose association of supporters, who were crucial in enabling him to maintain himself despite the threat of disapproval from others. Darwin's theories continue to be controversial today.[55]

Not only was Darwin's life an example of an effort to differentiate a self and be less reactive to social control in his family and in society, his ideas about evolution enabled millions of people to understand that humans, like other animals, are forced to either adapt or perish when their environment changes. At times, adaptation is possible but it always requires the ability to notice the changing environment.

Family units vary in the ability to adapt to changing environments. Selection may operate at the level of the family unit. More mature units produce flexible leaders, who can observe and promote adaption, while other units require more "sacrifice" from some and these people have less ability to grow and develop more independently of the unit.

Darwin and many others have been puzzled by the existence of altruism in family groups. Many explanations have been put forth. Some say it is the hierarchical arrangement in the family which promotes the level of self in the individuals. But others maintain that groups are selected for as there is clear variation among families. It should not be a shock that the family unit pressures on individual to function in ways that promote the survival of the group and secondarily the individuals in the group.

Darwin's Ideas and the Importance of Facts in "Thinking Systems"

Perhaps Darwin's most challenging idea was that given enough time, natural selection alone could produce the diversity seen in the world around us. The idea was heresy to some during Darwin's lifetime, who believed that God created the natural world only 10,000 years ago.[56] Today, 46 percent of people believe that God created the earth as it is today and 33 percent believe in evolution as a scientific fact. This is an example of how scientific evidence is not very compelling when it challenges long-held beliefs.

Darwin suggested that natural selection occurs through random mutations and the selection of what some referred to as the "fittest." He observed that differences in traits between animals living on different islands could enable some individuals to have a survival advantage over others. Herbert Spencer's phrase, "the survival of the fittest," described how well animals could contend with and adapt to changes in the local environment. Darwin noted that some differences (such as the size of a bird's beak) greatly enhance survival, but some differences, such as eye color, do not add to the survival benefits of an animal.

Darwin was an amazingly accurate observer of the natural world. His curiosity and detailed accounting of what he saw led to the accumulation of incredible amounts of evidence to support his thesis that traits that have enhanced survival in one era are selected for and maintained even in environments where they may no longer function as well. He coined the term "natural selection" to distinguish it from artificial selection.

Throughout his life, Darwin was fascinated with plants and was involved in detailed research on breeding animals that were artificially "selected" to produce desired and specific outcomes. During his voyage on the *Beagle*, he began to hypothesize as to how something like natural selection operated on the observable characteristics of an organism. Those animals or plants, which could sustain life, become more prevalent in the population. The others died off. Selection for the more adaptive was an idea he got from reading Malthus who documented that when more were born than could be fed, the population crashed.

More than forty years ago, Peter and Rosemary Grant returned to the very islands where Darwin studied finches and began to research individual differences in survival among them. Unlike Darwin, the Grants were able to return every year for twenty years and followed these birds over twenty generations. They recognized individual birds and noted the impact of selection on the types of birds that survived. This allowed them to offer reasons about how the fittest were able to gain predominance. They proved that, at least for finches, natural selection happens quickly, and not necessarily as slowly as Darwin believed.

Selection follows alterations in the environment. In the case of the finches, the rainy season produced more birds with small beaks because the seeds were plentiful and easy to open. During dry spells, these small beaked birds diminished in number, as the size of their beaks made it difficult to impossible to open the few remaining hard seeds. The difference between death and survival during the several years of drought was only one-half of a millimeter in the size of a finch's beak. The birds with larger, stronger beaks prospered because they could crack open the seeds and survive the harsh conditions.[57] Since the publication of *The Origin of Species,* we have learned more about the ability of selection to act on the actual physical characteristics of a population as it adapts to changes in the environment. This has implications for just how selection may be at work today in humans.

Differentiation of Self: A Selective Advantage?

We are living in the midst of vast changes in the environment—growing population, climate change, diminishing and sometimes unreliable energy and food resources, to name a few. These changes may be creating selective pressure on humans. Perhaps those, who are better able to adapt to the changes, will be "selected" to survive.

Consider this. We know that people under stress tend to lose their ability to perceive the environment accurately, to cooperate with others and to adapt. Could it be then, that an ancient orienting response towards togetherness, that is, to fit in or go along with the group, will dominate as humans face current and future challenges? Or will the balance tip in the other direction because it is more adaptive to be a more defined individual, capable of cooperating as appropriate, and not just unthinkingly react to the herd? Remember that herds of animals sometimes go off in the wrong direction and fall off cliffs. Lemmings are famous for this and it is the lack of food that triggers this response.

If people cooperate "appropriately" and are to be "selected" for, could the balance be altered in the general population between the forces of togetherness and the emergence of more leaders? In other words, can there be less suffering if people are more aware of the mechanism? Though this is highly speculative, it is possible that just as a family crisis can produce a family leader, so, too, may societal challenges can produce more differentiated and aware leaders, who do not rise up on the backs of others through blame and shame. Without this urge to become more differentiated, humans may well fall back to making decisions in a more primitive togetherness oriented way which can create polarization and intense divisions. To be more respectful and separate allows people to be closer without feeling threatened.

CHAPTER XIII
SOCIAL PRESSURE AND THE ABILITY TO REDIRECT ANXIETY

The Downside of Togetherness

Obedience is as basic an element in the structure of social life as one can point to. Some system of authority is a requirement of all communal living, and it is only the person dwelling in isolation, who is not forced to respond, with defiance or submission, to the commands of others. For many people, obedience is a deeply ingrained behavior tendency, indeed a potent impulse overriding training in ethics, sympathy, and moral conduct.

Stanley Milgram

Stanley Milgram's Question: How can we be so blind?

Stanley Milgram was a social scientist who conducted groundbreaking research showing how people's obedience to authority is automatic, even when it leads to the potential death of innocent people.[39] His goal was to study the conditions necessary in a social group to lead to an event like the holocaust. How can good and normal people be so blind to the consequences of their behavior? His work doesn't reflect family systems theory but it still gives us factual evidence about the nature of the togetherness force among groups of unrelated humans. His research demonstrates that a majority of people will do harm to others based on a command from an authority figure even if that command goes against a value not to harm others. We are tremendously vulnerable to certain types of social pressure and the more we can know about this the better off we are.

How can we understand this kind of automatic behavior to go along with authority to the detriment of an individual or the social group as a whole? If behavior in social groups makes no adaptive sense on a "local" level, then we have to move to the larger evolutionary stage to see how selection itself may have led to our species' sensitivity to the togetherness forces in the group.

The "togetherness" force is a deep part of the life force, an instinct so deep in the brains of animals that no awareness is needed for the behaviors to manifest. Togetherness has advantages and disadvantages. A flock of birds or herd of elk may be able to avoid predators as they keep an eye on one another's location, while for a group of lemmings, the togetherness force has deadly consequences.

For the human, the instinct to cooperate and the tendency to go along with coercive social pressure is also built on these same deep instincts about which we are totally unaware. It is difficult for us to know how we are being socially controlled and influenced to be "in the service of others." It is difficult to know if we are doing or even thinking things about our own individual viewpoints or if our thinking is simply a reflection of our deep connection to instinctive programming as part of a group. It requires both an awareness of these instinctive forces and the ability to carefully consider one's reactions and beliefs in order to pull a real self out of the mire of the togetherness forces.

Solomon Asch - Conformity raises questions: how to educate people in a democracy

We also know that for both humans and other forms of life under stress, the natural urge to go along with the social group decreases the ability of individuals to accurately gauge the reality of the situation. Solomon Asch, a social scientist, has run experiments that show people will doubt their own perception of reality in order to fit in with the social group. Reality becomes a "social reality" under pressure.

Here is how Asch's test went. A student signs up for a psychology experiment. Others arrive whom he assumes are also students but who are actually actors in the experiment. The actors' behavior has been carefully programmed. Two cards are placed in front of the subjects; the one on the left has one vertical line, while the one on the right has three lines of varying length. (See illustration.)[58]

The experimenter then asks each participant, one at a time, to choose which of the three lines on the right-hand card match the length of the line on the left-hand card. This process is repeated several times with different cards. On some occasions, the other "subjects" unanimously chose the wrong line. When this happened, it was clear to the real student that the others were wrong, even though they had all given the same answer. What would you do? Would you go along with the majority opinion, or would you stick to your guns and trust your own eyes?

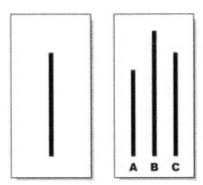

To Asch's surprise, 37 of the 50 subjects went along with the majority at least once, and 14 of them did so in more than 6 of the 12 trials. When faced with a unanimous wrong answer by the other group members, the average subject conformed on 4 of the 12 trials. "On average, about one-third (32%) of the participants who were placed in this situation went along and conformed with the clearly incorrect majority on the critical trials. Over the 12 critical trials about 75% of participants conformed at least once and 25% of participant never conformed."[59] Asch was disturbed by these results and said:

"Life in society requires consensus as an indispensable condition. But consensus, to be productive, requires that each individual contribute independently out of his experience and insight. When consensus comes under the dominance of conformity, the social process is polluted and the individual at the same time surrenders the powers on which his functioning as a feeling and thinking being depends. That we have found the tendency to conformity in our society so strong that reasonably intelligent and well-meaning young people are willing to call white black is a matter of concern. It raises questions about our ways of education and about the values that guide our conduct."[41]

173

When Instincts are Hidden as Values We Do NOT Question Them

Social pressure and a "togetherness" orientation to go along with the group are deeply instinctual and are incorporated into the psychological belief and value system of the human. Togetherness may usurp and hide under a pleasant sounding request like: "Can you please just *cooperate* with us?" We are urged to cooperate with others rather than to think carefully about how we can cooperate with others to manifest our individuality. There is no Self for anyone in going along with others in unthinking reactions to social pressure.

These more instinctive urges to go along with or to "cooperate" with others have been acquired over evolutionary time and spring from the more primitive parts of the non-verbal brain. Once verbalized, via our brain stem to our cortex, "cooperation" becomes a positive "value," forcing others to behave in the "right" way. The difference between one being mature enough to cooperate based on a principled position that values the action, is very different from being forced to cooperate by people using and/or giving into various mechanisms of social control. There are many numerous beliefs that reflect our more primitive urges to be for others and to give up self or to be for self and to abandon or even harm others. When instincts are converted into values and beliefs, we tend not to question them. Our beliefs reside in the emotional part of the brain, "far away" from the brain's cognitive center. Bowen believed that thinking (via our cortex) could gradually influence feelings, but that this would be a slow process because of the way the brain is structured.

Trying to be logical with highly emotional content may only intensify emotions, like throwing dry leaves on a forest fire. There is a distinct advantage for humans to become more aware of one another's different positions and at the same time, to take greater responsibility for self's decisions. The challenge is to "allow" others to be free to accept responsibility for their own actions and beliefs.

Bowen's Road Map

No one before Bowen described a road map allowing us to understand how to be a more separate and defined individual, and at the same time be able to be close to those who are different from us and even oppose our points of view.

Although the steps for defining a self have been mentioned earlier in this book, here they are again:

An individual states what he or she will or will not do.

The others in the system object to this change message. They begin to make demands that the individual change back and alter his or her stance.

In making a differentiating effort, individuals are aware of the resistance and make every effort to not react. Instead they make an effort to dampen down the fear since they have carefully thought about how to be present.

Strategizing before action allows one to interrupt, be silly, say nothing or keep in contact in a mild mannered way, while the system reorganizes.

The ability of one person to influence a system towards greater maturity by managing and focusing on Self is powerful. So, too, is the emotional fusion that binds people to one another. When the balance between individuality and togetherness is off kilter we see the use of the four-anxiety mechanism (distance, conflict, win-lose and projection) as a habitual way of binding anxiety. When the differentiating one takes a stand, usually the others cannot see the problem. They say, "Why would this person make such a stink about such a thing?" There is no pat on the back or love and approval for the person making the effort.

The differentiating one has to endure loneliness. The hope is that eventually there will be greater awareness and more respect between people, although this is not guaranteed. Differentiation offers the potential for human growth that nothing else does. By publishing his observations of the family as a unit and his thinking as to how one person can be less reactive and more principle oriented, Bowen highlighted the understanding of this potential in the human.

Bowen did his research effort in his own family during a time of relatively low anxiety. He found that often, unless the family crisis was big enough, few were willing to take on separating a self for the fun of it. The togetherness force is too strong. The differentiating one is perceived as cold or even heartless. Their response to cries for help from the group is with interruptive and challenging comments that confuse the group. But these kinds of challenges can, over time, result in more independent thought, less blame and often a more profound and mature way of acting in response to a crisis.

Managing Social Relationships is a Skill Based in Our Instinctive Nature to Adapt

We have inherited the cognitive ability to become better observers of our interactions with others. We have the ability to question others' and our own functioning and to question the way we relate to others and how they relate to us. This ability to increase our awareness and self-control is part of our evolutionary heritage. It conveys specific advantages to the social groups whose members have this ability.[42] The increasing awareness and self-control of humans is the evolutionary advantage that allows social systems to reorganize and survive. Evolution itself has applied selective pressure to family groups to promote the ability of individuals to define a better way to be for self and for the group. Moreover, selective pressure then favors those groups with more independent but appropriately cooperative individuals, who are able to adapt to the reality of situations, not just to social pressures.

There are reasons that social pressure to conform to the group has persisted. One may be that energy is conserved by conforming to past ways of functioning encoded in the "rules" of the social group. This may be useful when there is little change in the environment. It takes energy to define a more separate self from the group and such efforts can be disruptive and increase the cost to the group because each individual has to use energy to adapt to the changing individual. However, once the environment begins to undergo rapid changes, the group itself needs more individuals who are less sensitive to social pressure and more realistic about the environmental changes. Such people can, through their own non-anxious presence, enable others to be less reactive and more aware, both of which contribute to the survival of the group.

By increasing awareness through developing one's Mindful Compass, individuals are more capable of functioning effectively in relationships with others, even when they are under pressure. The conflict that occurs with the expression of differences in a healthy system decreases sensitivity and emotional reactivity and increases an individual's capacity to manage increasing anxiety. As a result, individuals learn to interrupt the status quo often by simply describing the ongoing interactions and defining what they will or will not do. These individuals have the capacity to wait, stand their ground without pressuring or impinging on others, and allow time for others to think for themselves.

It takes courage and the development of an emotional backbone to define a self in the face of emotional pressure from the group. As long as more individuals are capable of learning, reflecting, reasoning and correcting errors, the family (and work) system as a whole will have a better chance to adapt to the demands of the environment, not the emotional demands for "comfort" that maintains the status quo.

The Redistribution of Anxiety by Knowledgeable Leaders

Organizing self to deal with increasing threats or anxiety has allowed groups, from bacteria to humans, to survive. Here are strategies that people have found useful in managing anxiety.

1. Observing how systems function and how one's family has functioned over generations.

2. Understanding the mechanisms for absorbing anxiety (which can take the sting out of or depersonalize our feelings about the way people behave). One becomes more neutral as to how families distribute anxiety unevenly. A family leader can begin to alter relationship dynamics, finding ways to redirect anxiety by changing self.

3. Developing the ability of one or two people in the family to be less reactive and more thoughtful, interrupting emotional contagions.

4. Defining one's self to the family and being present and accounted for during important family events from celebrations to illness to death. Doing this over time allows one to be genuinely connected to people who are important to you in one-on-one relationships.

5. Using various methodologies to lower anxiety such as neurofeedback, cardio exercise and meditation.

If these efforts cannot be made, then the individual and the family will simply return to the automatic ways of managing anxiety—distance, conflict, physical or emotional problems, reciprocal relationships (the borrowing and lending of self between two) and projection of fear and anxiety onto others.

How is it that families do not see problems coming? It may be that the status quo is so seductive change must wait until a family crisis is large enough and/or one person is willing to alter their part in the relationship system. It is difficult and confusing to figure out how much energy one devotes for self and how much for others, and especially during times of crisis, as the instinctual urge for individual survival is to cooperate.

We have considered that there may be general tendencies in biological systems to organize in specific way. In social groups, there is a balance between the forces for individuality and togetherness. The force to fit in with the group should automatically create a counterbalance, which would increase the pressure to be an individual in one's own right. But these balancing conditions do not prevail when there is too much stress and fear.

The group think automatically pressures people to give up individuality for the group —"It's a threat." "Do it or else."—at its most primitive level. Too much pressure to be "for the group" can obliterate individual development.

This is what you see in war conditions or in some kind of intense perception of threat. Obtaining an adaptive balance, between being for the social group and being an individual, has evolved in many different species over evolutionary time. The work of a few experts in the natural and social science fields shows how at one end of the spectrum ants and bees are able to be for the colony in ways that are totally instinctual. Becoming one with the colonies has enabled these amazing creatures to adapt and spread over millions of years.

In contrast, social scientists such as Stanley Milgram and Solomon Asch show us how problems occur when blind obedience leads humans to (sometimes tragic) errors in judgment. Some humans have the ability to separate from the togetherness in the social group and this capability over time can impact the social group. The social group itself may need to become more oriented to providing ways to develop independence in its members, especially during times of rapid change.

In the human family a new pathway from other social animals has developed. Individuals can "learn" to become more systems aware. They can understand how relationship systems work and can learn to redistribute the anxious focus off the weak and vulnerable. Mature leaders seem to naturally know how to separate self and form coalitions. But for many of us, these skills have to be learned. It takes an effort to ignore the cues from the relationships system to fit in and to act in specific ways.

The reason this leadership skill may become more widespread has to do with the changing environment, that is, the increasing numbers of people in small and more isolated family groups and the possibility of threats to resources such as clean water and food supplies. Leaders in the future can be more aware of possible runaway relationship traps. By being less reactive to others, they then can promote greater responsibility both for others and for self. I speculate that if differentiation does confer an adaptive response during times of great change, we should see more of this ability become manifest in well-functioning social groups.

Below is a 1978 photograph of Dr. and Mrs. Murray Bowen accepting an honor from The Medical College of Virginia (MCV) for his groundbreaking work in videotaping families over many years.

The video series began at MCV in 1968 and continued monthly filming at Walter Reed Army Hospital. Two families were seen for fifteen years, until 1983. This represents the longest series of any videotaped family sessions. A third family continued for eleven years. These videotaped series on the functioning of three families was used as an educational tool to demonstrate the use of Bowen Theory in coaching. The series was a part of The Clinical Conference training for professionals at The Georgetown University Family Center. The videotapes and Dr. Bowen's professional papers are available for researchers and are archived at The National Library of Medicine.

CHAPTER XIV
INTRODUCTION TO
INTERVIEWS

One of Dr. Bowen's ideas is that being able to separate out a more mature Self, while staying in contact with others (the process of differentiation of self) is a natural phenomenon. People, over the centuries, have figured out how to lead. Leaders like Darwin and Lincoln were able to figure out how to bring their visions to life, both in the family and in society.

Bowen thought that motivated people could be coached and could learn how to understand the system and to be more *differentiated,* if they understood the process and the rational.

I was curious, was this fact? If I interviewed leaders, would they tell me how they were able to separate out from the pressure in their social system and be better defined in relationship to the important people in their family or at work? Would they tell me how others, both in the family unit and at work, would automatically oppose the growth of a "leader?"

To answer this question I asked friends who they would consider to be a natural leader. I then set about the job of interviewing these leaders. They told fascinating stories of leading under conditions of uncertainty.

The people I interviewed were local leaders. There were not famous, but each has been able to make a difference in some area of society without the useful aid of Bowen theory. Each one will tell you what he or she has been up against in trying to move forward through the social jungle. I was curious as to the kind of Mindful Compass they had constructed. After each interview there is a synthesis of the points on the compass that their story addresses.

Using the Mindful Compass makes it possible for more individuals to find and to define Self in the relationship system, despite the pressure in the emotional system. This ability to reflect on relationship pressure and to define Self is a process that reduces suffering and leads to more integrated thinking and a better ability to cooperate wisely.

More mature leaders have an ability to see emotional process and to respond creatively during times of great change. They have the ability to see the environment more realistically and to take difficult stands. It takes courage and the development of an emotional backbone to define a Self in the face of emotional pressure from the group.

Anyone can learn and practice this ability to be more differentiated in emotional groups using Bowen Theory. Systems theory is a completely new way to think about human behavior. No one knows what the outcome will be for those who are able to think and act differently, relate well and define a more responsible self. Few things are harder but more worthwhile to do than this.

The human brain is receptive to stories as a way to see hidden processes. We know that relationship blinders, stress, and information that "do not compute" can create reactions and the automatic overuse of defensive mechanisms. Increasing anxiety in relationships prevents us from questioning or noticing what goes on between people. So a critical goal is to learn more about managing ourselves in different types of relationships by listening to our own and other leaders' stories. People can give you a list of things to do—be nice, be positive, be joyful, argue thoughtfully, but any such list may not always help you change your behavior. On the other hand, real life examples show us the subtle ways that useful relationship networks are built and then managed by a person. If the individual is separate and secure, and best of all, systems-wise, their story will have an impact on the reader's brain.

The clearer people are about their experience, the easier it is to listen and even enjoy the adventure of the story. This allows us to see how others' experiences fit with our own experience. Stories add to our knowledge base. Armed with ideas from others and our hard won experience, we will be able to see just what is happening in social relationships. Eventually using only a very few clues, we will decide what to do about *our own* relationship patterns as we see them unfolding.

The ten people I interviewed talk about how they think their families may have influenced their ability to be a leader. I gave each interviewee a copy of the thirty-three questions listed in Chapter One, so that they had a preview of how I think about the influence of families on individuals.

Not all the interviews are structured in the same way, so the formats of each may be different. In the interviews you will read about those times when a leader could be clear and thoughtful as to the position for Self that they are able to take. You can hear the reactions, sometimes negative in the social group, and then see how others will eventually rise up, and the whole social group will function more effectively.

It is a privilege to hear how family relationships formed and influenced these individuals to become leaders. It is in their families that they learned early on, one way or another, to manage self in relationships. So, the focus of my interviews of these leaders was to see if, and then how, early relationships impacted the ability of these individuals to figure out how to function as leaders. After listening to their stories I linked their stories to the four points on the Mindful Compass, highlighting each one's ability to be aware of the leadership decision-making process. Each individual has a different way of thinking about being leader. These differences contribute to our knowledge about how an individual observes and understands systems, charts their own way, and gains strength and leads despite opposition.

After the interviews, these individuals reported that they had never thought about the events in their lives from a systems perspective. The ideas exchanged in the interviews seemed to help them see in new ways, their lives in their families and how they emerged as leaders. They saw the significance of crucial relationships that encouraged them to choose one path over another by putting their whole life story together in an hour or so.

No doubt each of us can learn from telling (writing) our own story and seeing more clearly how various people and events influenced us. The web of life emerges in each of our families. It takes courage to look into our deeper selves and to talk or write our story about where we have come from and where we are going. By reading others' stories, hopefully we can understand the impact of relationship systems on the challenges people face and provide some clues about how others have defined a Self to their near and dear. Perhaps the stories in these interviews will give you courage too.

Listed below are some of the ways I listened for the main points on the Mindful Compass as I reflected on these interviews:

- While listening to each individual, I asked myself whether the person told me what is important to him or her. I looked for "I" statements: "This is what I will or will not do." "This is what I believe." "This is important to me." These statements represent the first point on the compass, the person's vision and/or goals.

- When these individuals' "I" statements moved to some action, they inevitably had to predict and deal with resistance to their actions, another point on the compass. Such resistance is inevitable, occurring when the system comes alive to cope with changes. The response to such resistance tests the mettle of every leader.

- How well does the person understand the history of the family or work system they are in? Does it appear that they know their strengths and weaknesses in relationship to others in the system? Did the individual turn an "I will" or "I did" statement into a reality? Was his or her success based on an understanding of the relationship system? This is the compass point that reflects how well the person connects with others by using systems knowledge.

- How well does a person self-regulate when challenged and how do they manage self in triangles? One of the most difficult positions for leaders to take is to encourage others to separate out a Self without getting mad and reactive. Can any leader stand alone without trying to control others who differ?

The people I interviewed for this book fall along a spectrum of how they tell their stories. At one end of the spectrum are the abstract thinkers, those who can step outside themselves to relate their histories, analyze their experiences, and assess their impact. At the other end of the spectrum are individuals who can describe the details of their lives in such a compelling, intimate way that you can almost taste and smell their experiences. They show us how a strong commitment to self-knowledge leads to commitments to the well-being of family and the larger community.

The price of greatness is responsibility.
-Winston Churchill

INTERVIEWS

JIM WALSH

A former advertising executive, who moved to Hawaii in 1986, Walsh is the owner of Hawaiian Vintage Chocolate. He is dedicated to producing the world's finest cocoa using a process that begins with genetics and proceeds with love of trees and a growing concern for the environment on which we all depend.

Walsh has had many adventures that set him apart from the average person and he has deep memories of the details of his life that he tells in captivating vignettes. Few people can recall events from a very young age much less see how these events have shaped their later lives. Walsh can. His mind is very open and it was easy to enjoy the complexity and coherence of his story. During the transcription of the interview, I inserted comments to clarify either what he was saying or what I was thinking as I was listening to him. These comments are in italics.

AMS – One hallmark of a leader is the ability to be separate from others and think your own thoughts while still communicating with the others. I am always curious as to how people first experience being separate from others.

JW – When I was very young I had a sense of the sunshine, a golden sense of unity with the sunshine that made me feel like I was one with the universe. This is a very early sensation and memory that I can return to. Then, when I was two and a half or so, I had my first realization that I was separate. I was outside with the other kids playing, and did not want to do what my Mom wanted me to do—help her with the garden. So I went back to the house to play with the cat. I had my own agenda, but Mom sent my older brother to get me. When I told him I was not going back there, he said again, "Mom sent me to get you." I said, "Okay, I'll go with you if I get to ride on your bike." He agreed, but on the way my shoe fell off. When I got off the bike my foot got caught in the spokes of the wheel and my toe was cut off. This created the realization in me that I was different, separate. I had to go to the hospital and have the toe put back on. This was the beginning of noting how different I was from the others.

At five, I realized that I looked different from my siblings. My hair was a different color. Then when I was in third grade and bragging about my family and my Dad being a doctor, my best friend said, "You are not a Walsh, you were adopted." I went home and after my snack told my Mom that the strangest thing had happened—my friend had told me I was adopted. My Mom was putting a glass on a shelf and froze when she heard this. I knew it was true, that I was adopted, and that my entire identity, who I thought I was, was wrong.

My Mom said. "We were going to tell you when you were older." But after that life was very different. My relationship with my parents turned troublesome, and I was the only kid at home. I was wrongly accused of stealing at age eight. I can still remember sitting on the steps outside my house and promising myself that I would never let anyone else be in charge of my life again.

AMS – Would you say this last experience solidified a direction that had been building about the importance of being more independent from others?

JW – It was all part of trying to figure out who I was. I also recalled the early experience of the Dominican nuns, who would come over to our house. I am not sure if they were somehow involved in the adoption.

AMS – But naturally you were curious?

JW – Yes. When I was in high school, my friends and I decided to search my father's records for my birth certificate to find out more about who my parents were. We found a record that said a baby boy had been born to Ann Smith, with my birth date on it.

AMS – Did you ever meet your biological mother?

JW – I did not pay much attention to my biological family until my wife, Marie, was pregnant with our oldest daughter, Ashley. Then I became curious about the genetics of the family's health. I asked my Mom to arrange a meeting with Ann Smith, which she did. But then she (my biological mother) backed out. I decided to do it on my own. I found out where she lived, went to her home one afternoon, knocked on the door, and said, "I am Jim Walsh." It was 3 o'clock, school got out at 3:15. My biological mother had seven other children, whom she had never told about me. I pushed her to tell me who my biological father was. She refused to tell me. So I left.

My adopted mother did not want to tell me either, as the families were friends. No one wanted to tell on anyone, or put anyone in a bad light. My adopted mother is now 96 and I still do not know who my biological father is. From all that I know, when my adopted mother dies my biological mother will be free to tell me more information. My adopted mother is an intellectual, she thinks about things, and so there is still a secret that she is afraid of. She is not ready for it to come out.

AMS – I can hear the fear families have about issues they consider too difficult to deal with openly. Often families would just rather hide the information. This may make them feel better in the short term, but over the long run it makes things more difficult and closed. It can sever family connections, and it denies family members the opportunity to use their innate abilities to deal with difficulties.

What happened with your siblings in your adopted family after it came out that you are adopted? Did those relationships and their relationship with your parents change?

JW – I had three older brothers—one eight years older, Tom; one five years older, Bill; three years older and Mike, the youngest. After it came out that I was adopted, I was treated differently. My Mom would make two cakes on my birthday, one from my biological family and the other from my adopted family. There was a very real schism there. My brothers were sent to boarding school and I was alone with my parents for a few years before I went, too.

My mother had a difficult struggle. She was very involved in her identity as a small town's doctor's wife. And perhaps she had fewer opportunities to develop her own self because we lived in a semi-rural community. On many levels, she never really wanted to know what was happening. She was depressed for a while but recovered. I don't think she was happy in her marriage. She used to say that the happiest time for her was when she was in high school and thinking about being a nun. My parents were married after Dad finished medical school, and she said she was happy at the beginning of the marriage.

My reaction to both [*my adopted parents*] and their attitudes were to try to understand how things worked. And, of course, I wanted to be self-reliant and survive the tension in the house. I developed the ability to engage with others using my sense of humor. My Dad was also funny, and in the best of times I could play off of his sense of humor. Throughout my life, my dreams have been very powerful helpers, too. [*Jim Walsh has studied Jungian dream analysis.*]

After high school, I went to the University of Wisconsin and took pre-med. I wanted to follow in my Dad's footsteps. But, really, I had always been an entrepreneur. I was always involved in selling things. When I was 11, I helped run a grocery store. In college, my brother and I became involved in setting up musical events. He needed me to set up a club on the university campus so we could rent the University of Wisconsin's Field House auditorium. I was 19 when we decided to organize our biggest event. The dean of admissions was my uncle, so I asked him how I could do it. He said that I had to start a music club sanctioned by the university, and then I could rent the field house.

My brother and I had built up a war chest by putting on smaller events. Now we wanted to go to the next level and have a band from England come over. To make this work I needed $25,000. At the time, I had been dating Marie for about six months. I really liked her family and decided to ask them for the money. And, God bless her parents, they agreed. Her father went to the bank and borrowed the money on their house. The first concert of the national tour we were promoting was sold out. Marie and I drove up in the limo knowing we had made $60,000 on the first of what was to be 12 more concerts. I am telling her, "This is easy." Then the problems come. We see a mushroom cloud in the middle of the auditorium: The sound system has blown up. We try to patch it into the house system, but the tension mounts. The audience taunts and the lead singer throws a mike at a woman in the audience and knocks her out. She goes to the hospital. We tell people we will refund their money the next day, and then try to get the band to realize they have to pay for the woman's treatment. The band quits the scheduled national tour and goes back to England.

Now, here I am at 19 owing my future in-laws $25,000. I realized there was no medical school in my future. I needed to pay the money back as soon as possible. I knew I was good at marketing, so I got into the land business and paid them back in three years.

AMS – *[In the next comment, I was considering the position Jim Walsh found himself in, trying to become self-reliant as a way to deal with his parents' anxieties and the way his father had appeared to focus on him and blame him. The following comment was intended to connect my impression of the emotional process underneath the content that he is reporting.]*

Blame is a big, complex issue. Often parents are really just trying to make things happen right for their kids. They are over-anxious more about the children than about what they themselves are doing. So they push the children and blame them in an attempt to get the kids on the right track. It is often very challenging for parents to look objectively at their own behavior.

What is your Mom's sibling position?

JW – She was an only child. Her Dad was a grocery store owner, a big deal in the Knights of Columbus, and a Sergeant at Arms in the State Senate. He was married to Maggie, the oldest of three sisters. Talk about tough as nails—that was Maggie. Even my Dad was afraid of her. She lived with us for the last six years of her life. She had a knobby old cane, and when I would bring a tray in to her she would beat the bed with the cane and say, "Get out of here you devil!" I would run out of the room. But the sisters were always a very close family. My Dad and his uncle-in-law built a house so that the kitchen faced the way Maggie wanted it to face, even though the house was to be my mother's home.

189

AMS – That is a funny story! But you can see the threads of each generation being afraid of upsetting the others, and sometimes with good reason. Family loyalty is definitely a double-edged sword. It asks individuals to give up a lot of self to accommodate the dominant force—and that can be dangerous over the generations.

Can we refocus on your strengths and how you used them at work?

JW – Getting into land development got me interested in organizations and made me want to see how they worked. So at 23, I found a recruiter and told him I wanted a job with lots of exposure to other companies. He found me one—with an incentive company out of Minneapolis. After I worked there for a year and a half, one of their competitors recruited me. He said I could take over the company since the owner had no children. I enjoyed being with him and learned a lot, but then my mentor left and went to work for Green Stamps. This altered the dynamics. I decided not to wait, and went out and formed my own company.

J.P. Walsh & Company was a peer-recognition company. In many very large companies, the top salesmen win trips or other kinds of awards. I had good relationships with many of the top German companies, like Volkswagen and Mercedes. My overall goal at the time was to create a cash flow business so that I could buy a lot of other companies, kind of like Howard Hughes. By the time I was 30, I owned seven companies in Chicago.

Another turning point occurred when Ken Darby of the *Sun Times* interviewed me. I told him that since I had met my goal of becoming a millionaire by 30, my next interest would be how to feed the world's population using the oceans. It just came off the top of my head. But it stayed with me. About a year later, burned out from work, I decided to go white water rafting with my father-in-law in Chile. I suffered a serious head injury there. The doctor on the trip thought that I would never make it out alive, and encouraged me to write up my last thoughts to my family. I knew I was between life and death and that it would be grueling to get out of the Andes.

At that time I had been married to Marie for 12 years. I knew she would be fine and I could let her go. Ashley was three. She had a personality and was also fine. My brother-in-law was the number-two man in the company, and I could write him my ideas about what to do. Then I thought about choosing life. Marie was seven months pregnant with my daughter Camry, a child I had never met, and I knew I had to live to see this child.

Now, it so happened that my brother Bill had been doing some work with creative visualization, and I had just read a book about how to do it. So I realized I had a choice. I could die on the river or set things up so I could live. I started to visualize the injury. It was a big ball of blood, and if it leaked into my brain I would be dead. So I visualized a wall around it so it would not jar loose as we traveled out of the mountains.

We made it back, and I was in intensive care for a month. It took another year and a half to restore my cognitive abilities. Part of this was looking at how I consciously wanted to live my life. I wanted to give something back to the Boy Scouts, who had helped me. I wanted to live somewhere warm where I could see my children every day. So, that meant I would spend hours putting a Lotus spreadsheet together spelling out all my options. Marie was able to step up and sell some of our companies, and by 1984 I was back in the game again.

I decided I wanted to be in the food business, and did a survey to see what kind of food business I could add value to. I was still an entrepreneur wanting to solve my own problems. By chance I met the chairman of Hershey's and asked if he grew cocoa beans in Hawaii. He said no, but added that he would like to since Africa was politically unstable. I asked if he would be my technical partner, and in 1986 started a cocoa bean farm in Hawaii. Growing these trees is a 25-year process. But I had my dream—the warm weather, being with the children, and a natural crop that would give people energy. When our youngest daughter graduated from high school, my wife Marie, who is a four-seasons person, wanted to come back to the mainland. So, we came back home to the U.S. I had a successful business, Hawaiian Vintage Chocolate; so what would be my next step?

I needed to do some deep thinking about it. I took a year and I found myself getting depressed. But what came out of it was another entrepreneurial investment—using Hawaiian Vintage Chocolate's technical knowledge to make functional food. It would be delivered in the form of an easy-to-eat bar that is healthy, but still tastes good and delivers energy. We licensed the name SOBE from Pepsi. It was a great idea, but it took too long to get to the marketplace. We discontinued that bar in favor of one we called Z-Bar, for Zero Carbs. Now we are developing a full system of nutritional foods.

Hawaiian Vintage was the chocolate for people who have everything. It is the one you have to have. Clinton gave it to the head of China in 1995. The Dali Lama loved it. One day I got a call from this guy, Mark Hopkins. He told me he had been to a conference and met a shaman who said he had to find the American, who was raising cocoa trees in Hawaii. This man had to do a lot of digging to find me, but he wanted to deliver the message. The shaman said that the trees had a message for me. The trees say, "It is the cacao tree's role to heal the human heart and you have a role in that mission. Keep at it." Now, I have always had a special feeling for trees. I think that the trees are healing for me. We get this gift from the trees in a diminished form, chocolate. If you eat the bean itself you get more energy, more life. My investment banker, who had had a heart attack, came out to Hawaii and decided to use the cocoa bean to reduce his pain. This was an amazing incident for him and just further proof that I was on the right path. I am sure there will be many twists and turns in the years ahead, but the overall goal will be to give nourishment to people and life back to the planet.

AMS – I know you have to go. I've enjoyed talking to you and look forward to continuing the conversation in the years ahead.

Jim Walsh's Mindful Compass Points

(1) The ability to take ACTION and to define a vision: As a very young child, Walsh experiences himself as being one with the sunshine and the universe. This is a powerful vision that he has returned to, built on and used to focus his life goals through challenges and transitions. A painful injury to his foot when Walsh was barely three years old was a shock. He realized at that time that he was, indeed a very separate person and that he would have to look out for himself. Again, when falsely accused of stealing at age eight, he became fiercely determined to be self-reliant. Yes, it is possible to hear the edge in these stories, but the need to be self-reliant is a powerful drive that can be harnessed to promote people's ability to be more separate from the emotional system and to see that the system is not all powerful in

determining your fate.

By the time Walsh entered college, his goal was pre-med, following in his father's footsteps. As he went about making money and following his dream, he faced yet another challenge, erasing the dream of medical school. Again rising from the ashes of this broken hopes and goals, Walsh was able to recalibrate his compass and, with faith in himself, find another way to use his skills to repay his debt to his in-laws.

It often happens that when people become more financially independent, they are able to break the hold that the emotional system has on them and to establish new and different relationships with people that were once unavailable to them. Walsh found a way to follow a new vision in his relationships in both his family and his work—meeting his biological mother and establishing a company that that helps feed the world, a direction he found so inspiring.

(2) The RESISTANCE to change in self and in any system: Once we find a way to define ourselves in terms of what is important, we can be met with all kinds of resistance. There are the personal ones, such as when people close to you oppose you. This happened as Walsh tried to find and see his biological mother, and then again as he tried to make money in the music business. However, he also gives us a close up view of the resistance we can have in living life itself. After sustaining a major blow to the head, Walsh had to consider his own profound reasons to live. One of the deepest wells of resistance we may encounter in our lives occurs when we are forced to choose between life and death. There have been stories of terminally patients delaying death until all the relatives have had a chance to say good-bye, or until a child graduates from high school, for example. But not many of us have had to face an almost certainly fatal injury and decide whether to accept death or fight for life. There is a degree of peacefulness in accepting death as inevitable, and a degree of resistance to accepting the idea that our lives are shortly to be over.

Walsh systematically listed the pros and cons and decided that he must live to see his unborn child come into the world. He created a mental vision to help him resist the threat of death, and focused on what had to be done to get well. He also wrote to his loved ones to explain to them, and to himself, how he came to this turning point. Perhaps this exercise, like writing a last will and testament, frees people from a deeper level of fear and enables them to live. One lesson is that resistance will always be there. But one does not have to make a big deal of it. One has a choice, and can focus on the job at hand rather than the fear or anger about the situation itself.

(3) The ability to use KNOWLEDGE to connect: Walsh tells us of being determined to make contact with his biological family. It required him to gather the facts that were hidden. To do this he had to figure out how to use his alliances in overcoming the secrecy in his families. He also decided not to use his knowledge or his power to upset his adoptive mother and accepted that some information would not be available until after her death. This probably allowed him to be seen by others in the family as a more thoughtful person than if had he barged in and continued to push to get what he wanted. On a spiritual level, Walsh's early memory of feeling that he was part of the sunshine and a part of the universe is reflected in his desire to live and connect with all of life. On a business level, he enjoys selling things to people and connecting with them in the process. The obvious problem for a person, who naturally connects with others, is to learn to be separate enough to know and be true to his or her own values. Walsh seems to have established an enviable balance here.

(4) The ability to be STAND ALONE and to be more separate: Walsh had two painful wake-up calls when he was very young that showed him he was indeed separate and different. These were events not of his choosing. The first occurred when his toe was severed and the second was when he learned that he was adopted. In these cases, people can break or make their futures, either by a negative focus on how different and unfortunate they are, or by a positive focus on how to use that separateness to make one's mark in the world.

A person like Walsh, who has separated well from his family, but still knows he has more work to do in dealing with the tension between his biological and adoptive family, is not likely to become polluted by negative energy from others. Walsh was able to let go of the anger and disappointments that often accompany any realization that we are different and unique. How he will go about reconnecting with this family and staying separate will be another story. The significance of being with others and being separate from them is woven throughout Walsh's life story. This creates the sense of a man, who has learned to be self-reliant so that he can be productive in a highly value-driven way, while remaining a part of his family and society.

GARY RESNICK, PH.D.

Gary Resnick is Bioscience Division Leader, Bioscience Division, The Center for Homeland Security at the Los Alamos National Laboratory.

As a scientist, Resnick understands the importance of considering various ideas without becoming overly positive or negative about the assumptions, hypotheses or theories presented. As a scientist, he was the logical person to question some of my premises based in Family Systems Theory, which are the basis for my questions in the interview. For example, he was skeptical of the idea that there might be a link between his early relationships and his later leadership skills. This was especially intriguing to me, because in trying to establish a connection between relationships, life events and leadership ability, I appreciate knowledgeable but open-minded skeptics, who sharpen my thinking. For this reason, among others, it was a gift to be able to interview and be interviewed by Gary Resnick. He is not a first-born son who, according to standard theory, might be expected to inherit a leadership position. He has both an older and a younger brother (who died early), and he became a leader by choice.

I was introduced to Resnick by my friend Norman Johnson, who was working with Resnick on various security issues after the events of 9/11. The first thing I noticed about Resnick was that he was both "the boss" and an observer. Since he had leadership/management experience, I was somewhat surprised that he did not insert himself more forcefully into our three-way conversation. There was no trace of a "boss man" during our conversation.

Both Resnick and Johnson are internationally recognized scientists in the area of chemical and biological defense. At the time I met with them, they were working on modeling different responses to disasters, while I was trying to figure out how to communicate information to individuals without making them anxious. We had a common interest in understanding how large groups and individuals react to information. Resnick and I both understand humans and microbes as self-organizing systems operating in dynamic ways. We know that successful organisms learn and adapt to changing environments and understand that all living species must predict what strategies will work—or else!

When I asked Resnick if he would participate in a formal interview as part of an effort to understand the bridge between early relationships and leadership ability, he graciously agreed. He added the reservation, however, that he might be a disappointment since he was not sure how or even if his family had enabled his leadership ability.

Curious, I asked him, "How did you become a leader?"

GR – Even as a youngster I had no real interest in leading. Instead, I was seen as a leader and asked to participate as a leader. This may have had to do with my ability to solve problems. In fact, I even resisted being a leader, especially when pressured by a group.

Later on, when I started to study ethnology, which involves the concept of leaders and followers in other species, I began to form a concept about what humans are about. I knew what activities had to occur and what was needed for a social system to exist. I saw that even in ants there are leaders and followers, and most stay in their positions with some movement back and forth. I was interested in what roles were needed and how they were assigned.

My first real job came when I was in my early thirties, after my post doc. My work was headed down a very scientific path that did not involve humans, but somehow I picked my head up and noticed that there was a social system around me. So, I began to figure out how to use that social system well. Then I was promoted up and up. I started reading books on leadership at that point.

When I was about 36, in one of the leadership training courses I took, I noticed how the group influences leaders. In this case, a training group was put together with no rank used. All individuals there were to be equals. After a while, individuals were called into the middle of the group and given feedback on how the group members perceived them operating. Because I had not been given any feedback, when I was asked to go into the circle, I was surprised by the anger of various members towards me. They were mad. They said I was tuning out during lectures.

"So what?" I said. "My job is to get the point. After I get the point, I tune out until the next point comes up." The group members said, "If you tune out, you diminish the perceived value of what is going on."

AMS – *[My thought is that Resnick immediately understood that the group wanted him to act as a leader, in spite of the ground rule stating that all members should be equal. Resnick objected to the pressure the group was putting on him.]*

GR – I called them on it and said, "How can I be a leader, or have that role, when we are all to be treated alike?" This was another awakening moment for me. The pressure was on for me to behave differently, because they "needed" me to be a leader. It was clear that the group had expectations that I would assume a leadership role. When I did not comply with their expectations to act as the kind of a leader they needed, they were critical of me—until I pointed out this entire sequence to them.

AMS – *[Listening to Resnick, I realized that this was a clear example of how the "group mind" can easily over-influence individuals, often to the detriment of both. Although in this example cited by Resnick, he resisted their efforts. It is good to see these kinds of reciprocal relationships in which group members assume less responsibility by trying to force one individual into an overly responsible position.]*

GR – A leader needs cognitive smarts. Leaders also need to be able to solve other people's problems. I am a bit unusual in that I have the ability to solve problems to meet others' needs. I give people good advice. This attitude is close to what is described as the abundance mentality. "There is enough for everyone. I can work hard and always get what I need." This is in stark contrast to the scarcity mentality that says, "There is not enough. I have to beat other people out. Someone is going to lose."

AMS – *[It's interesting to speculate that this "abundance attitude" enabled Resnick to maintain a broad viewpoint, both intuitive and detached. It allowed him to resonate with an individual's dilemma, and yet deliver rational advice. Resnick noted that when he advises people about career choices, he often sees many sides of an issue, many ways for everyone to win. His approach is - "There is an institutional need, and here is how you might fit into the future of this organization. And, we can also consider your personal need and what might be in your best interest." This is a good example of a leader increasing an individual's personal responsibility by allowing him or her total access to information. Individuals treated this way are going to develop their brainpower to think broadly about their decisions.*

As we turned to his family dynamics and looked at the types of influences that might have enhanced Resnick's leadership ability, he said, "I don't see how my family influenced me. My family was not communicative."

I responded that some people learn by identification, while others look at what's happening around them and learn what not to do. Family research demonstrates that individuals often find other ways to manage self rather than follow strategies that do not appear to be working. Children, in particular, who see that their parents' coping mechanisms are not working, accept that as a fact without blame, and move on. When there is no blame, an individual has more opportunity to build coping mechanisms that are rationally based.

Resnick considers personal information in an objective way, without defensiveness. For example, he listened to my ideas and tried on a few. He was able to think scientifically about how past family events influence one's current life in indirect ways. After listening to my thoughts about the ways people learn within the family, Resnick noted the following.]

GR – What does fit is that when I give my analysis of why I am doing what I am doing, I probably over communicate. And it may be that I do this because my parents did not communicate very well. I am making sure that you cannot say to me later that I did not give you every opportunity to do what you needed to do to succeed. I think my job is to let people know what they are up against. In my way of doing it, I am giving them personal responsibility for their own salvation. I've given them many pictures of the situation so they can make an informed decision and take responsibility. I grew up in a family where there was not a high level of communication about major changes in family life.

AMS – You may have grown up with a bit of an advantage in that your older brother might have had been more pressured to continue any family tradition, even non-communication. As the second son, you might have been freer to grow up in your own way. *[Resnick agreed saying that he did feel free to grow up in his own way. He added that in his family, people simply did things, saying only that those things "just had to be done." There was little discussion about how and why things were done.]*

[In my head at the time I was thinking as to how to point out another viewpoint. I knew from precious conversation that Resnick had a younger brother who had died early. I wondered aloud if this lack of communication in his family of origin might have been influenced by the early loss of his brother. I also noted that Resnick was 27 before he began thinking about the importance of relationships. Perhaps, I added, when Resnick discovered novels (which he did later in life than most), he picked up clues about how relationships work at a subliminal level.]

[We don't really know which events in a person's life motivate them to move in a new direction. As noted throughout the book, the general direction of one's life can be seen as a series of probabilistic events but no one has come close to being predictive as to events in future social life. After college Resnick went on to do graduate work. He then spoke about that time.]

GR – Doing my Ph.D. in Rhode Island, in microbiology was an exciting time. This whole world of analysis, of cause and effect, was opening up. It was about how you interact with everyone.

AMS – We know that you had a big change then in terms of thinking about relationships, but let's take a broader look. How would you account for such a shift in your thinking? What was changing in your family and in society? It was 1976 and the Vietnam War was over. Your brother had been in Vietnam and he came back. What impression did you have of your brother when he returned?

GR – I did not have much contact with him. It took him a few years to settle down. He was obviously affected by what had gone on.

AMS – Could his going to war and his return have influenced you in some subtle way?

GR – I don't know. Just to give you a feel for how out of tune I was, I got my bachelor's in 1971 and did not take a final exam at Cornell until my senior year. This was because the protesting students would shut the school down. During the shut downs I would just go bass fishing. I had no interest in the war.

AMS – Could it be that, since your younger brother died your interest in exploring or thinking about relationships was essentially shut down until your older brother returned from the war?

GR – I don't recall a triggering event. I was not part of the social network. The change was abrupt. I just started noticing other people and how they interact. I changed my reading habits. I read voraciously—*Dune, The Hobbit*. Until then I had only read science books. I became enamored of the idea of consilience, the convergence of knowledge from both the hard and soft sciences.

AMS – If we go back to your family to understand the kinds of leadership traits you developed, how might your father's career have influenced your career decisions?

GR – My dad had an escapade going into business with my mother's relatives, and the business failed. He had left the construction trade in Connecticut to try his hand at retail in New York City. When the retail business failed, he returned to the construction trades, but was forced to take a lower position as a helper, which is under a mechanic. It took him years to regain his old position.

When I think about my mother, I see her as having talent, but being born at the wrong time and place. Because of her family's financial status and the way society was structured then, there was little chance for her to have a professional career. She would have enjoyed being able to contribute in the workplace at a leadership level. She would have liked to be an accountant and be successful.

AMS – There is a theory that states that if a woman's husband does not live up to her hopes and dreams in his career, these expectations will go into the son and he will become more successful than the father.

GR – There was a fellow, who was a very effective group leader. Then he was promoted so that he had three groups under him. Instead of seeing these as three groups that each needed relatively autonomous leaders, he tried to treat them as one group that he would lead. If you cannot delegate authority and power, and instead treat several groups as a "one," there will be too much complexity to manage.

I can see this dynamic and apply it to my family situation. I can choose to intervene and solve my son's problems by dealing directly with his teachers. But if I treat my son like a subordinate leader, I override his ability to handle his own problems. On the other hand, if I coach him to deal with people, who are creating problems for him, he will do better over the long run.

AMS – I wonder to what degree knowing your grandparents and their stories influenced your ability to be analytical. You know the story of your grandparents in Russia.

Knowing one's family roots is evidence of a person, who is better connected to his or her family and is a less cut-off individual.

You may not know the details of the family story three or four generations back, but most well-connected people know something of their family over the generations. The hypothesis is that you learn something from the failures and successes related in family stories, and the more you know, the greater the complexity that your brain can handle.

GR – I can see the motivation to not fail coming out of my family.

AMS – You may also have a motivation to help younger people, since your younger brother died. And you may have a strong motivation to help women, since you saw your mother as worthy of many opportunities.

GR – Yes, I can see that. I was given an award for enabling women to do well. But, if I do not see a good outcome, I cannot lead. If I do not believe in what I am doing, I will leave or turn it over to someone else. I would say it is still hard for me to make a bridge between the family's influences and one's leadership ability. But there are three things that I hear that could contribute to my leadership ability. I would agree that these traits may have been influenced by my family: (1) that I over-communicate, (2) that I will strive to do well since I may have a fear of failure, and that (3) I do enjoy enabling others to do well.

AMS – This has been an interesting interview, and we will see what each of us gets out of it on reflection. I know there are many ideas here to think about. Thank you very much.

Gary Resnick's Mindful Compass Points

(1) The ability to take ACTION and to define a vision: Resnick talked about two aspects of his leadership vision. The first was how he as a leader needs to have an "abundance mentality" so that he can give individuals access to the information they need to make good decisions. The second relates to the idea of consilience, the convergence of knowledge from both the hard and soft sciences. This idea allowed him, as a leader, to investigate various ways of understanding people and to maintain a more accurate view of human nature. Overall, Resnick's principle was to give adequate feedback to others. For example, he told people what their opportunities were within and outside the work system and didn't pressure them to do something in support of the work system that might disadvantage them as an individual. He was committed to being a good communicator.

(2) The RESISTANCE to change in self and in any system: One reason I enjoyed this interview with Resnick is that he had an easy, non-defensive way of explaining that, for him, the connections between early family relationships and his actions later in life were missing. By the end of the interview, however, he was able to move past this resistance and see that there were some connections. He was able to listen to his doubts and give

them space, and then overcome those doubts when a connection made sense to him.

(3) The ability to use KNOWLEDGE to connect: Resnick saw his father struggle with his work and the unfulfilled potential in his mother's life. Because he did not have to deal with blame and anger associated with these two situations, he was free to explore other ways to connect and work with people. He discovered that people value his problem-solving ability, and he was able, early on, to use these cognitive skills as a leader. He connected with the generational stories in his family, even when he was not sure they were grounded in total reality, and he had an understanding of the trials and successes of past generations. Later, he became curious about how humans and other species work together and discovered that successful organisms learn and adapt to changing environments. All living species must predict what strategies will work, and Resnick has been very good at doing just that.

(4) The ability to be STAND ALONE and to be more separate: During the Vietnam War, when Resnick was at Cornell, protesting students shut down the school at exam time. Resnick's response was to go bass fishing. His ability to be alone was more a pleasure than a trial. Being alone is a very important means of adjusting to changes, and this may have been what was happening at a preconscious level for him at the time. After the Vietnam War, Resnick began to read fiction with a passion, and we know that reading and thinking requires time alone.

ARTHUR HOUSE

Arthur House is Managing Director, Public Affairs at Webster Bank, the largest independent bank headquartered in New England. He has worked in the academic world (Assistant Dean of the Fletcher School of Law and Diplomacy at Tufts University), and in government at the World Bank (1971–1975); as a White House Fellow (1975–1976); as Special Projects Officer at the National Security Council; and in the U.S. Senate. He has also worked at several corporations.

Art House is the oldest and only son in his family, with an older and a younger sister. First-born sons are often said to be natural-born leaders.

Having a competent older sister can decrease the family putting all their bets on the son. In many cultures, sons inherit the family farm and title, and are often pressured to "manage the farm well" for future generations. But many oldest sons can, for many reasons, fold under this kind of pressure. Sometimes, they have parents who were not oldest or who did not do well themselves and so they get many mixed messages as to leading and being responsible. At other times, there are added outside social pressures that can derail a so-called natural born leader. Art House fit with the natural role of a leader as his family expected him to become a leader, to be responsible, and to give back to his community. They encouraged behavior that would serve him well as a leader.

AMS – It's been interesting to me, after giving my interview subjects the list of questions about relationships affecting leadership ability, to listen as individuals talk about their different experiences. It has been almost a Darwinian process. Many questions go unnoticed, drift into extinction if you will. Other questions seem to live on because they prove to be relevant. People hear something. A light bulb goes on; an idea builds and becomes a theme that is part of that individual's life experience. But that theme is also interesting for the rest of us. Dr. Bowen would say something to the effect that the wisdom of the ages is in each individual. You just have to create the right environment to allow the person to explain it all to you.

This has to do with the way the person is with the other, and how the person thinks. It's not just about the questions that are asked. Anyway, right now, I'm interested in any thoughts you have about leadership and the impact that your early relationships had on you in that regard.

AH – When I was in graduate school, one of my professors said that a good predictor of leadership, in terms of world leaders, was a talented individual from a prominent family, whose mother had married below her station in life. The child, he said, would often live up to the expectations that the mother had known in her own family. She would inculcate the leadership expectation in her son. My professor had a long list of historical figures that fit this description, but it did not really apply to my family. I think of leadership not so much as success or triumph, but rather as *trying*. Leadership to me is the effort, the will and the work done to accomplish something—which can be inspired by either parent.

AMS – Yes, I agree that inspiration can happen with either parent. The child becomes the subject of the mother's or the father's investment. And sometimes the marriage might even benefit. It seems to work out as long as the parent's expectations fit well with the child's natural talents, desires and capacity to be disciplined. One of the big issues is that the parent must be able to maintain his or her own identity and not become confused about who is who.

AH – There was a somewhat subtle example of leadership that came from my father. He was a very good public speaker, ran for elected office and won. After becoming a State Senator, he went on to become a judge, and later was the Chief Justice of the Connecticut Supreme Court. He was a recognized public figure, a modest and a self-effacing man. He did not trumpet his accomplishments in any way. Leadership in the sense of effort was kind of a given. And, therefore, I was aware that public accomplishment was possible. That was the setting in which I grew up.

My mother's family was well educated. My mother went to Wellesley College and became a career person after graduating. It was unusual to do that in the 1930s, but she wanted to go to work and was professionally accomplished. She had one sister, who worked in State government and three brothers: a medical doctor, an educator and an economist. There were a lot of Ph.D.s in the family.

And there was a sense of security in my family. The overall idea was that it was okay to go out and try things. Venturing out was fine if you were serious about something, and you always had the family to fall back on.

One particular situation helps explain why I was determined to lead in my own way. I come from a rural area where everyone knows everyone. As a youngster, I enjoyed the outdoors and sports. Then my family and I decided I should go away to prep school. But I quickly discovered that I just did not fit in. I found the school to be arrogant and elitist. I gave it a try, but just did not blend with the culture. I was a bit hurt about this, but I simply did not like the values of the place and was not going to change mine to be a popular person and fit in. That was profound experience at age 14.

In my senior year, the school made a serious mistake and sent the wrong grades to the colleges where I had applied. I was rejected everywhere, including my "safety" schools—which is how I discovered the error. The school at first lectured me about being an underachiever, but when confronted they admitted the mistake and agreed to sort it out after a rather tense meeting with my father. Ultimately, I was accepted at Tufts—which turned out to be a stroke of unbelievable good fortune. I instantly liked the culture. There was a large, diverse group of people and a healthy rather than elitist atmosphere—a complete contrast to my prep school years. I was class president a couple of times and eventually headed the student government. I helped establish a program in Africa and led a group of Tufts students to West Africa one summer. I also won some leadership awards as an undergraduate. After that I went on to an outstanding graduate school and was pleased to be able just to study—nothing to prove or vindicate. I think my family provided a subtle but powerful influence by being encouraging and supportive. By surviving the experience in prep school and then thriving in college, I learned that I could make it in a difficult situation and hold on to my core values.

AMS – This is one of the better stories about being a strong, separate self and why it is so important.

AH – I can still recall very vividly going out one night my freshman year at prep school to sit on the bleachers and sort things through. I was clear within myself. I did not like their values and was not going to become one of them. I should have told my parents at the time and just gone home, but I was not able to do that. I just decided that I would do all that I could to remain different from this culture. It was a very lonely thing. It was a trial. Years later, my parents expressed great sadness when they found out what I had gone through. They felt I should have told them.

AMS – Often that is more difficult if you are an only male or identify strongly with your father, who is a strong man. Tell me about your family and your parents' families.

AH – I have two sisters, an older one and a younger one. My mother was the second oldest of five siblings. My dad was the middle child between two sisters.

AMS – The social pressure is often great, and may not even be from the family, for the man to be strong and silent. One who does not complain can be an unspoken rule. In addition, within the family, an oldest son is programmed to live up to expectations and to follow the parents' wishes without complaints.

AH – I can say there was an expectation to do well and not take the easy path. That was especially true with my mother, leaving Wellesley to become a professional woman. She worked at a corporation in Boston, while a friend of hers helped start a program for women at Harvard Business School. This was in the thirties. Later a "headhunter" recruited her to be personal assistant for Mrs. John D. Rockefeller Jr. She lived in New York City before marrying my father. Dad had graduated from Harvard Law School and evidently had a challenge convincing my mother to leave the bright lights for Manchester, Connecticut.

Our family dinner table was fun but also an institution unto itself. The conversations there were inviting but challenging—they were a formidable part of growing up. You had to discuss and defend your view. My parents encouraged us to read the newspaper, and we had to pick a subject and say something that made sense about it. We also learned to respect others' opinions. We could tell jokes and have a good time, but diversity of thought and interesting conversation were highly valued.

I say this because later in life I became a Democrat (as did my two sisters) while our parents were Republicans. What was most important was to have a rational argument for defending a viewpoint. It was perhaps strange that all three children became Democrats—coming from a family that was "Rockefeller" or liberal Republican. Years later, when I ran for elected office, a reporter asked my father how the son of a prominent Republican had become a Democrat. He said, "His mother and I taught the boy how to read, and he has been on his own ever since."

The influence of the dining room table was very positive. It was not pressure, but rather an expectation that you know and be able to discuss, in a rational way, the current events in the world.

AMS – Promoting diversity of views is crucial to families, nations and businesses. You were allowed and encouraged to think for yourself, and that is something that certainly should be part of an ideal family environment. But I am not sure how much of this can be taught or encouraged. How about your grandparents?

AH – My maternal grandfather was the middle child of seven. He was the headmaster of Harrisburg Academy in Harrisburg, Pennsylvania, for 28 years, helping develop the faculty and bringing students in from overseas. There were always people visiting the school, so my grandmother both managed the family and entertained visitors to the school. She was an only child and I remember her from my childhood as very kind and loving. My grandfather died before I was born.

My paternal grandfather was an only child born in Manchester, Connecticut, and the first in his family to go to college. He was a Harvard engineer and worked for the New York Central Railroad in Pennsylvania. My grandmother, also an only child, came from a prominent business and real estate family in Pennsylvania. After they married, he decided to return to join his father in the family retail business in Manchester, the oldest and largest store in the town. He was also head of the Chamber of Commerce. My grandmother died when I was a youngster. She was a warm and gracious woman, as I recall. My grandfather was very sharp and prospered in difficult times, but was warm toward his grandchildren. He enjoyed seeing my father thrive in politics. He always insisted that we come together as a family for holidays.

AMS – You still have contact with your aunts and uncles?

AH – My father's two sisters have died. My mother's older brother and one younger brother are alive. The older, Philip, was my Dad's roommate at Harvard, which is how Dad met my mother. Philip received his doctorate in economics and served as an intelligence officer in World War II, then subsequently wrote for the *Washington Post* and set up his own economics consulting business. He is extremely well read. Now, at age 97, Philip still reads three newspapers a day and occasionally plays squash. I used to spend hours talking to him when I lived in D.C. He is very tolerant and genuinely interested in what others are doing and thinking. But if you ask him about his life, you have to draw him out.

Philip recently told me about long conversations he had with his grandfather, who fought in the Civil War and was a prisoner at Andersonville. When his grandfather returned home to the family farm in Ohio, the family did not recognize him because he had suffered so considerably. There are not many people alive today who have talked to people who fought in the Civil War.

My mother's younger brother was in the Pacific during World War II and returned to earn his doctorate at Yale. He spent his career as an educator and became provost of a college in Pennsylvania. He has been a mentor to many educators, including my older sister, encouraging her to get her Ph.D. and pursue her career as a professor.

AMS – Families that place a high value on supporting one another can often tolerate and even promote a greater diversity of ideas within the group. Family support between the generations enables people to do far better when difficult times arise. In general, they do not cut off from one another. This provides what you have talked about as a feeling of security. People are able to go out and try new things, knowing there have been generations of people who have been supportive of one another. I think this builds a stronger overall family group.

The same principle works for religious groups and even organizations. People tend to support others who share most of their deeper values. Of course, there is always a balance between getting along by embracing the group's values, and being able to explore and be slightly different from the group.

AH – Yes, but there can be too much security, too. Security is one thing, but a family also has to demand accountability and seriousness of purpose. I thought of that when I spent an evening with President [George W.] Bush while he was running for Governor of Texas. We had plenty to connect on. My father as an attorney had represented Prescott Bush, the President's grandfather. And I had worked with the first President Bush when I was at the National Security Council and he was head of the CIA. George Bush and I talked about the people we knew in common, and he was clearly secure within his family background. But he was also clear that he was very much his own person. He felt no obligation to be consistent with his grandfather or father's political viewpoints. He seemed to be saying that they were great men, but that he was his own man, going his own way to fight his own battles. He showed almost no interest in the issues of their day. I got the sense that the only tradition he seems to want to uphold is to run for office and win. Perhaps he has had too much family security?

AMS – From what you are saying I gather that the ideal is to be thoughtful about the various alternatives and the costs/benefits of going this or that way. They may get in office for one reason and then emerge with other values as for political people the judgment of history may be more meaningful than the current polls.

AH – I have three children, all girls, and each of them has a willful streak. My sisters, who are both psychologists, say, "There you have it, leadership in the making." For them, sticking your neck out, trying new things and even being headstrong is not rebellion but rather seeing how well they can make decisions and discover the consequences. This is real trial-and-error learning.

AMS – Often it seems that the dialogue between parents and children is the important ingredient. People, who stay in good contact and listen to different ways of thinking, seem to learn and respect more about one another. How do you and your wife communicate about your daughters?

AH – My wife is the intelligent one. She is a medical doctor. The children call her the "real" doctor while I am "Dr. Dirty," specializing in splinters and scrapes and things like that. As for communication, it really does take a team to rear children. I listen to my wife, and her insights usually make good sense to me. She has been more intensely involved with the girls at most stages of life to this point, but I try to find areas where I can be close. We tend to agree and work well with each other. I am amazed at how very different three individuals in the same family can be. I try to stay as involved as I can and talk to each of them about what is going on in their lives.

AMS – How did you and your wife meet?

AH – My wife and I met in 1984 when she was starting medical school and I was running for Congress in Connecticut. Her brother is a very good friend of mine, and she volunteered to work on my campaign. I lost in the Reagan landslide but probably won something more important.

AMS – That seems a similar pattern in the way your parents met?

AH – Yes, brothers can help, but this one certainly did not go to any extremes to let me know about his sister. It was actually my campaign manager, who brought us together. Rita, my wife, is the youngest with two older brothers.

AMS – You also have a younger sister so your sibling positions fits very well. This can make for a marriage where people can understand one another almost automatically. When the families are friends, that is a great combination for a good marriage.

I am curious, also, to know if there have been other mentors, who helped you learn about leadership skills.

AH – There have been two, Abe Ribicoff and Mike Walsh. For me, the most important aspect of leadership is seeing what needs to be done and having the courage to do it. Doing what you think is right can often cost you the disapproval of a lot of people. I was Chief of Staff for former U.S. Senator Abe Ribicoff, a man who was true to his moral instincts. He had the courage to make the tough decisions and see them through. I have never met a man with a better political sense and more guts to do what he thought was right. Another person I became very close to was John Gardner's protégé, Mike Walsh. They worked together as the founders of Common Cause. Mike became a CEO at an early age. He revolutionized the Union Pacific Railroad, changing it from a utility to a deregulated, competitive transportation company. Then a large conglomerate called Tenneco crashed and the Board of Directors hired Mike to straighten things out there. Mike convinced me to move to Texas to work with him. He set up adjoining offices and we quickly became close friends. Mike was one of the most compelling leaders I have ever witnessed and he faced a massive challenge. The company had about $13 billion in annual revenue with six businesses ranging from aircraft carriers and gas pipelines to tractors and plastic bags. Mike had to figure out what went wrong and bring it back to prosperity.

Mike went with his instincts, but he also set explicit goals. He believed that a good leader makes him or herself vulnerable and gathers others in to share the vulnerability and then win. He was a remarkable example of leadership. He understood people well. If you are to be a leader, he said, "Tell people where you are going. Plant the flag. And then once you get a team assembled you can rationally figure out how to get it done." He was a powerful speaker and motivator. He was loyal and also demanding. I had seen leadership in public life, and now I was able to see it at the corporate level. He would set a goal emotionally and rationally and use his powerful intellect to get where he needed to go. Unfortunately, Mike's life was cut short by a brain tumor. He believed that he had exhausted himself in this hard work and that this state of exhaustion had allowed the brain tumor to take over. We were together for two years, and for the last six months he was dying. But in both his living and dying I learned a great deal about life and values.

AMS – I have found that the people, who are important to you and who die, often live on in various ways. Some people tell me that such people will come and sit on their shoulder and talk to them and keep on encouraging them.

AH – I think that is accurate.

AMS – There are probably at least seven factors that go into aggressive cancers. I look at how many people have had cancer in the family, the genetics, the emotional atmosphere, the burden people feel they are under, etc. If someone feels he or she has used up their life energy—well, that has to be one of the big factors.

AH – My experience with Mike underscored both the promise and vulnerability of life. And you are right. Mike's influence will be there forever.

AMS – One other question I had about leaders in general is how accurate they are at predicting future events. How are you at that?

AH – In certain areas I can do that, and in others, no. My predictive ability is strongest in areas in which I have both an educational background and experience like international affairs and the media. Frequently, I feel confident in seeing where something is going to end up. But there are a lot of areas where I am simply ignorant or inexperienced.

I sat on a board with Elliot Richardson, the Attorney General, who refused to comply with then-President Nixon's order to sack the Watergate Special Prosecutor, Archibald Cox. Richardson understood the public sector so well. After all, he had four Cabinet positions. I once asked him, "What makes a good President?" He replied that one thing any President needs is a thorough understanding of history; the other is the ability to understand and predict what might happen if a particular decision were made. I thought that was a remarkably insightful set of criteria. None of us is as good at this as we need to be. Anticipating what might happen has to do with your understanding of the past and of the circumstances affecting you in the present.

I wrote a piece about Iraq before the United States went to war in which I expressed great trepidation that we would end up exactly where we are, isolated from our allies and bogged down in an area of the world that has been subject to brutal dictatorship, is not prepared for democracy, and faces profound internal divisions and chaos. Unfortunately, that was a pretty good prediction. There are other areas where I have no idea what is coming next. I do not understand nor have any sense of where rap music, tattooing or body piercing as social trends are headed.

AMS – Another question is about being strategic versus being authentic. As a therapist, I have to challenge people to look at their behavior, behavior they cannot see. Then, even if they do see it, it is often difficult for them to change. Therefore, I have learned to think strategically as I coach people. How will my interactions with this person be experienced? I need to understand the individual and what he or she might be able to hear. If people get stuck, I often make paradoxical statements, or do or say absurd things to make some kind of difference. Some people say I am being manipulative, but I say it's thinking strategically. Political and corporate leaders, too, have to think about how to deliver a message that makes sense to people. So, I was wondering about political strategy, balanced with the need for transparency.

AH – The authentic individuals without guile are few and far between. Who are the people who are there for you no matter what? Often your old friends are always there. They know you (and often all your mistakes), so you have nothing to prove and nothing to defend. But that ability to accept another completely and totally, without condition, is rare. You need people like that in life, and I am blessed with a few such friends. But they are remarkably scarce.

AMS – Yes, it very difficult because as soon as you need people to approve of you, or at least not to react negatively, you are taking a risk if you say or do anything controversial. This is a constraint on openness. But on the other hand, if one's main fear is upsetting the others, then the skill of being strategic can be practiced. Gregory Bateson, a scientist and biological philosopher, used to say that information is like a grain of sand. A small amount given to an oyster can create a pearl, whereas a large amount just gets spit out.

AH – Yes, I agree. Even in your family, where people generally love you, you have to assess the cost of openness and set limits. Parents often face this with their children. We know there are difficult issues, but you still have to raise them and then manage the reactions.

AMS – I have really enjoyed this time with you and will look forward to thinking about all these ideas and hopefully seeing you in the future.

Arthur House's Mindful Compass Points

(1) The ability to take ACTION and to define a vision: At a young age, House was forced to define his values and stand by them. He saw himself as an open, accepting person interested in the differences between people, not as an elitist determined to embrace an exclusionary, discriminatory attitude. This view of himself was based on deep values that he later applied to the public and private sector work he undertook. In order to live out his vision, House had to learn to tolerate being alone—not an easy task in the prep-school years. Living his values and allowing others to live theirs, without trying to change them or allowing them to change him, was his first lesson in becoming a leader. Knowing that he could stand by his principles without flinching allowed him to emerge as a leader in college. There he became class president, headed the student government, and helped establish an exchange program in Africa.

His early experiences around the family dinner table, where conversations were based on rational argument and respect for others' opinions, very likely prepared him to defend his ideas and to respect the viewpoints of others. Throughout his career, House has valued diversity of thought.

As he noted, a mature leader must be true to his or her moral instincts and have the courage to make the tough decisions and see them through. To maintain the courage of one's vision, one often has to be tested emotionally. House's story is one of the best examples of how the coercive power of any group can undermine leadership potential or ability, and how resisting that power can lead to emotional growth and strength.

(2) The RESISTANCE to change in self and in any system: The primary lesson in House's story is his ability to embrace his vision and to maintain it. The second lesson in his story is that one can sometimes ask for help, even when it makes one vulnerable. As an adult, House says he wishes he had told his parents of the difficulties he was experiencing at school. But it's easy to understand the reluctance of someone just 14 years old to open up to his mother or father on such a sensitive subject. However, he was able to learn a great lesson from that reluctance. He saw his parents' sadness when they discovered what he had been through, and he knew that he would do it differently and be more open next time. Being open with parents and other authority figures is not always seen as the best thing to do. It takes a different kind of wisdom to realize that talking to important others about difficulties is not a sign of weakness, but rather of willingness to handle challenges in a transparent manner. Many people are concerned that if they tell others about anxious events, they will have a hard time handling the others' reactions and maintaining their own decision. It would be better if, instead, these little sparks of fear led people to the "emotional gym" where they could learn to deal with the anxiety, rather than try an end run around the anxiety in the form of avoidance. It is almost always worthwhile to go to the emotional gym and practice being open with those who are important to you.

(3) The ability to use KNOWLEDGE to connect: The family that House grew up in had been very well connected for generations. Because his father was an important figure in the political landscape, all kinds of fascinating

people came to his home and talked about interesting things. In addition, his family stories were well known to him, and his contacts with his extended family very significant and meaningful. Given this setting, it was natural for House to feel at ease with important people and to make others feel equally at ease. In fact, it is reasonable to predict that those families that maintain a wide and open relationship network will have a strong legacy going forward. Someone for whom it is natural to maintain a complex network will not have to spend much effort doing so, the effort may just go into observing and seeing how relationships function. For those who not have a large family of social connections, they will have to be more like a relationship pioneer. They will enter into a more foreign emotional system to just see what happens. This is what Art House did when he went to boarding school. Any of us can learn a great deal by creating a large network of family and friends. One take away is that as long as we are curious to see how people impact us, and how we manage the interactions with other, we will build our emotional backbone, just as Art House is doing.

(4) The ability to be STAND ALONE and to be more separate: As we listen to Art House's story, we see how the his early life of being exposed to different ways of thinking allowed him to be able to place a great deal of importance on knowing and despite the cost, being true to your own values. One of his major experiences at being a self came about in how he handled the intense social pressure from his school peers, and then using that ability to maintain himself in the midst of intense social pressure to conform. These kinds of early experiences prove to be very valuable in all relationship systems, where one has to be one's best self and resist going along with the group. Art House's experience has enabled him to see and recognize the usefulness and challenges of relationships, enabling him to stand alone in a variety of different cultures and work environments.

ROBERT DUFFY

Robert Duffy is the former Mayor and Chief of Police of Rochester, New York. Currently, he is serving as the Lieutenant Governor of New York State.

Frank Staropoli, a consultant in Rochester, introduced me to Bob Duffy during the time he was Chief of Police. Frank accompanied me to the interview and asked Bob a few questions.

AMS – Two questions: What was it that made you want to be a leader? And how early in your life did you start thinking, 'I can make a difference'?

RD – I didn't think that much about being a leader early on. I enjoyed being on sports teams, and was a co-captain once or twice. I enjoyed being depended on. I liked having a position where I could make a difference. And I have loved what I have done with the police force from the first day. By my eighth year on the police force, I started looking at what I could do if I were a sergeant, or if I were the lieutenant, sometimes out of frustration. I worked hard and I wanted to have responsibility. Then I became a parent and I felt more responsible, not just for myself, but for other people. I wanted to have responsibility where I could make a difference.

AMS – How does that fit with your position in your family?

RD – I am the youngest, with two older brothers.

AMS – That is unusual. Perhaps your Dad was a youngest and you learned some skills from him?

RD – Yes, he was a youngest. And my mother was an oldest. Among the siblings, my oldest brother took few chances. He was very intelligent and did well in school. My middle brother and I were never able to do as well as he did in school. My middle brother was the rebel of the sixties. My parents said I was always respectful and did not challenge their authority, but I got to do what I wanted to do. I learned from watching my brothers and avoided the interactions that my brother engaged in with my parents. My parents responded very strongly to challenges to their authority and/or to disrespect, and so I learned what not to do. I learned not to challenge them.

AMS – What kind of work did your father do?

RD – My father was payroll manager for a technical company. My mother taught fourth grade and later on kindergarten. When they were younger, my father studied to be a priest and my mother to be a nun. My father had an older sister, who lived in the convent. She played matchmaker for my parents. My parents were inherently good people. We had dinner at six every night. My father walked in at five every day, my mother was home by 4:30. Every Sunday we went to church and had to kick in with chores. There were certain strong values I saw with my parents. They were organized and did the right thing. As a kid you might have wanted different parents, but now I know I was lucky they had strong values.

AMS – How about your parents' extended families? How did they influence your parents?

RD – My mother's mother died from a virus or flu when my mother was nine months old. Her father died when she was 11. She had a couple of half-sisters, who were born in Ireland. But she was born in the U.S. My mother was handed around to different relatives and came out with the feeling that staying together and having strong values were extremely important. Her father worked for the railroad and drank, so my mother also had a fear of alcohol. She had certain other fears. She never let us play football. She had seen someone become paralyzed and didn't want that to happen to us. Her fears made sense. My parents didn't come to our basketball games until my senior year, and then my dad became a real fan. We had to stick together. My mother would be very upset if anyone forgot to send a birthday card, for example. You always sent cards and remembered your family. That was what counted. Your friends were important, but it was your family that took care of you.

AMS – Have any of your parents' values influenced how you operate as a leader?

RD – My mother had a spine of steel. She was the clear leader in the family. I have some of that in me. If I believe in something, I will hold my position even if everyone else is going in the opposite direction. There were times when I did not like that about my mother, but she could hold the line. We had to do our homework. There was no TV and there were no excuses for bad grades. My parents were very disciplined, very conservative people. I never heard them talking badly about other people. I never saw them fight or argue. I am sure they did have disagreements, but they did it in private.

I often tell the story of when I was eight years old. Another boy and I were playing around, throwing rocks at each other, and my rock broke a window in his house. I ran home. A few hours later his parents came with the rock and I was grounded for one month. I kept thinking that my mom would let me go out and play after two or three weeks, but she believed in truth in sentencing.

What it taught me was respect. I knew I could not get away with things. Her saying was, stick to your guns. When you believe in something, you have to hold a line.

When people on my staff come in and advocate, for example, I'll listen. But if it goes against what I believe, I don't worry about taking a stand, even if it's unpopular. I will support a better way of doing things, but on issues of principle I have to hold my ground and stand for what I think is the right thing to do. I listen very carefully and want everyone to have his or her say, but in the final analysis I have to define where I stand. Learning to hold steady in the face of reactions, well, you learn this from standing up and determining your own direction. In my family I learned to do things without being rebellious.

AMS – If parents can deal with their own families, they can do well with their own children. It sounds like your mother and father dealt with their own families. Did they have good contact?

RD – My mother had a sister we were closer to. My grandfather died when I was three, and my grandmother when I was a freshman in high school. We had good contact with them, but they did not pop in on us. We went to see them on a more formal basis. It was not a real close contact like in some families. We became people more like my parents than different from them.

AMS – Did you hear any stories about your relatives you admired?

RD – My mother talked about her family positively, but always acknowledged the difficulty of not having had a mother to raise her. My father and his brothers were veterans of World War II, and they all settled around Rochester. Change comes in many ways. There are people in the family who march to a different beat. My middle brother was born with a cleft pallet, which made me aware of how I wanted to protect him and how mean kids could be to people who were different. My youngest daughter wore glasses growing up, and when she went to contacts she blossomed. It's difficult to be physically different from other kids.

AMS – If you have people in your family with problems and differences, you develop more understanding. You learned how to accept differences as positive and not as negative. This may have made a difference in how you dealt with a big city population as diverse as Rochester's.

RD – My parents were always good to the other kids on the basketball team, who were different. Even if kids had been in jail, my parents did not demean them. I notice with my own kids how easily they notice and are puzzled by differences. Accepting people as they are is a strong value that I saw lived out. I see that people are shaped at a very young age. It's hard for people to rewire themselves unless they really want to. I see this in the schools and here in the police force.

AMS – Do you think that a positive identification with your father makes it easier to have the right wiring, or is it more than that one factor?

RD – Hard to say. But I know it's easier for some than for others. My middle brother has been married three times, and my parents married for 56 years.

AMS – Would it have been more difficult for your brothers than for you to identify with your father?

RD – Perhaps I see in my family, where my wife is also a youngest, that my oldest daughter is very different from my youngest daughter, who just fits in with us easily. My youngest daughter might be home till she is in her forties, but the oldest already wants to be independent.

AMS – These are all important ingredients in the person you become. There are probably many factors influencing people to move in certain directions, and each one of us has to choose. Families are not cause-and-effect machines. They are living and adapting organisms. Some people have an easier time living in a system than other people do. Some people feel they just do not fit or are not understood or—whatever.

Frank Staropoli – I see that you, as a leader, use these talents for holding your ground and not letting relationships become contentious. I see you have done that with the head of the labor union. Perhaps your relationship with your middle brother also helped you to have more compassion for people, who were different?

RD – Sometimes I tell the story about when I was a young high school kid. I was five feet, seven inches and weighed all of about 120 pounds. One of the guys in school, who was a little different, was pushed down by one of the big football players. I said, "Leave him alone." I am not sure why, the teacher was not there. I did not know anyone. The guy said, "Who are you talking to?" He comes over and hits me, and without thinking I hit him back. So he said, "Meet me after school." I knew I would get beaten to a pulp, but I went there and the guy did not show up. I never knew why.

AMS – How do you see your family relationships helping you function in your role as the Chief of Police?

RD – I have been able to have a relationship based on respect with the Mayor. I listen very carefully to what he says.

FS – You seem to have a similar way of dealing with him as you did with your dad. You seem to maintain your own opinion, but do not get into confrontations with him.

AMS – I was also thinking about triangles and how people communicate in large systems. Is the relationship just between you and the Mayor, or do others get involved?

RD – He keeps his communication with me very straight. We have had few, if any, negative exchanges. There was one, on an issue about which neither of us was right or wrong. It was just that each of us had a different position. Just as in my family, I do not come back and complain about what the Mayor is doing. I know where he stands and I appreciate that.

AMS – Another individual I interviewed, Bob DiFlorio, talked about the triangles with the School Board, the Mayor and the press. He had to practice keeping one-to-one relationships with each of them.

FS – I think there is a triangle relationship with Bob and the union chief for the loyalty of the men in the police force.

RD – A couple of years ago the union chief had a heart attack. I went down to the hospital and his wife jokingly said, "You might make him worse." We laughed and had a good time. We have great respect for each other. We feel very strongly about our positions. I am not saying I am right and he is wrong. Therefore, we have a very strong relationship. I am never one for public fighting. We are trying to find common ground. It's not perfect, but it seems to work. If you are a leader, you are an ethics teacher for your generation. We have had people come in here and teach courses on leadership, like *The Seven Habits*, and I have seen that this is very effective. People cannot always listen and learn from their families. Any kind of course that helps you see and respect others' values is very important.

AMS – The biggest challenges are in the future.

RD – What do I want to do here? The Mayor will retire in a year or so. I can walk away. But the city has great problems and it's hard for the people to understand the price they need to pay to make this a better city. We live in a culture where people want to eat hamburgers and sue the hamburger company. We smoke cigarettes and want to sue the tobacco company. How do we bear the responsibility for the lack of responsibility in others? Families and churches are in positions to effect change. We have a great city, and we have a great struggle in the future. There are a finite number of people. Our country will face many challenges, and yet the changes will have to happen on an individual level. I want to do something to make a difference. If I can address a small number of issues and work on them, we will have less to worry about in the future. I have a passion for what I do right now, and I think that is the key—to keep the passion alive for what you can and will do.

AMS – It sounds like what you are asking is, "How can I change myself to make the world a better place?"

RD – I always try to focus on the strengths of any individual and work with them. But if I see that people are not behaving correctly, I do not reward them. We are trying to focus on the high performers in the police department.

AMS – Every system has rules. It doesn't matter if it's an ant colony or the human family. The participants in the system are guided by their interactions with others. If the system is set up to reward a specific type of behavior, then more of that behavior will surface. If you can get away with threatening others in order to rise to the top, then that is the kind of system that will emerge. Dr. Bowen used to say to individuals, "I will be straight with you if you are straight with me, but if you trick me then I will trick you." An individual's behavior brings consequences based on their actions. Yet, often, people do not see the connections. Leaders have to hold people responsible. If you let people get away with too much, your organizational ship will stink or sink. If people stay responsible for their actions, the organizational ship will be well run and will sail straight. Again, thank you for the time and all your good ideas in this interview.

RD – You are welcome, and I also learned a lot. One of the things I had not really thought about was how my relationship with my middle bother influenced me in so many ways.

Robert Duffy's Mindful Compass Points

(1) The ability to take ACTION and to define a vision: Wanting to make a difference and seeking the responsibility to do it are two drives that have shaped Robert Duffy's life. His need to make a difference has been fuelled in part by frustration with the status quo. But a deeper motivation may be rooted in the fun of the game, which he learned by leading and playing on various sports teams. In addition, his vision was influenced by his experiences with deeply held values that made a difference both in his family and in his organization. When defining himself to the larger group, Duffy keeps in mind and balances two skills—remaining open to others and keeping a clear vision of what he wants to accomplish. Welcoming challenges is likely a talent he developed. Sticking to his guns is a value his mother passed on. One of the values Duffy clearly stated is to increase personal responsibility while cutting down on the culture of blame. Before

making decisions, he looks into the history of the individual or the issues. Organizationally, he focuses on the positive and rewards the outstanding people. Having person-to-person relationships within his organization enables Duffy to develop deeper connections and stay in touch. When someone is hospitalized, for example, he understands the value of going to visit, not just sending flowers. Person-to-person relationships also encourage the development of mentor-like relationships, allowing the people in his organization to take their cues from real people, rather than from rules or slogans.

(2) The RESISTANCE to change in self and in any system: Duffy tells two stories that are perfect examples of how we learn about our reactivity and, if lucky (or reflective), we can use those lessons to find better ways to function. He first told about throwing a stone through his friend's window, and then hiding out at home until the inevitable call came and he had to face the facts. In the second story, he tells about seeing someone being bullied at school, then defending the boy by punching the attacker—all without thinking about the consequences. Who among us has not been surprised by our reactions to threats? But, the important question is, how do we use this awareness to make better adaptations in the future? Generally speaking, whatever path we choose will be shaped by our history.

(3) The ability to use KNOWLEDGE to connect: Duffy's family encouraged him to be a thoughtful observer of the social forces that operate inside a nuclear family. Growing up in a family that has experienced early loss marks one as different. But people can compensate for early losses when there are mature individuals within the family system to fill the gap created by the loss. If someone in the family steps in and takes over the functioning of the one who died or left, the child will be able to grow up relatively secure. At the extreme, having a system that is well connected can make the difference between life and death. True as that is, people often do not see the significance of relationships as long as they are there. Or, to put it another way, "You don't know what you've got till it's gone." Family history has an observable effect on people who grow up in a system that is not the norm. Duffy certainly saw the significance of people staying connected, especially through the hard times. I assume that this history influenced him to develop a leadership style that puts him in personal

contact with a larger network of people. Even in contentious relationships, (for example, the contract negotiations with the union leader) Duffy remains connected and supportive during difficult times.

(4) The ability to be STAND ALONE and to be more separate: When we can't get anyone to take our side, we are left alone to contemplate what is really important. After Duffy broke his friend's window, he was unable to get his mother to back down on the punishment meted out. Being grounded for a month meant exactly that—a month. Duffy's inability to influence his mother to be more lenient gave rise to his own values about truth in sentencing and the importance of sticking to your word.

Superior leaders get things done with very little motion. They impart instruction not through many words, but through a few deeds. They keep informed about everything but interfere hardly at all. They are catalysts, and though things would not get done as well if they were not there, when they succeed they take no credit. And, because they take no credit, credit never leaves them.   *Lao-Tzu*

DIANE AND NED POWELL

Diane Powell – Chairperson, Des Plaines Publishing and a former vice president at NBC.

Ned Powell – At the time of the interview, he was director of the USO, a private, non-profit, non-partisan organization whose mission is to support the troops by providing morale, welfare and recreation-type services to those in the armed services.

One of my goals for this book project was to find a husband and wife team, who could explain both how their leadership was influenced by their family histories and how they each managed having a dual career family. I met Diane Powell through my book club. She stood out because she's a very tall, outspoken woman. She's full of fun, a leader that asked personal questions that connected each of us to the book's topic and allowed the people in the group to know one another at a different level. I asked her if she would like to participate in this project since I knew she was interested in the special challenges women leaders face in corporate America.

Diane was interested in reflecting on how her relationship with her family over the generations might have predisposed her to becoming a leader. I also knew she admired her husband Ned Powell, who was at the time of this interview, the director of the USO. Therefore, I asked if he would also participate in the interview. They each liked the idea, and many fascinating concepts emerged with these two engaging individuals.

Ned Powell began the interview by reflecting on how family relationships sustained each of their wishes to contribute to the larger community. We all agreed that the family has some role in how individuals function in the larger society. And that, in turn, society has some influence on the functioning of families.

Ned believes that both social and family expectations set the stage for how children view challenges and opportunities for leadership. He acknowledges that families frequently cannot overcome the obstacles in society, such as the low average life expectancy for inner city school children. Societal forces impinge on positive expectations and outcomes for children, despite a family's best intentions.

NP – What happens if your family has certain expectations for you? It's in the air you breathe. What are the expectations you learn in your family? Those expectations are behind the scenes, setting a stage for your future. In our society, we are surprised when there is a mismatch between the way the family is operating and the wishes, hopes and expectations of how we want our society to be. When my Uncle Lewis, died I became the oldest male in the generational line. It was then that I began to realize the importance of family influence. The patriarch had died. It's a shock to know you are now the oldest. You are it.

[Uncle Lewis was Lewis Franklin Powell, Jr., an Associate Justice of the Supreme Court of the United States from 1972 to 1987. He developed a reputation for moderation and was known as a master of compromise and consensus building.]

He was my father's oldest brother. My father also had a twin sister. Both my Dad and his brother served in World War II. My uncle went to law school and my father to business school at Harvard. My family comes from a long line of teachers and contributors to society. We have been in Virginia since the1600s. The expectation was that you had a role and you were to contribute to society.

The expectations go in both directions—encouragement and restriction. They involve many levels of pressure that can be very subtle. For example, when I was living in Boston after my father died in 1979, I got a letter from Uncle Lewis who had stepped into the parental role, even though I was in my thirties. He wrote to ask me 'What are you doing leaving the Commonwealth of Virginia? No one in the Powell family has ever left the Commonwealth except to go to school or to serve in the armed forces.' The family values were clear. Contributing to society is a privilege and an honor, not a choice. Being a leader simply enables you to do the job better, to leave the woodpile better than it was when you found it.

My biggest disquiet is when people talk about inner city school kids. I can see how disconnected people are with the actual lives of these kids. What are the expectations these kids have for life? People ask how can you get inner city kids to do this or that? The answer is process. The dirty little secret in schools is families. What is going on in children's families and homes has everything to do with what is going to happen at school.

The reality is still family expectations. When you talk to inner city school kids many of them will tell you that their friends are dead. They have no future they can count on. For these kids, having a family member, a coach or a mentor that makes him or her think they can do better, is invaluable. The reality is that due to my family's social position I could do just about anything I wanted to do as long as I am willing and able to pay the price of success with hard work.

DP – In my family, I, too, was given the message that I could go to Harvard. All I had to do was get a loan and put in the hours to achieve in school.

I also see the expectations in society, especially as they operate on women. For women, society was **not** able to meet the family expectations for opportunity as far as work went. For women born in the 1940s, expectations for them were to find a good husband and have children. My grandparents were all immigrants. They had to learn the English language and make their own way. I had other challenges. I could go to Harvard but then what? Society was not and is still not ready to enable women to do well.

Families' expectations did not prepare me or other women for hitting the glass ceiling. Our grandparents had come to this country with all kinds of dreams for a better future, but in my grandparents' day women supported men's careers. Women in the board room are a relatively new phenomenon. I am not sure how family dynamics, like sibling position, plays into preparing us to become leaders. It is easier to see what happens to a defined group like women and the social obstacles that still exist. Ned, do you know if the people on your executive team are oldest in their families?

NP – I have not thought much about succession roles in families and a possible transfer over to work roles. I realize there are logical associations with family positions and family dynamics. But I have no first-hand knowledge of how sibling position might operate at work. I could guess, and I would assume, there are some logical correlations. Functioning positions in all kinds of groups make an impact on any individual's ability to perform.

I would guess that the numbers in families might also make a difference. Odd numbers might not work that well, because it's easier to gang up. It's like *The Apprentice* over and over again. And as Bill Cosby said, 'the parents who have one child do not know what it's like to be a parent.'

In my family of origin there are four siblings. I have two older sisters and a younger brother. I am close to my brother and my older sister. The sister next to me and I are a lot alike physically. The physical characteristics are interesting. Both my parents were brown eyed and two of the siblings have recessive traits with blue eyes.

My brother is much more introverted than I am. He's into mountain climbing and is not afraid of physical risk. I have no interest in that, but my business life is far more risk-prone than his. I like to talk to people and he likes to read books. He is more like my mother and I am, in general, more like my Dad. I was close to my Dad but I know I gave him heartburn. Our personalities are alike.

Mother was into the arts. She was very bright, personable and the president of her class at Wellesley. She was the youngest of five. Even though my Dad went to Harvard Business School, he did not like to read at home. I like to read like my Mom. Dad likes to read about airplanes and so did I. We had a common interest in airplanes. I still like reading about planes. Dad was a Navy pilot but my vision was so bad that I couldn't go in the service and fly. But I wanted to be a part of the effort, so after college, at age 21, I enlisted in the Naval Reserve. That was an important decision for me. I will cogitate on something then I will do it. I do not agonize over the decisions that I make. I have to focus my attention on getting things done. Mother will agonize over decisions. I am sure this gets in her way. It's interesting to think about the diversity in families—who was influenced by what behavior and where the overlaps are.

AMS – Often people in families learn just as well by positive identification as they do by seeing certain traits as negative and not wanting to go in that direction. Overall, it sounds like you identified more with your Dad but respected your Mom and, of course, you have the two older sisters. It would be very important not to agonize about decisions if you're a leader, so that's an important skill to pick up.

DP – I think the decision to enlist was a very important one. You earned more respect by enlisting because you learned more about relating to all kinds of people and making your own way. The fact that you became an executive in the USO after enlisting gives me a different viewpoint on how to think about issues.

NP – Yes, and I can see the problems for women in society due to seeing the personal experiences of my sisters. My sister Kathy is very smart. She did very well working for a bank and then she married and had children, and this was a kind of death for her career. Once you get off the track, if and when you come back to work as my sister did after fifteen years or so, you find yourself far down in the hierarchy.

DP – The problem is clear, but women still must compete with men and put a similar effort in to achieve a similar reward. Women should not use their family duties as an excuse not to do as well as men.

NP – That may be, but the legal system does not allow you to say to a woman "You have to remain on the job in order to compete with the men." Unfortunately, there are stereotypes and if a woman needs more time away from work for her family, she can get written off as not a serious contender. On the other hand, if women try to keep up with men, their children can pay a price. I try to teach people to consider the risks and rewards and the far-reaching consequences of decisions. Often, one of the partners can make a decision to have a career and the other can stay home. But for some families there is no choice and both parents have to work. I would hope that having children is a choice, so I say to people, 'Be mindful of your choices. If you have children then that is your first commitment.'

In her book, Judith Wallerstein talks about second chances. She seems to think that it does not matter if the men or women stay home with the children. But we know there are issues that have to be resolved. After all, we do not have the ability to change the biological fact that women are the ones that have the babies and this causes some angst if the mother has to leave the children and go to work.

DP – The traditional way is that women are more often the nurturing ones for the family and the men are the breadwinners. In my family, what I took away was that the father had the better life. I am sure there are a lot of different influences in order to answer the question, 'Do I want a career or do I want to be a caretaker?' There is some kind of a biological push, and then there are the family hopes.

In my home, it looked like the men had the more interesting life and the woman had the chores. If a woman identifies positively with her Dad's path over her mother's, then it may be that the woman has almost self-selected to choose a career over having children.

I am a first born with a younger brother and while Mom and her friends were in the kitchen cleaning up, I preferred to go and sit with Dad and his friends talking in the den.

My mother is a bright woman, who had a career in modeling, but then gave it up to have a family. I think she may have also wanted me to have a career because she never taught me the things she knew about makeup and was more interested in my doing well in school.

But, she was also definitely interested in my getting married. I can see from my family history where some of these influences began. My maternal grandmother, Flora, was able to figure out how to leave Poland/Russia at the very young age of thirteen. She decided she was going to Kansas City to live with her uncle. She had heard her parents would have to sell the family farm to raise a dowry for her. She was the youngest child and the only girl. She did not want that to happen so she wrote her uncle in Kansas City and said she would come and work for him as his servant if he would pay for her trip to the USA. Flora never saw her family again, but she did create a family of her own. She married five times and my mother has four older stepsiblings. In her later years Flora lived with us for six months and then year after year, she would get on the bus and go visit her other children in California. I guess from her own mother's life, my mother got the idea of the importance of finding a good husband and she hoped I would find one, too, and now I have one in Ned.

But, overall, I identified more with my father and thought he had a more interesting life. My Dad's family was well known in the business community. My paternal grandfather was one of thirteen. He and his brothers started a Chocolate Company in Wilmington, N.C. and eventually moved to Philadelphia. They produced candies like *Goobers* and *Raisinettes.*

My grandfather died on my fourth birthday. The Yahrzeit candle replaced my birthday candle. He had divorced my grandmother years earlier. He was said to be the nice one and she was the mean one. Indeed, she didn't like any of her children's spouses and became very isolated from the family. My father and his brother helped support her. After her death, we went to clean up her place. It was a mess. But there were all kinds of very expensive jewelry hidden away. She left the jewelry to me. Who knows why? But, again, it reinforced in me the idea that I have to be careful to be self-sufficient.

All of this sensitivity finds its way into my marriage. Sometimes Ned and I laugh that he is my cricket and I am his ant. I make sure if it's a cold winter we will survive and he says listen to the music and let's dance.

The sibling rivalry with my brother also played into my doing well. My brother was like the prince with blond hair and blue eyes, more like my mother. But both my parents were focused on him. I was perhaps trying to say I was as good as or better than Mark and this competition turns out to be another factor in my doing well.

AMS – Yes, sibling position is a good one. You have your natural intelligence and then you have the conditions around you that support or handicap you. What your parents' sibling positions are (and even their parents' sibling positions) makes a difference in their ability to relate to you. In your case, your mom and maternal grandmother were both the youngest and you're an oldest. Therefore, it may have been more difficult for you to identify with them.

DP – I made my choice to have a career and be self-sufficient. My first assignment after Harvard Business School was to be the publicist for NBC's Saturday Night Live.

NP – I remember one time Uncle Lewis made the comment, 'The women's movement in this country is a luxury of the upper class.' In the lower classes, both men and women make about the same wages and are hard working. When we were in Kenya, there was no question of a women working. The women's way of contributing is to have children. In many cultures, women are valued as child bearers.

In industrial countries, women began to be valued for their intellectual contributions to knowledge. Some say that the largest single factor for the economic failure of Muslim countries is they have kept women out of economic life.

There is still a struggle between women, who work outside the home, and those, who stay home and raise children. You can see a kind of old-fashioned ethic in the way Hillary Clinton is judged by far right conservatives. It is as though one feels that the other is too different from what has been, and is, therefore, threatening the status quo and the future.

DP – My mother did often seem desperate for me to get married.

NP – The biggest problem for men is their fathers and for woman their mothers. It's about the expectation that you will follow in their footsteps.

DP – There is something that depreciates your choice if your children do not follow in your footsteps.

NP – I met a football player. He was telling a story about his son getting better than he was and so now, to get his position back, this father said he had to beat up his son.

So, in some families there is the element of a child doing well that the parents need and in other families, parents can resent a child's success. Both parents and spouses have a way to reach in and push the button to downgrade your life effort. The parent-child relationship continues on in many different forms throughout life with all kinds of people.

AMS – We are always vulnerable to the feedback we get from others that can influence and determine our path. This is why it's so important to have some kind of a compass so you can guide your own self through the jungle of sensitivity created in the past.

DP – The women I worked with, who had reached the VP level at NBC, still try to get together for lunch once or twice a year. Many of these successful women, who choose to have children, did so late in life. When they pull out the pictures, I can feel badly because I didn't have children. But, I also realize how much they sacrificed to have and raise these children. It is really curious about how many of these decisions, career vs. babies, are real choices and how much is programmed into us?

AMS – We do have instincts for procreation but our brains are also hardwired to notice the changing landscape and adapt. The evidence is that the changes in society are very radical now compared to how we humans lived for millions of years as a more tribal species.

As population exploded and we moved from an agricultural to an industrialized society, we were forced to adapt to more social demands.

These changes, adaptation to pressure, occur before we have time to reflect on them. No one decided that we needed to have women in the work force or that we needed smaller families in industrialized countries. These are just trends that reflect our adaptation to changing conditions.

DP – You can see how many instinctive patterns still play out. Put a bunch of women into a group and it will not take long to see there is no question about who is in charge. There is an almost instinctive knowledge about who will be in charge.

NP – Now if you insert a strong man into the woman's group it will alter the dynamics immediately.

I am not sure how this relates, but I heard some people in a restaurant complaining and the other person saying we just have to rewrite your childhood to solve the problem. Perhaps it's more than your childhood you would have to rewrite. There are larger forces influencing us.

DP – If you watch dogs, you see how the alpha dog keeps reinforcing his/her position. Within groups, people seem to know their roles and their positions almost immediately. Men seem to have a definitive pecking order that is more of a command and control operation. Women's pecking order is based on something else. I found it difficult to navigate the women's pecking order, but then I had one brother and women are more of a mystery to me.

NP – There is a different dynamic among men.

The group has to have trust that you know where you are going and you have to have a connection to your followers. They want to know where you are going and how you will get there and that you care about them.

Look at Clinton. Even though people knew he lied to them about his personal life, and that this was a bad thing, they did not feel personally betrayed. They looked around and saw that their life was better and felt he had delivered on his promise to them and, therefore, Clinton left office with a 63-percent approval rating.

With men, looks do not matter significantly or make a tremendous difference. Leadership is more intellectual. I am not sure that is true for women. To some degree we are still hard wired to our biological heritage.

To be a leader, people have to be able to break the code of their group. The question is how men and women work it out to rise above the crowd and lead. We are hard wired to go along with the group. It may be more difficult at work to differ with the group. A small percentage of people can rise above and lead others because they have some talents and social skills the group needs.

DP – Is there a skill one can develop to have a more independent mind, remembering that any leader has to be able to "soothe" the group when he or she differs from it?

Some people learn to joke and enjoy turning aside the "digs" from other females. While someone like me learns to ask questions and find out more about other people. These are all social skills useful in being a leader.

NP – For men in high school, there are two distinct leadership tracks, the athletes and the smart guys. Both win the awards.

When they go to college, very few of the jocks know how to keep going, but the more intellectual types do well. When you get to graduate school it is even more focused on intellect. I am not sure about the trends for women? The cheerleaders do not have to change. They can continue on their track to get married. This is the path for the majority of women—find a spouse.

DP – Sometimes you see that the women, who are leaders, have become the sons in the family. Their brothers do not do well and the sister seems to take over and excel.

AMS – One question to consider is whether the parents directly or indirectly select the brightest one to focus on to be the leader of the next generation. There are probably a lot of factors that go into a woman becoming the chosen one in the family.

NP – As my family went, it was handed down to me. It's my job to go to work and be responsible rather than to be the nurturing one. In general, there is probably more awkwardness when it comes to men who take on the nurturing female role and look after the children while the wife goes on to be the career person.

AMS – How do you all manage your career choices and how do you balance out the two careers in your family?

NP – Choices always have consequences. There may be doubt and uncertainty at first. My brother stayed in the family business while I went on to graduate school and was determined to do it myself. It looked early on like my brother was going to be more successful in the real estate business, but I took more risks and now both of us admire the other's choices.

DP – The way I see our careers is that we trade off. When I was able to get a job that was fabulous, we moved for my job. About the time Ned had a great offer, my media company was bought out. President Clinton challenged Ned to get involved and so we made a move here. Now, the next move might have been for my career but Ned was given this wonderful opportunity with the USO. I can be with him and travel and be useful to the organization so it worked out for each of us. We talk these things over.

NP – Both of us have been blessed with great, wonderful mentors that are a bit older.

One of the men I admired walked out of Poland and came to this country after the war, and now I want to give back to younger people, as he did. This is another significant aspect of leadership. Who do you invest in that sees potential in you and invests in you as a future leader?

I also knew that I wanted a spouse that is intelligent. Diane is one of the first women I have known, who I do not have to explain things to.

DP – There are good things and challenges about the fact that I have been in the business world. I often have opinions. I have a strict sense of justice. Once I was serving on a board as a member of the investment committee and found out that three of the board members had conflicts of interest. I stuck it out for two years during which time the facts came out and the various people resigned. This was good example of staying with your group while managing to keep factual and true about your values. It is not easy to do. Women in management positions face a lot of resistance, so they cannot slip up.

I was fortunate to work for Grant Tinker, "the man who saved NBC," when he served as the network's chairman and CEO from 1981 to 1986. His vision was to hire the best creative people and let them work without interference from executives at the networks. He lived his values. Once I was at the airport waiting for my bags and he saw me and asked me if I wanted a ride. The cost of the ride was to answer a lot of questions he had about my take on the company. I was a low person in the organization and was amazed at how interested he was in what I thought.

I have kept this kind of attitude with all the people I run into. You never know what you are going to learn from the people around you no matter their position. One of my strengths is that I will stand up for the people under me and defend them to the end. The downside is I do not find it easy to sell myself to the bosses.

NP – Another important aspect of being a leader is that you need to know your strengths and weaknesses. When people ask me a question and I answer, they tell me that they learned a lot from me. Finally, I saw that I was able to mentor people.

As a couple, one of the fun things is that we almost simultaneous think deeply about things and are willing to talk about our life experiences.

DP – I am still thinking about the issues for women. I think one of the biggest challenges in business is how caught up women are in the social approval game. Women can be other women's worst enemy. Often they want other women's approval for looking good rather than for work well done. My experience is that it almost seems more natural for women to do in another woman in order to help a man, than to help another woman.

AMS – I wonder if a woman's natural role has been to find a husband and raise children then in that circumstance there is little overt competition with women in the neighborhood. People cooperate easily to raise children. But once you put unattached women together, without children nearby, you alter the cooperative dynamic. Once you introduce a man into the mix, there is competition at an instinctual level. How that is handled depends on the women's level of awareness and their ability to see it.

It would seem there are many things we can learn about that will make it possible for men and women to work cooperatively together. A current trend now is that more women than men graduate from college. This will force more pressure for change. There are many questions about how people will cope and adapt with all these larger trends occurring in society. I want to thank you each for your time and your treasure trove of ideas and experiences.

Ned Powell's Mindful Compass Points

(1) The ability to take ACTION and to define a vision: Ned was clear that his family values are important to him. His vision of giving back to the community is based on these values. One could make the case that he has absorbed his family's value of contributing to the community by performing well in every job he has taken on.

Ned has worked in the public and private sectors and was clear about the importance of values in making decisions. He said that a key skill in implementing a vision is to consider many factors without overworrying any one issue. It is hard work to filter ideas and develop a comprehensive plan or solution to bring a vision to reality.

His wife pointed out that Ned has the ability to relate to all kinds of people. He learned a great deal while he was in the armed forces, gaining the opportunity to test his skills and to know a diverse population. Understanding people is a prime requisite for any leader.

Leaders often say that they take in a lot of information and try to be as efficient as they can about their time. Few would disagree that it is important to have a variety of ideas in order to make good decisions. But it takes a special talent to enable people to feel safe and valued so that many ideas present in a group will surface.

Ned has spent many years in different arenas, making tough decisions and keeping on his path, even when people around him object. He related well to the people around him, communicating his vision and enabling that vision to become reality.

The calmness and certainty of Ned comes across whenever you meet him in both informal and more professional settings. When talking with him on almost any topic, he seems to have thought carefully about many different viewpoints. This ability to think carefully helps move the group forward and is reassuring to people when they are faced with uncertainty.

The ability to see group dynamics and also connect with people in the group enables Ned Powell to move forward with confidence. It is clear that in his case these social skills were learned very young, by noticing how people over the generations in his family related to others.

(2) The RESISTANCE to changes in self and in any system: The story Ned tells us about his uncle's very subtle influence to reinforce the generational norms is both instructive and endearing. He did not tell us the details of how he handled the pressure but we can assume from how he told his story, that it wasn't a very big deal.

Being able to handle even subtle pressure to change self for another is a leadership skill that is very important. How do any of us avoid creating more reactivity when people put pressure on us to change for them?

Both members of a social group and a family can have undue influence on a leader. If the leader reacts negatively to interpersonal pressure the whole situation can deteriorate. Ned Powell demonstrated that he kept a sense of humor with his uncle. This gives us one example of his ability to have perspective when faced with resistance.

(3) The ability to use KNOWLEDGE to connect: Ned comes from a family with three siblings and a long history of living in one area. He learned from watching his sisters that women often have greater difficulties than men sustaining a career decision. The conflict with family needs and the needs of

the job are often at loggerheads. He has taken this knowledge and used it to enable women in his organizations to do well, recognizing without judgment what women are up against. He helps people see the facts so that they can make a thoughtful cost-benefit analysis while making their own decisions.

As a young man he enlisted in the service where he had the opportunity to build on his ability to relate well to all kinds of people. He enjoys being in personal contact with a large network of people, as he has been since he was young. His family connections led to his larger community connections, which in turn helped him remain connected to a larger network during his career.

One other connection that Ned Powell mentioned was the skill of teamwork learned in sports. Sports are a proving ground for teamwork and leadership. These skills are evident now as he plays golf. Golf allows him to get to know people in a competitive situation. There will be a winner and loser today but that can, and often does shift, in the future. This is good to remember in business. Not taking sides and watching what happens in the moment are skills that golf encourages. Golf is also a game of risk where one's physical skills, values, and ability to relate well to the group are equally important.

Leadership can be learned in many different ways but it is an advantage to be able to play and to think well in our daily life.

(4) The ability to STAND ALONE and to be more separate: A short interview cannot demonstrate clearly each point on the compass. But to make choices that go against the family grain, for example, by leaving Virginia as Ned did, can force any of us to experience a moment or two of separateness. This builds one's emotional backbone.

Noticing how you are different from significant others and allowing that to exist without being upset about it is important to a leader's ability to relate well to others. Being separate gives any of us an opportunity to consider what our deep values are and how to live by them without impinging on others. Managing a marriage is a skill. Both of the Powell's have great respect for one another's talents and differences.

Diane Powell's Mindful Compass Points

(1) The ability to take ACTION to define Self: Diane talked about her early need to be self-sufficient while remaining true to her deeply held values. She had positive family expectations that fit with her talent and desire to achieve. Growing up in an intellectually stimulating environment enabled her to enjoy learning and translated into performing well in academic settings. As she encountered challenges as a woman in corporate America, she used her personal learning experiences to consider the bigger picture. Her question was and is, how can women help other women do well? In her view, women need to have a realistic picture of the costs and benefits to their personal and family lives to do well in business. Some women may naturally understand group dynamics while others may need more mentoring. One question she asked was: if there were more women, with greater awareness on corporate boards, would that provide more opportunity for the corporation itself and also for many other women to live up to their potential?

(2) The RESISTANCE to change in self and in any system: The story that Diane tells us about how she served on a board where she found out that several of the directors had conflicts of interest was a good example of how a leader can know the problem but must be patient and strategic since it can take a very long time for change to occur. She sees problem solving as a process that requires the leader to be neutral and able to relate well to others. She had to sit with the opposition and the tension in the group, while nothing seemed to be happening. It might have been tempting or even easier to quit the board or the job rather than stick to dealing with the slow process of change in the group. Change can take a long time since it often happens one person at a time. Seeing the big picture and having patience are two traits of successful leaders for whom resistance is another challenge and no big deal.

(3) The ability to use KNOWLEDGE to connect: Being able to build networks of supportive people is important to any leader. It is not necessary that these networks be directly connected to one's job or current career. Overall people need to have balance in many relationship systems so that if one is uptight the others might be welcoming.

Diane talked about the group of women, who have been vice presidents at NBC. They still keep up with each other as part of staying connected to their own history. Just as people like to have knowledge of their family history, so too keeping in touch with one's co-workers adds depth and genuineness. She described her own growth in relationship to the different paths other individuals had taken. It is always good to be able to question one's decisions and wonder how your life might have been different had you chosen a different path. At the same time there is satisfaction in being pleased with one's choices. Often people say. "I do not want to go to this or that reunion because it would be too painful to see so and so." Many miss the opportunity to go to the emotional gym and have a good workout. The people who have known us the longest often hold us to a higher standard. There also may be some correlation between long-standing relationships in one's family and long-standing friendships in one's working world.

(4) The ability to STAND ALONE and be separate: Diane is one of many women leaders who commented on being separate from their peer group growing up. She noted that her Mom did not encourage her to use make up and that she found it difficult to figure out how to be at ease with girls her age. If you do not fit in with your social group then people often fall back on their skills which are often more intellectual or athletic. These kinds of skills are not as subject to group pressure. Yet as Diane also says, "You have to unlock the ability to relate well to groups of people in order to be their leader." Her ability to ask good questions and really listen to others is grounded in her ability to be separate and relate to people as separate individuals. As a bonus, Diane noted that her ability to understand her husband was part and parcel of her ability to listen well and to risk being open with all kinds of people.

GERALDINE MACDONALD

Geraldine MacDonald is retired Senior Vice President, Global Access Networks, America Online, Inc. For 25 years, she was responsible for computing and networking at the State University of New York at Binghamton.

In his book *Serious Play,* Michael Schrage identifies a leadership trait he calls "retrospective sense-making." It is a trait that enables leaders to link the past and the present to the future. Individuals so gifted automatically use their relationship knowledge to build future success. If you ask them, they can reflect on how they got from point A to point D and can assess the probability of getting to point E by doing X, Y or Z.

Most people don't easily link their preferred ways of working as leaders or team members to situations in their early lives. But one can learn to do that. When you think about your early experiences, about what happened and why, look for links between those early events and patterns in your life today. You will probably have to spend quite a lot of time thinking about this to see these patterns as they take shape, but it is time well spent.

MacDonald is a leader in technology, able to reflect on the early relationships and events that made significant impressions on her. There may be certain kinds of experiences that reinforce the traits needed to be successful in different fields. Changes in technology occur ten times faster than in other industries. A leader in technology has to be able to let go of past ways of doing business or producing products. The product life of soda drinks, for example, is very different from the product life of cell phones.

MacDonald is an oldest female with a younger sister and brother. As an oldest sister of two younger siblings, she would be more of a natural leader—as long as the family expectation for women was that they become leaders. She recounts her early experiences with her father and the dramatic stories of her family's escape from Eastern Europe in the late 1930s, a history which has had significant impact on her life.

Leaders often notice small changes and can see how they might become future trends. When the group does not see the trend or get the message, the leader must have that special ability to stand apart until the group catches up. MacDonald talks about how families and mentors can enable young adults to develop the skill to be aware of the group's direction, while also articulating a different way of proceeding. She also sees in her earlier experiences practical application for leadership training in schools and business.

Kathy Wiseman, a long-time colleague of mine, joined me in the second of two interviews with MacDonald.

243

MacDonald used her knowledge of math and science to participate at a high level in the technological changes of the 20th century. This is extraordinary given the many impediments to women in the sciences that were the norm throughout most of that century. Now, society would like to bottle and sell encouragement for women in these fields. How did it happen for her? There is something to be learned by listening to her story.

GM – My Dad said, "Just worry about math and science, which is the only thing that is important." He was Jewish and came from a large family with perhaps eight or nine siblings. He was one of the younger ones. Many of them did not survive World War II. He was alert enough to see how society was changing, and escaped from Eastern Europe before the worst treatment of the Jewish people had begun.

MacDonald's father knew the situation in Eastern Europe was deteriorating when all Jewish people were required to report where they went every day. Seeing how movement was becoming much more restricted, he took steps to get out of the country. He had a passport that made it possible for him to leave Eastern Europe and go to France without as many problems as others had, but it was still extremely difficult. By comparison, the financial burden of leaving his business was no doubt a welcome risk, considering the personal risk of staying in Hitler's Europe.

MacDonald's mother's family was divided in their ability to see and react to the changes in society. Her mother was the middle of three girls, and appeared to be the one most comfortable remaining with her parents, despite the threats around her. Her older sister was in her twenties at the time and was able to get a visa to the United States. The younger sister was part of a "kinder transport," a program designed to save children under the age of 15, who were caught in Eastern Europe. A movie called "Into the Arms of Strangers" was made about this program.

GM – When I asked my Mom why she, too, did not flee, she said that she and her family just could not believe that their friends and neighbors would betray them.

Her mother's youngest sister was determined to get her parents and middle sister out. She and every other child in the program had been told that it was their responsibility to see that their families escaped. This sister worked on a plan to sponsor the rest of her family. She camped out on the doorstep of a potential sponsor with her request, day after day after day, until he finally agreed to help her. The sister's determination saved the lives of members of this family.

AMS – It is very difficult to change basic assumptions about how safe the world is and how secure one's position is in it. And it requires great courage to let go of past comforts. But if we want to consider different mental models of the world, we have to let go of the old way of seeing. And I assume that those, who in the 1930s realized that the world was changing and would never be the same, might have passed on this ability to "see" to their offspring.

GM – Well, I am not sure about how all that influenced me, but I am an oldest and am used to pushing the envelope and constantly striving.

AMS – Global uncertainty and unrest can destabilize family functioning—that's clear. But a family with a relationship system that incorporates a thoughtful view of the outside world can give realistic feedback about what is changing in society and what needs to be done now. Your family clearly demonstrates how the ability to see the possibilities in the future can lead to success. My general thesis is that people emerge from their families with higher levels of functioning if the family relationship system is calm and reasonably focused on doing what needs to be done. This is much healthier than thinking fearfully of the past or about the future. It's not that people don't experience fear. They often do, but then they can let it go and not use fear as nightly entertainment.

GM – Children learn very early the difference between what is acceptable and what is not. As they grow up, they continually push those boundaries. For a creative person, the key is to be able to push the boundaries without having the parents—or, in later life, the boss—crack down too severely.

AMS – One of my favorite stories is about Jane Goodall's early life. Jane was missing for hours. Unaware of the fuss, she was happily watching how chickens laid their eggs. When her mother found her, Jane was not punished. The mother understood that Jane was a budding scientist and an observer at heart. She had just pushed the parental boundaries a bit, but not to the point of anger.

GM – In the best cases, children will risk and the parents will form a kind of management team. I think there are many similarities between these informal family "rules" and the ways organizations are run. Let me give you some of my ideas:

1) Feedback: In well-functioning families and organizations, individuals receive immediate feedback for boundary infractions. They are also given positive motivational rewards for good work. In a family, a child can earn a dime for doing good work, and can also lose money or privileges if he or she is disrespectful or breaks the rules. In companies, the feedback is much more complex, of course, because it includes input from customers.

2) Expectations: Both parents and bosses can be guilty of setting unrealistic expectations. This creates problems in corporate America, just as it does in families. I think it's best to give newer people a chance to prove how well they function, realistically, before hoping or deciding that they will be the next leader.

3) Assumptions: The needs of the corporation and the needs of the family can become so great that making an accurate assessment of any individual's talent is difficult. Workers, like children then might try to become something for "*the other.*" This type of pretending to be what one is not, eventually leads to disappointments and frustration for both.

AMS – Another assumption that people hold is that before five years of age children are primarily influenced by their relationship with their parents. After five years of age, children become more and more sensitive to how peers view them. Many youngsters' values are a result of their orientation to peer group standards—a process that results in conflicts with their parents during high school. Eventually, each individual will select the more personally meaningful set of values. Some will be from the parents and others from their peers. This means that some young adults will emerge with a tilt more toward just accepting the peer group's values, while others will be more stabilized from within self because their values have been well integrated into who the individual is and is automatically reflected in their behavior. Individuals, who reflect on their family's values and take what they need from the family, often find it easier to stabilize self during the hectic teen years. Individuals clear about their own internal values are more likely as teens to be more independent, creative and flexible. To reach this point, however, each individual must run the gauntlet of peer pressure.

GM – Often peer approval is more important to girls than to boys. Boys may spend more time learning team values. The highest value for girls is often more about looking good and fitting in with the group. Boys can be athletes or smart and still be accepted. Accurate feedback from parents and the parents' ability and willingness to support the child's natural talents can make a difference as children approach their teen years. This is one of those areas where companies and families are similar. When companies give accurate feedback, it reinforces and sustains individual accomplishments while enabling diverse individuals to work productively inside the system.

As individuals climb the corporate ladder they encounter more responsibility and tougher rules. Long-term goals are crucial for a CEO, whereas new employees have short-term projects. Leaders are concerned with the long-term vision for the company, while new people have shorter term goals, like needing to have the right tools to get the job done. At each level, success is measured differently.

Organizations used to have more of a relationship model for teaching and learning. This was a time when taking on an individual as an apprentice, being a mentor, was popular. Now some companies look for the "knowledge worker," the ones who come to work with the tools and know what to do. No serious mentoring or training required. This is very different from how people have lived for thousands of years. In the agricultural economy, jobs were similar from generation to generation. There was less need to specialize.

AMS – Does this imply that the boss or the management team has less impact on the worker because there is a feeling that no matter what you do there is less overall company loyalty? One piece of evidence is that companies are investing less and less in their employees.

GM – This differs from company to company. The parent's job with the teenager could be seen as similar to the job of an aware CEO, who is looking for a replacement. You want someone to take over a role. It is not to be yours forever, so you have to invest in the future performance of your new people.

AMS – Let's consider what part schools play in this leap between the family and the job. If the families fall down on the job or fall apart, we can be sure that the school's job will harder—perhaps impossible. Schools become a hoped-for replacement for the family. Similarly, the organization becomes the next "replacement" for the family. A solution that many religious and coaching organizations have suggested is renewed focus on values and character. To the extent that this makes people think about the long-term consequences of how they deal with one another, it can be useful. But if people disregard their family members and become more isolated, then they become more and more sensitive in relationships at work and elsewhere. The bottom line is that each segment of society has to deal with the relationships. Organizations can make rules about harassment, discrimination and other issues, but they fail to address the deep nature of the problem. What will probably happen over time is a slow recognition of the nature of relationships and their impact on the business environment.

Another question: Are men and women moving toward more cooperative relationships at work?

GM – Women have been in the workforce in large numbers since World War II. Women are probably better at trusting their instincts. Men are about teamwork. You learn on teams what cannot be taught in classrooms. Men learn to cooperate on teams. Women have a harder time, especially if they did not play sports.

Every company has teams that are formed to solve intellectual problems. Now high school teams are being encouraged to solve problems. For example, there is a program (Odyssey of the Mind) that gives the students one year to solve a particular problem. In solving the problem, the students learn to work together as a team and to exploit the skills of their teammates.

AMS – One question I have asked is if families are thinking about preparing children for teamwork? Do they allocate tasks that allow kids to succeed? Without some focus on teams and an individual's responsibility to contribute to the whole, people will tend to follow the leader, no matter where he or she is heading. We see a herd mentality then in the followers.

Some people say that teaching teamwork and leadership is not going to help, since it's "obvious" that entrepreneurs are just born into the right times and even the right neighborhood where experimentation is going on. But I see a great need in schools to teach the skills needed to become a leader. After all, only a few young adults can get to be the football quarterback.

KW – What are the qualities you are seeing in leaders?

GM – First of all, you have to be intelligent. I enjoyed the TV program *The Apprentice* because it shows how people use all kinds of smarts to do well. Initially, the women went overboard, selling a kiss with the lemonade. Then the producers had a more mixed team between the men and women, and more sexualized behavior fell out. One woman took the blame for the failures, but Donald Trump told her that he wanted her to fight with him about what had gone wrong. People often misread their bosses and then do not deal with them directly. What is the skill set you need to teach? Relationship awareness might be a skill that can be learned more easily when you are young.

AMS – Can you teach an introvert to be an extroverted leader?

GM – Perhaps it is easier to learn to be a follower and go along, but if you want to be a leader you have to be willing to take a risk and live with success and failure. To summarize, I would say there are four points: being aware of your natural strength; having relationship skills, such as knowing who to trust and who not to trust; knowing when to take a risk; and having the confidence to go with your instinct, to go with what you think is right.

KW – Is there an example of when you took a risk?

GM – In 1968, when I was 19 and a half years old, I graduated from college and made a risky decision to go into computers. I could have taken a safe job for a woman and been a teacher. Another interesting fork in the road was when I interviewed with AOL. I had been teaching and building technology systems for 25 years when a friend told me that there was a job at AOL and asked if I would be interested. This was early 1995. AOL was a distant third in online services. But I saw the potential. I thought that I would be crazy not to take the job, even though it was a big risk. But I was right. Six months later AOL was leading the Internet revolution. We really did change the way business was done, and I am so pleased that I made that decision.

KW – Are there times when you have to define yourself to the team and you get a push back?

GM – Yes. When I was line manager at AOL I had to do this every day. In fact, I also had to say to my boss, "You are not paying me to say yes to you on everything. If that were so, then you do not need me."

If you have an acquired skill set it is easier to make risky decisions. Making decisions about softer things, like when to get married is a different kind of analysis. In business, you have measurements and a series of checks and balances to see if you are making the right decision. I like to use the football analogy. The quarterback leads the plays, but the team's performance is what is really being measured. In the same way, the company's leaders set the goals, and then each department has to see that it is on the right page and that there are goods metrics to measure success.

AMS – Do you think being able to talk more openly with your father helped you in business?

GM – Yes, it helps to be able to talk to your parents, but it also helps if your parents are providing a secure environment. I had parents, who were willing to trust that I was making the right decision. You need someone who believes in you, not someone who is constantly questioning you. The parents have to be willing to believe that the children are making the right decisions and can live with the consequences. The parents, who criticize too much, are eroding the child's chances to learn from their experiences. The parents become too powerful. They make it so the child's opinions do not count. Both parents and children should have a right to be heard.

KW – Would you say that leaders are looking for ways to build maturity or foster maturity in an organization?

GM – You do this by observing how people operate in teams. You see who the contributors are, and you reinforce their achievements by saying, "You did a great job with that, now would you like to try this?" By keeping them in a feedback loop and giving them more responsibility, you help them to learn how to be successful. Of course, you can learn from your failures, too.

If a company wants to grow leaders from within, it has to create a way to see who these leaders are, how various individuals function in the group. If you ask middle managers to identify potential leaders, they might point to their best friends. So, you have to set up work groups to see who will be able to contribute. It is up to the senior people to look for potential leaders and figure out how to bring them along. It also depends on the company. There are companies that, in times of slower growth, develop leaders from within. When there are mergers, then new leaders may be picked from outside. Then you have to focus more on integrating the two cultures.

Young adults also need opportunities to do something different. Both schools and families could be more conscious of who gets to do what. Being more inclusive would require an effort on the part of schools.

MacDonald switched her emphasis on leadership building and teamwork to a look at the ability to spot trends and the influence of family.

AMS – You got to see your father's genuine interest in taking things apart.

GM – When I was at college, my Dad loved going to auctions. There was a clock he wanted a part for, but to get the part he had to buy a box of these clocks. There were probably 50 of them. He put them all around the house, and at night there was symphony of clocks. I will never forget that.

AMS – Do you think you learned to see future trends from your Dad?

GM – I am not sure that there is a direct correlation. Individuals, who can really see trends, are not always leaders. They tend to be more removed from people, tend to be more thinkers than doers. But my Dad and his clocks helped me see more about how things work, and that got me over some of the technical barriers. I think being a woman in a technical field is a real issue. There are lots of men, who will not hear what you say just because you are a woman. But if you ask them if they would want that to happen to their daughters, well, that can be an eye-opening experience for them. In certain parts of corporate America, fighting for what you believe in as a woman is not appreciated. Women have more passion. Donald Trump noticed this and recognized that there is a difference. But, in general, corporate America is not there yet. I think that as there are more and more women in the workplace, the different ways of communicating strong opinions will become more accepted.

When you are woman and doing something by yourself, you think you should get credit for it. But I think that if you are moving up in a company, you don't have to worry about getting credit. Instead, if you reinforce what others are saying that is close to what you think, suddenly people seem to be able to hear you. Then you can get things done.

You also have to be aware that there are people who want your job and who will try to do you in. This is just the nature of corporations. Helping people understand who to trust is very important. You have to figure out how to get realistic feedback from people you work with. What is dangerous is not the personal criticism, but the negative messages that float around you.

AMS – Do you think that having a more open family helps you to deal with criticism at work?

GM – I think most families are loyal to one another above all, and that in families you do not experience the political backstabbing that is in corporate America. Perhaps your teenage peer groups are closer to what goes on. There are cliques in corporate America, just like there are in high school.

KW – Are there skills as a leader you would like to acquire?

GM – I am working on ways to socialize my thinking. When I have a project that I want supported, I go around and have one-to-one chats with people about my research and what I am thinking. This is something I think I had to learn—how to get people you're working with to put some of their own skin into the project. If you can do it, you have a better chance of success. How you get a team to work well is a big part of a leader's job.

AMS – I hear you as saying that there are skills you pick up in your family, and that you then have to develop them when you get into your job. There are things that no book can teach you—there's just your ability to observe relationships and to notice what works in the moment.

Thank you again for giving us so much of your time and being willing to continue to think about these ideas. It's been fun.

Geraldine MacDonald's Mindful Compass Points

(1) The ability to take ACTION to define a vision: MacDonald highlights the early influence of her father on her career choice. Her father loved and had a great curiosity about technology. She built on his encouragement and embraced her own dream. The ability to build on your family's intellectual resources facilitates taking a calculated risk with your own vision. When MacDonald saw an opportunity at AOL that fit with her long-term vision of connecting people through the Internet, she took the risk. That decision ultimately enhanced her ability to make a significant difference in opening up a new market and changing the way people around the world do business.

(2) The RESISTANCE to change in self and in any system: MacDonald also told us about her father's coaching in regard to the pressure to fit in with her peer group versus following her own dreams. ("Just worry about math and science, which is the only thing that is important.") For MacDonald, that advice has stood the test of time. She used this idea when her mother could not understand her career choice. In addition, MacDonald was later able to step back and let her own daughter find her own career path. Like most of us, MacDonald has experienced those "odd person out" feelings that can be associated with being a woman in business, or with having ideas that are not well understood by people who are important to you. Being able to stay centered, without reacting or taking a passive or revengeful stance, as those people try to catch up with your thinking, or as they reject you and your ideas, is a key ingredient to working with teams.

(3) The ability to use KNOWLEDGE to connect: MacDonald is very much aware of and grateful for the courageous people in her multigenerational history. Clearly, she is knowledgeable about the impact of looking after family members. But the degree to which building and sustaining her family network has helped her in building her business network was not clearly addressed. Generally, however, people who maintain good connections with their families find it natural to sustain a well-functioning network of friends and business associates.

In her nuclear family experience, MacDonald saw her father's sincere interest in doing well. This was transmitted to her. He had his own business and could see the impermanence of trends. Therefore, as he predicted the future in technology, he stressed to his daughter the importance of math and science in preparing for a future career in that field. As a seasoned observer of how people pressure each other in social ways, he was able to warn his daughter about the dubious benefits of trying to fit in with the girls her age by rejecting the "boys' subjects" of math and science.

In addition to talking, he walked the technology walk. Very probably, her father's love of mechanical things gave his insistence on the importance of math and science a more realistic base. This is an example of the genuine strengths in the father-daughter relationship—coherence between what is said and done, and it probably enabled MacDonald to take the more challenging, less popular road.

While her father was obviously very aware of the changes happening in society, it is unsaid, but assumed that her mother fully supported his position, encouraging math and science for her daughter.

Finally, because the ability to have a respectful relationship with one's boss is often related to one's ability to have an open relationship with one's first authority figure, the father-child relationship can influence one's ability to connect.

(4) The ability to STAND ALONE and to be separate: As a youngster, MacDonald saw her father disassemble motors just so he could understand how they were made. As an adult, she watched him put together a box full of clocks. He was interested in making things work and in getting a good price.

His example retains a firm and fun-filled place in her retrospections about her family experiences. Her father was also convinced that he could see the way the future would turn to embrace technology. He saw the introduction of TV to the American home and concluded that Americans were in the early stages of a technological revolution.

Parents, who communicate easily, often have a genuine interest in the subject rather than an agenda to make the child "do the right things." Learning by identifying positively with a parent's message makes it easier for children to learn both by imitation and by listening to stories. Although her parents influenced MacDonald to stay in science, there was no undue pressure to go in a direction that did not fit with her underlying strengths. Most important is that her father saw MacDonald's strengths and was able to support her ability to make the most of them. Having had a positive mentoring relationship with her father probably made it easier for MacDonald to relate to men in authority. She could also see the importance of men and women working in cooperative relationships and noted that men with daughters were more likely to enable women to be successful.

Knowing the way systems operate as natural phenomena makes it possible to stay separate and not overly react to the way things are. Being a good observer without reacting also enables people to make small changes when there are openings for changes, rather than trying to force a system to be more ideal.

LADONNA LEE

Ladonna Lee is a strategic communications consultant, who has worked with many of the top political leaders and committees in Washington, D.C. As of this writing, she is employed at Foley & Lardner, LLP, a law firm in that city.

Ladonna Lee is the second of eight siblings and was raised with them on a ranch in Colorado. Sibling position is an important fact in developing an understanding of the patterns that emerge in a family system. Different sibling positions have different advantages and disadvantages. Many leaders, for example, are oldest children, since responsibility is thrust on them at an early age. However, if the oldest child does not take to a leadership role, that responsibility can fall on the next willing child.

In most families, the oldest child initially takes up most of the mother's time, while the second child often spends more time with the father. In families that emphasize careers and education, the second child may have an advantage in being closer to the father, who often has a career outside the home. And, true to form, Ladonna Lee was special to her Dad. He was special to her, as well, and over time she became a family leader.

In my interview with her, Lee was able to convey a feeling of the forces that her family contended with by giving me just a few well-chosen thoughts and memories. This was enough to create a background understanding of the times and influences at work in her early family life.

LL – My parents lived through the Depression. My Dad was sent away after eighth grade to herd sheep because there was not enough money to get by in those days. The money he and the other older children earned was given back to the family."

Ladonna's Dad had a clear influence on her choice of career. Here is how she explained what she heard about his beliefs and saw in his actions, and where she differed from him.

LL – My Dad's political responsibility was to influence his situation. He believed that parents could influence their children. His believed that children's philosophy and values were largely formed by the time they are six years old.

Ladonna believes that there is further shaping and influence once a person leaves the family unit. Politics, we know, is one way you can influence people.

LL – My Dad was interested in local politics first. There was no high school in our rural area. My older sister had to go live with another family so that she could attend high school. School was important to Dad. He decided to run for political office so he could make sure there was a high school locally so that the rest of his kids would not be sent away.

In talking about her unique skills, Ladonna said that in her family, it was expected that the children would do their jobs without being asked. Her father would brag that, "Ladonna could grease the windmill, and be ready for Church in 20 minutes." With eight children, the uniqueness of each was valued—but to receive individual recognition was special.

LL – By the time I was a senior in high school, Dad ran for the State legislature. When I was a freshman in college, he asked me if I would be interested in working at the Capitol during the sessions. It was great. I loved it—and I got to live with my Dad. I got to see up close how the political system worked. What I found compelling about politics is that there are so many ways to let people have their voice. You are exposed to a lot of ideas, and there is a definite measuring stick to see if the ideas are workable: People get elected—or they do not.

Thinking about the progression of her work life, Ladonna said she made many choices on her way to finally selecting politics as a career.

LL – One that stands out occurred when I was asked to interview for Vail Associates to be a corporate secretary to, among other things, wine and dine investors. Vail was a hard and fast lifestyle. It had some appeal to me at age 25. But I knew it was not the place to be if I wanted to raise a family. It was not my values or my lifestyle. I knew they appreciated me for being a blond and interesting woman, but this was not the talent I wanted to build on.

There are many situations like this where one has to choose, to ask which of the choices represents a deeper value. The bigger driver for me was to move to another environment. I had spent time in Colorado and I wanted to know more about the broader world. My career decision was practical-driven. I was working for the Governor of Colorado when he lost the election. Then, I got an offer to come work in D.C. for the Republican National Committee. This was post-Watergate, when very few people would publicly admit they were Republicans. I knew that there would be many opportunities here to solve problems.

Ladonna Lee's Mindful Compass Points

(1) The ability to take ACTION and to define a vision: Ladonna's story

suggests that she is more on the side of the importance of work itself rather than winning approval from others. The ability to do one's job without "needing" approval is crucial. You know that's true if you've ever worked with someone who constantly sought your approval or with someone who would either become paralyzed or mad as a hornet if you did not approve of what he or she were doing.

Politics was appealing to her as it gave the ordinary person a chance to express ideas and stand for a point of view and be elected or not. She wanted to give more people that kind of an opportunity and become involved in the political process. By seeing how things were accomplished in a political system, she was able to use her relationships with others to take action, as her father did, to make a difference in her community. She recognizes how she has been influenced and can address the pros and cons of various opportunities before she articulates her own goals and makes a selection, which she will see through

(2) The RESISTANCE to change in self and in any system: Sometimes resistance appears in the guise of an easy way out, in Ladonna's case a flashy job at Vail. Easy money, easy life—how many of us have been tempted to take a job that offers lots of benefits, but that could derail our long-term goals? Two of Ladonna's values were clearly stated—Let other voices be heard in the political process and pick a task where success can be measured.

(3) The ability to USE knowledge to connect with others: Like many successful women, Ladonna had a sound relationship with her father. Having a role model whom you admire early on makes one's life a lot easier. Women, who have been fortunate enough to have positive relationships with their fathers, find it is easier to build trusting relationships with men, to see them as allies, and to expect that men will do well by them.

In addition, we can assume that Ladonna's father encouraged her to build a working network of relationships as he himself had done. Once again, life is easier on those people who have positive experiences and can identify with their parental figures. They can build on that identification rather than struggle to figure out who to trust and how to build networks.

(4) The ability to be STAND ALONE and to be more separate: In her story, Ladonna described how as a child she showed leadership ability, "no one had to ask me to do things." The windmill story exemplifies her Dad noting her leadership ability. This brings up an interesting question about a leader's ability to be emotionally separate and to do things more for self rather than to please others. Where is the motivation found to be wise and thoughtful for the long-term future for self? People find values for the long term to be refreshing once they are named. The confusion can come over the short-term consequences of staying with your long-term values in the face of opposition or conflict. It can get tricky if you like both pleasing people and doing a good job for yourself. This is a dilemma that many people may not even recognize. The problem is that pleasing people can be dangerous; it can cause you to lose sight of your own direction and goals.

People, who care more about the work they are doing than about pleasing others, are often called loners, idea people, or introverts. These people usually stand out and do not fit in. And because they are not easily influenced, the group can react negatively to them. However, a person, who can be in a relationship with others *and* withstand the lure of those oh-so-good feelings of being popular, is a person who can be free. This person stands out *and* fits in. Do you fit this pattern?

One way to answer that question is to gauge how comfortable you are spending time alone. Another is to inject a few minor differences into your relationship with someone with whom you normally agree, just to test how well you can swim in choppy waters.

In Ladonna's case, the feedback from her Dad was not so much about approval as it was about expectations that you carried your weight and did the right thing no matter who was watching.

A short story such as Ladonna's can give us a good look at the big picture. It's up to the individual to build on any insights or appraisal given by others—or, in the case of Ladonna, assess the feedback from her Dad about her ability and then use her talents in the service of a worthy windmill.

The Importance of Feedback

After submitting the write-up of Ladonna's interview to her, I asked if she had any other stories that could attest to the importance of being more emotionally separate as a leader, yet still in touch with others and able to function at a higher level. This is the story she kindly added.

LL – When I was about 15, we arrived home on the school bus one night and found that our folks hadn't gotten back from town yet. Shortly after dropping us off at home, the school bus driver roared back into the yard. He was hysterical and said that there had been a bad accident involving our pick-up and our folks were dead.

When I asked, dreading the worst, specifically who was dead, the man said he wasn't sure. He was incapable of functioning. I told my sister to call the ambulance, knowing it was over a 30-minute drive from the nearest town. I was getting ready to drive over to do what I could when our hired man, who was the driver of one of the vehicles in the accident, drove in and said help was on its way and that our folks weren't back from town yet. Thankfully, I was saved from personally dealing with the carnage and finding out if my folks were the ones who had been killed. It was the first time for me that an adult hadn't measured up to a major crisis, and I knew I had the capability to step in and deal with a terrible situation. Fortunately, my role then turned to one of calming my siblings and the bus driver and caring for our injured hired man.

If individuals' intellectual functioning can retain relative autonomy in periods of stress, they are more flexible, more adaptable and more independent of the emotionality around them.   *Murray Bowen*

The Individual and the Influence of the Social Situation

Inevitably, when the successes and/or failures of individuals are discussed, the question of their various socioeconomic backgrounds arises. We know that different people have different constraints. That's a fact. How people manage and overcome those constraints is the key question. Yes, it is ever so nice to be born into money and privilege but it not a requirement for success.

The stories of Bob DiFlorio and the interview that follows with Steve Waite are examples of the possibilities in adaptation to a loss in the family and illustrate what it takes to manage anxiety in self and in others around a loss of a leader. The interview with Bob DiFlorio, who lost his father as a youngster, shows us how the family as a system changes after such a death and how the functioning of young people is altered. Steve Waite, on the other hand, lost his father as an adult. The opportunity to be closer to his father as his death approached, gave Steve time to reconsider his life direction. This open relationship was a gift for Steve.

Obviously, loss within a system provides evidence of the emotional glue that either does or does not hold people together. In addition, loss can propel people to function at better levels despite the losses. The loss of parents will alter a life course. Each individual will figure out how best to carry on and compensate for the loss. Fortunately, the family emotional system often has plenty of other relatives, who can step into the situation and provide emotional resources after a loss. In addition, since old patterns often reside in specific interactions, loss can also bring forth new behaviors by family members. Loss can also spike fears and a gathering storm of symptoms will appear. Leaders need to understand that loss will require more creative responses to the anxiety that inevitably will appear in the system. If the family leader is able to manage self in the group through the changing circumstances, the family will function better. Loss then represents both a challenge and a window of opportunity for change.

My hope is that reading these stories will give people a few more ideas about coping well with change and loss.

BOB DIFLORIO

Bob is a retired school superintendent from Syracuse, New York.

I met Bob DiFlorio through his niece, Liz Sollazo, a friend of mine. When I asked her whom she admired as a leader and who could tell an interesting story, she suggested without hesitation her husband's uncle. She asked him if he would participate in this project and he agreed. Bob is a retired school superintendent from Syracuse, New York. When I first met him, I loved his friendliness and warmth. If I were a kid, he would make me feel safe and listened to. Perhaps his warmth comes from his Italian roots or from his youthful experiences on the streets of Syracuse, or from his more than 35 years in the school system thinking about and being a teacher.

We sat at a kitchen table and it felt just like old times, even though this was the first. His story unfolded as soon as we met, without much prodding on my part.

AMS – I left my questions in the car since I assume you've read them and have an idea that my interest is in how you think you became the leader you are.

BD – Yes, I think there are many factors in becoming a leader. I come from an Italian immigrant family. My father died when I was six. My mother had to work and she needed help. My oldest brother was 16 at the time, the next sister 14, then a 12-year-old sister, a 10-year-old brother, and me at six, and an 18-month-old kid brother.

DiFlorio's father, a fruit and vegetable vendor, was 46 when he died. His mother was 38 at that time. DiFlorio's mother was still alive at the time of the interview, and at 89 continues to influence the family.

BD – When I was seven or so, I would have to leave school, get my baby brother from the babysitter, then bring him back home and baby sit. I can still remember climbing up the snowy hills with him. We were taught to look out for each other or else.

My Dad's death changed our family. We were all a lot closer to my mother. She gave us a lot of independence, and she was positive, not critical. We all had to work to make the family go. At 13, I was working in a bowling alley three or four nights a week. We all had to bring money home to help out Mom. There were no thoughts of college. We had to get a good job and get married and carry on the family. Mom encouraged us. She saw that it was necessary for us to get a trade. My brothers all have a trade.

My mother was the eldest of seven children. She grew up knowing about responsibility. My Dad was the eldest of nine. Now, my kids have 50 first cousins.

Throughout our neighborhood, and even in our school, people's cultural backgrounds were very similar. We were Italian. Therefore, most of us had the same values. Families stayed together. You might sometimes want to kill your brother, but if anyone came near him it was your responsibility to protect him. It was my responsibility to look after my brothers even if they had angered me. These values lasted. Even now, every Sunday my three brothers and two sisters and I get still together for breakfast. We did not have a father, but my mother told us we had to have that unity despite our differences and fighting. We had to learn to get along, and now we enjoy it.

Another important lesson my mother taught us was that if there was dissention, we had to clear it up. This also worked to keep us together. We had to resolve our problems, and the way you did it was with direct confrontation.

Later in life, this was the strategy I used in my administration. I was not afraid. I was direct. I was not intimidated by people being different or by those who had opposing ideas. I can remember one superintendent I was worried about. He was intimidating. But I thought, "So what? I can get a job somewhere else." Later on this superintendent brought me into his office and said, "I need you because you can get along well with people and deal openly with tough issues."

After high school, I went into the Army, and when I came out I taught diversity. A guidance counselor in high school had encouraged me to go to college. He said, "You can be a teacher." He told me I was going to go to Oswego State on a scholarship. That made a difference to me. I was the first in my family to go to college. I cut hair all through college and thought about being an electrician.

After a stint in the Army Reserve, I taught drafting and driver education, and then got my Master's in guidance counseling. It took from May till the last week in August of 1963 for me to get a job in a school where no one wanted to work. This job was in an all-black school. The school district was so tough they gave you a $500 bonus for joining the staff. They called it "hazard duty pay." I was not intimidated and I did not want to fail.

I was picked as one of 30 guidance counselors in the country, after my second year as a counselor, to attend a Syracuse University summer symposium. There was a trend in counseling of being non-direct, but I was not that way. I was direct. "You are going to college; you are going to do it."

I didn't mind listening to anyone, but it did not take that much listening before I knew what they needed to do to be successful—and I would tell them. Finding success has a value for each individual, and I knew that. It is the right thing to tell kids the truth and put the facts on the table. Yes, there will be kids, who are bad. But what I saw was intelligence. They may act badly, but if you push them the right way they will go for it. Two years later, at 25, I left counseling and became an administrator. And I have been in administration ever since.

AMS – You seem to handle conflict well. I'm curious about when you first ran up against your Mom.

BD – I would be out late, or something like that, and she would say, "What are you doing?" She never really hit us—she just told us that we have a responsibility and we knew it. I had respect for her. She worked hard. Her job was to help out immigrants, and she loved that. People from all over would come to our house, and she would teach them English as a second language way before it became popular.

AMS – Your Dad was an oldest and you are one of the younger ones, and one of the most successful, so I would guess that your older brother must have had a harder time with his father's death. How did your older brother do?

BD – He had a hard time in school. Later on he straightened out and became a plumber. My next brother went to work right away, and he took a lot of responsibility for the family.

AMS – How much did your extended family help out?

BD – My mother's family was involved. My maternal grandmother lived with us for 30 or so years. My uncle was very present. When my Dad died, one of his brothers, Joe, lived upstairs and looked out for one of my brothers.

I am not sure exactly how I got out of my neighborhood to do well. A lot of things were involved besides the family. There were teachers, who also really made a difference. You need to find people outside your family, who can make a difference too. It's important to find a sense of trust in your family, and then you can use it outside on the street. I learned how to get along with all kinds of people. I think being able to be independent helped me learn to think, think, think. I would have been dead in some situations had I not known how to think on the streets.

My junior year in high school there was teacher who said, "You better start turning this around. You have a brain and you better use it."

AMS – How did you learn to be comfortable with confrontation?

BD – I trusted myself and I was not afraid to make a decision. I did not worry about it being right or wrong. If it's wrong, then you just correct it. I always thought to myself, "What are you worried about, losing your job, being beat up, or the media being negative about you?" I said to myself, "I had nothing when I started. If I lose it all and have nothing, so what? I will just be back to where I started."

This attitude paid dividends for me. I was not going to back down and do things I did not believe in. I knew there were things that you had to do that would be hard. I knew you had to bow before the State legislators to get things done. I also knew it was not worth being too proud to ask and badger people. There were too many children, who were hurting, and the politicians did not and still do not want to put resources into the schools. I had a big job and knew I needed to surround myself with very bright and competent people.

AMS – I am also fascinated with charisma. You said that on the street you were able to be wise, and then you mentioned talking to your son about how you learned to really listen to people.

BD – When people tell you their concerns, you try to get into it and figure out what it is they are trying to tell you. Later on in life, this paid big dividends for me. I could listen to principals and find out their deep concerns. I think that because there was a deep level of trust in my family, combined with the freedom that I had, that I learned to listen—and in my family, you had to make the effort to listen. In my family, cut-off was not allowed. You had to listen. There was no running away.

In my job, I wanted to convince people, the city counselors or the mayor, for example, to use resources more effectively. The main thing was to encourage them to think about what they were doing, and then how they were going to become more effective. I learned the importance of thinking things through before you make a decision, and not being emotional and reactive.

My main concern is still the rising level of poverty in the school system. About 75 percent of children in elementary school are on free or reduced lunch. I ask myself, "Where do we want to go as a society?" A leader is just one person. We have to understand the big problems and then take a position that people can understand. Then we can make things happen. We have to think carefully.

I left my successor two envelopes. The first had the message "Keep your chin up" and the second "Blame me." In any job in life you will encounter lots of problems. But for me, I came in fighting and I leave fighting and that is the way it should be.

Bob DiFlorio's Mindful Compass Points

(1) The ability to take ACTION to define a vision: Often a question informs one's vision. DiFlorio's question was, "How do you teach?" School administrators know that there is a set of skills each child must learn. That's a given. Less obvious is how to provide an environment that encourages the children to learn those skills.

DiFlorio's vision was also informed by his experiences in his family and on the streets of life. He had learned the importance of independence and the value of hard work and direct confrontation. Also, he had developed a deep sense of responsibility. As an adult, he understood that the students would do well if the school system was working well. He also knew that to make this happen, to improve the school system, he had to involve everyone—no part could be left out. To develop understanding between the parents, the children, the teachers, the political people and the media, DiFlorio had to deal with tough issues. But as a leader willing to be direct and confront problems, while also listening carefully, DiFlorio was well prepared.

His goal was to use the school's resources wisely in order to help all the children learn needed skills. At the same time, he wanted to make sure each child was seen as an individual, who might learn differently from others. The school system's resources had to be organized so that both students and teachers were treated in a way that encouraged excellence. This meant that all parts of the larger social system had to be engaged by DiFlorio in order to move the school system forward.

(2) The RESISTANCE to change in self and in any system: For many people, the most difficult thing to overcome is fear—fear of loss, fear of future loss. DiFlorio explained that he directly confronted that fear, accepted the risk, and used that acceptance as way to build his courage and character. He said, "I trusted myself and I was not afraid to make a decision. I did not worry about it being right or wrong. If it's wrong, then you just correct it. I always thought to myself, 'What are you worried about, losing your job, being beat up, or the media being negative about you?' I said to myself, 'I had nothing when I started. If I lose it all and have nothing, so what? I will just be back to where I started.' "

(3) The ability to use KNOWLEDGE to connect with others: DiFlorio's mother made sure he understood the value of staying the course and maintaining connections. He was forced at an early age to deal with issues in the open rather than avoid them. He saw the value of having an extended family around during his growing-up years, saw that his uncle made a difference in the life of his brother, and was most positive about having his grandmother nearby when he was young. It is a guess, but there is some research indicating that complex social systems enable individuals to develop an awareness of how to operate at an intuitive level. It's also possible that DiFlorio was born with a personality that easily connects with

people. There may be a gene for sociability and if so DiFlorio has it. A big and friendly guy, who has no fear of others, he automatically relates easily to people and puts them at ease.

(4) The ability to STAND ALONE TO BE more separate: DiFlorio was a default leader in his family in terms of sibling position, but easily took up the banner of personal responsibility and led. Able to step back and see the nature of a problem, he is more interested in solutions and getting things done than in winning friends or doing what pleases people in power. His ability to take a separate stand and fight with his brothers, and then reunite and deal constructively with them, may have established the groundwork for DiFlorio's adult understanding that it is critical to fight for the things you believe, while maintaining and working within the relationship network during and after the fight.

STEVE WAITE

A creative musician and among other things Founder of the Graphene Stakeholders Association, a new force aimed at uniting key stakeholders for the benefit of everyone in the graphene marketplace.

I met Steve through my son-in-law, Michael Mauboussin. I had asked Michael who he thought was seriously interested in how leaders emerge. Michael suggested talking to Steve. As you will see, talking to Steve is like spending a Saturday afternoon at the library. This was a warm and intellectually stimulating exchange, made all the more fun as Steve cannot help but bring music into any discussion. Steve savors ideas like a chef delighting in each new ingredient. Yet, when it comes time for action, he is able to do what needs to be done despite great emotional difficulty. His story is simple. Yet, he asks the most profound question—What do you do when the leader of the band dies? Despite the good meal and the joyful afternoon, we, too, must face the problems of succession and death. There is no hiding from the storm when a system transforms. If you want to go on a ride with Steve don't forget to bring *Zen and the Art of Motorcycle Maintenance: An Inquiry Into Values.*

AMS – I am interested in what age people are when they first start thinking about leadership?

SW – I recall thinking about leadership and being aware of Peter Drucker. No doubt, Drucker was a seminal influence on my understanding of leadership.

It was 1984, and I was working for the American Bank Company. I was fresh out of graduate school when I read Drucker's view of how to manage yourself, not just at work, but in your life as well.

One of the things he said that resonated with how I thought was, pick out the right heroes. I always tried to pick out the best people to learn from. I was also fortunate in another way. I admired my parents. They were the very best.

When I was very young, nine years old, I saw firsthand how important it was to have a positive attitude and a great coach. My dad took me to a football game when Ohio State was number one in the country. No one thought they could lose. But Michigan State was fueled by a different kind of a coach. He was a great leader and his team believed in him. I will never forget that day when a low ranked team came from behind and beat the number one ranked team in the country. Without that coach, the guys might not have played as such a great team. Sometimes one leader can make the difference in people pulling together to overcome the odds.

There are other memories highlighting the importance of heroes. When I went to London I read about Churchill. There, in his country, I understood more deeply how he faced adversity and rose up in the face of overwhelming odds to lead his country to victory.

A third example would be Charlie Munger, who also emphasized different aspects of leadership in his book, *Damn Right! Behind the Scenes with Berkshire Hathaway's Billionaire Charlie Munger.*

AMS – To bring this back to you, do you think your position in your family influenced your way of being a leader?

SW – Perhaps it influenced my style. I am a middle sibling with two brothers.

AMS – Yes, and as I recall your Dad is also a middle sibling in his family.

SW – Perhaps I got his good genes. I admired him but we were different. My Dad was a doctor, and he had a love for medicine and a curiosity about health and physical problems.

I had a love more for social problems and how they came to be. I also always loved music.

My career was as a macroeconomist on Wall Street. This might be something like a general practitioner in medicine. My Dad also had to know a little about everything so he could decide what to look at in detail.

I love being able to delve into the various disciplines and subspecialties, and put knowledge together in an interesting way to bring new insights into any problem.

AMS – I hear how you identified with your father and now I am wondering how old do you think you were when you begin to be a more separate individual in your family?

SW – I knew you might ask this question, so I asked my Mom what she recalled about me having my own mind. She told me the following story: When I was six my mom was trying to get me to go to church. I told her, no, I was not going because it wasted my time. She laughed about how important it was for me to be engaged in deciding at that young age what was really important, no matter what others thought.

AMS – Religion is an interesting area to define personal beliefs. Often, families have traditions and people follow these traditions. Perhaps, it might be one indicator of a more open family system if children are able question the religious beliefs and expectations of the family.

SW – I am still a more spiritual person than one who thinks I should follow the beliefs of any one church.

In addition to being different about my spiritual life, my parents always said I was my biggest critic and too hard on myself.

I listened to people's criticism but don't believe I took it in too deeply. It is important to consider criticism because we have so many blind spots. In general, I enjoy thinking about things at deep levels not just assuming things are true at face value.

I have continued to develop the ability to wonder if I and other people are thinking about things correctly. This has helped me handle criticism. If the criticism comes from someone I have enormous respect for, I will be tuned in 100 percent. But I am very analytical and consider carefully who's telling me what and how much of what is said is factual.

AMS – From an early age, your Mom valued your ability to stand up to her authority and to have an independent mind. She did not laugh or criticize you when you opposed her about going to church.

SW – Another factor giving the family more freedom about religious issues was that my Dad did not often go to church. He was always on call and so did not make church attendance a priority.

AMS – I am also interested in what your Mom and Dad's extended families look like?

SW – My mom is the older of two daughters. Her mother was a tough Italian and was married to a kind and warm German man. My maternal grandmother was never able to tell my Mom she loved her and that was hard on my Mom.

It seemed like my Mom was more emotional or as I like to say, all limbic, and my Dad was all cortex.

AMS – I know it is very important to control that limbic and very hard for most people to do. Most people run on automatic. It is challenging to be aware of how we are automatically programmed to react. Our past experiences leave a trail of sensitivity in the brain. We are sensitive to repeating patterns. The past provides information that can trick the brain into over or under reacting to perceived threats that are often just worried chatter in the brain. If one's mother was too cold, then over generations, people in the family can dread coldness rather than figure out ways to have fun with the supposed "threat."

SW – Great poker players and great investors can control their limbic responsiveness. I was also drawn to this way of being by watching my parents interact.

AMS – I would guess your Mom would have had a more difficult time relating to men since your Mom had a sister. Was your Mom able to relate well to your Dad as a partner?

SW – Actually, Dad was good with my Mom as he had sisters. In fact, they were very close. When he died, in 2000, a big part of her died.

I think about their relationship as part of quantum entanglement. They were deeply connected or entangled at a deep, energetic level. I think quantum entanglement is the most underrated concept.

My parents were very young when they met and yet somehow knew they were made for each other. Neither had another boy- or girlfriend. They were a fit from the beginning. They fell in love immediately and married in 1955. My dad then went in the army and after he came out, he went to medical school.

AMS – It is interesting how people are attracted to one another so fast and sometimes the bond they create works, while for others the attraction fades. What is the difference? We know that more than 50 percent of marriages do not hold together over time. Perhaps, a marriage that works gives people not just personal comfort, but it may also offer many solutions to problems created in the past generations.

I am not sure exactly how it works but John Gottman, a well-known researcher on marriages demonstrated how easy it is to predict which marriages will last based on how couples fight and make up or do not. Many of the ways we are socialized as young people carry over into adulthood. There are many areas and topics that people are sensitive about by the time they are preparing to find a long-term marriage partner.

SW – So you are tracing excellence in leadership and marriage back to family dynamics? Well, I can see in both situations that one has to be a self and take responsibility for managing relationships and solving problems. Overall, I think being a leader is a simple task. First, you have to foster teamwork and create a family-like atmosphere of trust and cooperation.

I think you have to also lay down a few ideas that people can rally around and then let people do their thing. G.E. is a good example of this kind of leadership. G.E. is a great company because they also think about succession. The great leader surrounds him- or herself with others who are capable and can take over.

There is a market for psychological profiles for leaders and their executive teams. Another characteristic I would list is the ability to connect. Michael Dell is another one of my heroes because he is responsible and personal. He returns every email I send him.

If you follow the personality profiles developed by Myers Briggs then I am an ENFJ. I naturally like to help people.

AMS – If you created a leadership spectrum, at one end you would have leaders who were aware of their impact on others and saw their fundamental job as enabling others to become the best they could be. This would put dictators like leaders, who have less and less respect for individuals, at the other end of the spectrum.

SW – Some people need dictators. They do not like to think and they let other people lead them.

AMS – Bowen described two forces—the togetherness force, to be more like others at whatever the cost, and the force to be an individual, at whatever the cost.

There is a mid-range of autonomous functioning, where a leader can be concerned about the good of the group, and about his or her functioning, without becoming selfish or bullying others.

SW – You asked a question about strategic leaders and degrees of transparency so I wondered, do good leaders lie?

AMS – It is clear that a great leader has to be a great communicator. This becomes more complicated depending on size and the politics within the group. That may mean that at times a leader will put a certain spin on information or even withhold information believing this will help her/him manage the group.

SW – I helped created a technological company based on swarm intelligence. We created a forum for finding out what customers thought and sold that information. We knew people would be more productive with more information. The goal was to allow people to function at higher levels using the best information we could obtain.

AMS – I hear you on that point. However, total openness can be an idealized value. Think about a small group, like a family. The family leader has to think about how and when to communicate different subjects depending on the age and stage of children, etc.

The anticipated death of a family leader from cancer might be one example. How do you talk about transitions in a way that allows people to cope well? The leader does not want to scare people or at the other extreme deny reality. A thoughtful family leader would ideally recognize that change is a process and keep working on staying open.

I have watched family leaders, who are able to talk openly about death by having small conversations here and there about the possible changes so that others are prepared but not alarmed.

I do think one day we will be able to demonstrate with more clarity, that how one emerges from the family of origin influences us to be or not to be a leader.

SW – If you are lucky enough to be born into a family with a father who is a great leader, perhaps it is easier. There is so much we need to know that no one person will be able to give us all the knowledge we need. Therefore, no matter how great your father is, you also need other heroes to learn from.

AMS – How far back in your family would you have to go to see where people learned from the people who did not do so well? Perhaps you might have other examples of leadership emerging where people had to overcome stress or early loss?

One way of learning about being a leader is to positively identify with someone in your family. An interesting question is how does one learn from bad examples in the family?

As I recall another of your favorite books is *Lila*. In this one, Phaedrus is sailing down the Hudson River when he meets Lila Blewitt. She is a psychologically unstable woman, but of course he considers her to be "a culture of one," as he discerns in her an unexpected "quality." Therefore, he is driven, beyond logic, to learn from her, perhaps satisfying his driving curiosity about what made her tick. In this pursuit, he lost his intellectual curiosity and began wanting only to control her. Once he fell into the "controlling the other to help them," he lost her. I think this book contains two wonderful lessons, which may allow us to learn about ourselves—one, the pitfalls of learning from those we do not deeply value and two, the importance of giving others freedom.

SW – It is hard to keep that process in mind just as it is hard to unlearn what you have learned. I think there is an old Zen question, 'How do you keep a beginners mind?'

As an investor, I teach students by letting them do it (analyzing companies) their own way first. Only after they reveal their ideas do I teach them what will happen if they consider learning to think differently about companies. As an investor, I am always looking for new information to frame a problem in a different way.

Many of my heroes study nature and find a different way to think. Bill Miller does this. He is always looking for new information to help frame certain situations. This ability to be open and think broadly is fostered in certain environments like the Santa Fe Institute.

AMS – I also think maintaining a beginner's mind and questioning old assumptions, relates to the ability to respect and yet to question authority.

You were respected in your family when you questioned, at age six, your mother's authority. The family did not squish you because of your different viewpoint.

SW – Overall, there was a sense of love as a major part of my family environment. When my Dad died, I dedicated my life to love because that is what he was. I view myself as a loner and value my friends more because they are great thinkers and that is how they have influenced me.

My older brother turned me onto music and Jimmy Hendricks. I have played guitar since I was young. My younger brother is like my twin. We are inseparable even though he lives in Detroit. He has the best of my Mom, and I am the best of my Dad. My older brother lives in Texas and is a geologist paleontologist. He married and divorced and remarried and has two boys. Brad has three daughters. And I have two girls.

AMS – So you have never had to define yourself as a separate person with different ideas to your brothers? You have never had any serious disputes?

SW – No, we are all pretty much on the same page. My older brother spoke at the funeral. I was so proud of him. Now my mom lives near my older brother.

I am a fan of Peter Drucker's concept that the future has already happened. Most people do not know how to tell what has or is happening.

I think it is more important to read books than to be entertained by CNBC. But look, I wrote a very dense book that very few people read, but it is important to get these kinds of ideas out, even if you know few will pay attention.

AMS – We can agree that popularity and responsible leadership are not always compatible. But a leader does have to communicate his/her vision to people and then be able to deal with the resistance to his or her ideas. This process has been the main focus of developing your Mindful Compass. You have a better opportunity to manage self in the social world if you have an idea about the impersonal forces that exist in social systems.

SW – I wrote a piece called, *The Leader of the Band.* After my Dad died, I wondered what you do after the leader of the family/band dies? In my family, my mother went into a deep depression. I moved to Connecticut and isolated myself to write my book. But, then, I realized that my Dad would want us to stay together and do the best possible job we can do. In thinking about him and what he would have wanted, I realized that my Dad did not die.

My Dad told me that my compassion was lost on Wall Street. I have had to figure out how to maintain my compassion. The central question is 'how does the team or band reorganize to keep on going?' I wanted to keep my father's good ideas going. I am not sure how I have done the things I have done, like write my book in just three months after Dad died. I just had new energy.

AMS – I think what we are doing here is to look at the deep values and how and when they are generated. One way of doing this is by telling family stories and finding the embedded values.

I was wondering about what skills leaders think are worth cultivating? How about the ability to bring up difficult topics and have open conversations with people, family members included? Is this a skill people should practice?

SW – My Dad was very approachable and liked to answer questions. I would consider him open.

AMS – What are the factors that might encourage openness in a family or in an organization?

SW – In my family, there was a high family value on being curious and learning. But the greatest single asset might have been my parent's sense of humor. I notice now when I am filling out forms for graduate school for my students, the schools often ask about the candidate's sense of humor. Lots of great leaders have or had a sharp sense of humor—Bill Miller, Warren Buffet and political people like Winston Churchill.

After my Dad died I took care of my mother for a while. I saw a little girl in my mother again and watched her grow again. I have not seen mother in a while, although I do talk to her on the on the phone most days. We have been able to talk about death without getting too emotional. This makes being open less threatening.

At first she would say, "You can never understand my pain," and I would say things like, "I am trying to understand the pain that Jesus suffered." And "I think you suffer because you do not have the physical presence of your loved one. You might find it easier to think about the love you shared and to share that with others. If you want to be alive you have to spread the love, if you want to be dead then you can sit home and not share the love that your husband gave you." As soon as I told her I wanted to try and understand her pain I think that really helped us out.

The other thing is she is a caretaker and really wanted to be able to take care of someone else and so when I talked to her I tried to key in on her own gifts.

AMS – I think it's a good example to show how you offered your mom choices. You did not "should" her. You also allowed her to see the consequences of her choices. There are always consequences. Giving people options and not forcing them is an important guiding principle. I call it, "no demands thinking."

SW – My Mom came from an era where the man took care of the woman and so now, we, her sons help take care of her to some extent. But I also want her to be more independent and I coach her. I stayed with her for a week. Once she told me she woke up scared and I said, "There is no need for you to live in fear. I am here for you and you can take care of yourself as you get back on your feet." It's like at this time our roles are reversed. Her children are like her parents in a way. When the leader dies there has to be some period of adjustment, to get over the little humps. After I was there for a week she said she felt much calmer.

Perhaps, there was not enough role exchanging or diversity in my parents' lives, and so when my Dad died, my Mom did not know how to do all the things that had to be done. Now I am trying to bring diversity back into my Mom's life through love.

AMS – Love to me is the willingness to remain optimistic and open while trying to hold people responsible.

SW – A lot of my music is all about love. I have no idea how these ideas come to be but they do come up and I try to let them live in my music. I see that in society it is hard to know what personal responsibility is all about. Now we are living in an age where we have a problem and so we sue Burger King.

AMS – It seem like we are living in an age where it's hard to know personal responsibility if we do not know the consequences of our actions.

SW – Hopefully, more and more people can learn that by being responsible and loving they can build a better future.

AMS – Thank you for your ideas and I will look forward to listening to your music.

Steve Waite's Mindful Compass

(1) The ability to define a vision: In order to have and maintain a vision that is important to one's self, one has to be able to separate out a self and to know one's own values. Steve Waite tells us how early on he began to state his "truth" to his mother about things that seemed important to him. This early interest in religion has sustained him over his lifetime. Many abstract concepts, such as love and compassion, are difficult to trace into lived out actions. However, we can see his actions as reflecting his deeper vision lived out in his adult relationship with his parents and in his career path. The death of his father helped him to reevaluate his goal and to alter it into one that reflected more of his values. His father was able to be open with him about how he saw Steve's life unfolding and this openness allowed Steve to reconsider his vision.

In his story, as Steve tells us about his relationship with his mother, we can also see and feel the "love" that he experiences towards his mother as she makes a new life for herself. In his work, he has chosen to stay on his own track with an emphasis on nanotechnology and ideas that can radically alter the way we live.

(2) The resistance to change in self and in any system: Steve Waite found himself in a lucrative career that did not match with who he was at a very deep level. This happens to many people. The status quo offers security and comfort. It is very difficult to face one's self and to make changes more for self than to keep others happy.

If people change their career paths, it can often wreak havoc in their family life. For these and many others reasons, it is rare to find individuals who, like Steve Waite, are willing to quit their job, write a book and change career paths.

(3) The ability to connect: Perhaps due to the fact that Steve Waite's father had just died, I did not investigate much about his relationships with his extended family. He and his brothers seem to be sticking together to help out his mother. Sometimes in a tight nuclear family people can have more problems reaching out into the extended family. This can become a problem in future generations if contact with the larger family is lost. However, for many families it takes two or more years to reorganize after the death of a family leader.

Since Steve Waite describes himself as an introvert, it may be more difficult for him to build a large and close extended family relationship network. Often this kind of relationship job is given to the wife, who is often more extraverted. Steve Waite seems to have no problems communicating well with a large number of people on an intellectual or emotional level. He understands more than words.

(4) The ability to be STAND ALONE and to be more separate: For Steve Waite, the ability to examine his values is an ongoing responsibility. Driven by curiosity and love of explanations, he is a seeker. His enthusiasm might sweep the reticent person up. His overall respect for all things different allows him to create a very deep conviction for his own way, all the while, maintaining openness as to the differing values of others. Since at one point the "songs" of great wealth and success overly influenced him, he is very cautious as to being overly influenced by others. His father words, "Find

your passion" ring true to him and seem to fuel his ability to build his basic self. This encouragement also seems to be at the heart of his ability to be a more separate person from others. In working to be more of a knowledgeable individual self, he can then allow his warmer feelings of deep compassion and love for others to surface, most especially in his music. This more idealistic self is where he returns to deal with the challenges of heartbreak, misunderstandings and conflict.

SUMMARY

The public is curious — what goes on in families that give rise to amazing leaders and/or terrorists? How do relationship form and disintegrate? What does it take to "see" the "pressure" in the system and know how to manage being one's best SELF in any social matrix? This book shows us how each family has an *emotional system* that is fine tuned by evolution and "values" its survival as a whole, as much as the survival of any individual in it. Families snooker us, encouraging us or other family members to take sides, run away, get sick or just become difficult to deal with. There are ways to navigate the hard to see relationship minefield that is part of everyone's life. The research of social scientists shows what we are up against in social situations. They show us how we are all, to different degrees, regulated by relationships. Stanley Milgram, Solomon Ashe, Philip Zimbardo and John B. Calhoun, detailed the vulnerability we share to being duped and deceived. Misperceiving relationship cues results in our inability to make thoughtful decisions.

In the 1950s, the psychiatrist Murray Bowen, M.D., hospitalized a number of families with a schizophrenic child for up to three years at the National Institute of Mental Health. Bowen was observing and studying what these families actually *did* rather than what they said. Through this effort, he was able to describe how family members overly influence one another; a factor that distributes stress unevenly and can result in severe illness or other symptoms in selected family members. Armed with knowledge from the sciences, stories from real people in their own words and specific guidance through the "Mindful Compass," readers learn how they can alter the automatic trajectory, which relationship systems impose on each of us.

At times, all of us are confused by our relationship with others. People do not come with signs that warn "I am an emotional creature, living in a social jungle." Each of us is born into complex worlds beyond our understanding. It is in our best interest to be seekers of knowledge and wisdom and to maintain some kind of psychologically aware filtering system. We are bombarded in our relationships and by the media with the mundane, the seductive, the fearful, and simply wrong-headed information. In addition, our near and dear can believe whole heartedly that if we love them we will agree with them. Having a Mindful Compass enables us to orient to a different way of thinking, offering a way to be less vulnerable and more able to find useful guideposts through the social jungle.

By developing your Mindful Compass, you can clarify that the road to greater emotional freedom is a continuing focus on integrating and balancing the forces for individuality and togetherness. Once any of us sees the playful innocence with which social pressure and fusion influences us, and recognizes that the challenge of being more separate is always with us, the sooner we will settle down to develop "our way" to deal with the upsets in the social jungle.

"Thinking systems" can open the doors of perception to allow you to experience the world around you in a different way. Our basic physiology has inhibited our ability to see the world of social forces influencing us. The brain produces cortisol under conditions of threat. Our mind constructs a cause for the fear and a "systems viewpoint" is lost. Often, we are reacting to the physiological cues and looking for the lion, it is then that we are truly immersed in the social jungle.

There are no shortcuts to rewiring our emotional system. It takes moving through the social jungle with a different head set. "No short cuts" requires a certain amount of discipline to "think systems" and to have the courage to be a more defined Self in relationship to our near and dear.

Murray Bowen was the first person to observe and write about this ability of the human to, over time, be able to alter their functional position in any social system.

The ability to know emotional systems well enough to take a position for self and to be more differentiated will always be available, as it is part of the natural way humans, who are aware, can cope. To be a more separate, mature and more functional individual, while remaining in contact with even the most difficult people in our lives, is not easy. The key is to practice (to experience the fear, the seduction of the fusion force, the ease of giving in) and to just stop, breathe and take the time to see what really is going on.

The waves of fear or the pull of togetherness will slowly diminish and you will find that you did not die. In fact, just by stopping and watching and seeing the system around you promotes your being more separate, while allowing you to get hold of your emotional backbone.

Since there is a great deal of intellectual explanation in this book, be aware that you can also lose yourself in overintellectualizing. You might then fall into the fusion pit and start to "teach" others as to the benefits of "systems thinking."

To deeply respect others is to allow them to find their own way, while being open to your way.

It takes time to see that you can influence others just by being more authentically you. You can tell them all about your adventures and that might be useful. Who knows what people learn from our being a self or even by telling our stories?

I have simply seen that the less intellectually and emotionally fused a person is and the more independent/autonomous a person is, the less he or she will be influenced by irrational elements—whether in relationships with others or in how their brain itself functions.

Whatever forces come along demanding a change in you, it is important that you be able to change and adapt in your most thoughtful way. Otherwise, the good times will deteriorate as you cling to old ways of doing things, under new and challenging conditions.

Bowen would say, "We have just scratched the surface of 'systems thinking.'" If you keep an open mind and build your ability to be a more independent observer, amazing new worlds will open. This will allow you to see a very different social jungle, which will be more fun to navigate with your Mindful Compass.

We are emerging from the influence of many complex systems to manifest nature's way, each in our own way. To the degree we are aware of the forces impinging on us, we can see and move about the social jungle with greater ease, taking challenges and even rejection less personally. The effort to be more neutral and objective to the forces of life around us enables us to be more deeply connected to our near and dear, while still maintaining the ability to think and understand our feelings and be thoughtful about emotional issues. When we are more aware and less vulnerable to emotional pressure, we automatically manifest more of our deeper Self. Developing your Mindful Compass will enable you to find your best way through any turmoil or even perils if and when they occur in your social jungle.

ACKNOWLEDGEMENTS

Writing as one must - as gratitude - for the ancestors,
for knowledge, for the future.

Andrea Roth Maloney Schara

Memories are often a blur. One need not recount in great detail the storyline that remains. Our personal history weaves it way connecting one generation to another. The facts of the story are like the bones buried in the forest of our memory. We dig up the facts with our personal, subjective taking on all that has happened. And this is the story that is passed on to the generations to learn from or to ignore.

I was ten, almost eleven, on that hot August day in 1952. People react differently to seeing one's parents fall apart. In memory, there had been the year or so of drinking, the hospitals, the war stories, and then on that hot day in August the yelling persisted until the neighbors called and the police came, and then the world changed. Three days after this event, my maternal grandparents came to Florida, removed us from the orphanage, where we had been secured, and eventually were awarded custody of my two younger brothers and myself. We lived with our kind but confused grandparents. Surrounded by comfort, in a contained and quiet oceanfront home, who was to ask what had happened? Who could explain the chaos? Was it important? Who knew to ask as we drifted in comfort, seemingly far away from the sharp memories of the post-war chaos that had haunted our parent's lives?

My grandparents knew little about the downward spiral of my parent's lives. After the war, we moved to another state and the distance hid the reality of the situation. Neither of my parents had much of a voice. They were shuffled off to other places. My father lived with his parents and grown siblings. My mother traveled the states, living in modest quarters supported by my well-to-do grandparents. The one message from my father to one of my grandparents was hidden in a book of photographs, only to be discovered long after all their deaths.

My father, Andrew, had addressed the note to me, perhaps knowing I would have deep curiosity as to what he was trying to say or to explain. The mysterious note and the book of photographs have tried to let us see what he thought, but for me these only added to the mystery. What kept my father from talking? What was so mysterious?

Almost twenty years after my father died (1967), my cousin Liz Eitt brought me a photo album with a cryptic note from him on top. Inside were the black and white photos of my father's early life—his family, his awards at work, his marriage and two young children. Then came the airstrip and buildings on Saipan where he was stationed during World War II. There were black and white photos of the men standing half smiling beside their planes, the nose art on the B-29, the planes flying over Japan, the bombs dropping, the prisoner of war buildings with "POW" taped jaggedly on the roofs, pictures of graveyards, and the bombed out buildings in Tokyo and Hiroshima.

The mysterious note attached read:

If your substantial arguments as a militarist do not convince the recalcitrant, perhaps this tome presented to you by your granddaughter, Andrea Roth Maloney, will enable you to deal more effectively with the most difficult thing in the world: "The opinions of an ignorant man."

What was he trying to say? Was I to give it to his father or to his father-in-law? Someone was ignorant, or perhaps we all were? Perhaps he was misunderstood? The guessing continues as the past has buried the ones with the answers and left only the clues. I read the note and remember my mother, "Puddney," in her confusion and anger about the cost of war. She found comfort in music and would play the piano for hours, singing and smiling as if to say, "Despite the war and the ignorance, *love remains.*" For each of my ancestors, I acknowledge all their love and care and I will always be deeply grateful.

Once upon a time as a naive, eager beaver, somewhat argumentative and stubborn teenager, my grandfather, Walter Maher, said, "Slow down, look around, see what's going on. Perhaps you will make a difference when you are older." That seemed silly as "older" was a million years away. Now his basic message appears timeless. Slowing down to see what is going on, acknowledging that your impact will be limited but worth doing, is as hard now as it was back then. As she grew ever more frail, my grandmother, Anna Maher, one day turned to me and said, "How will you deal with your grandfather after I die?" I had to bumble my way to the answer to that question. There was no book to explain how families are automatic systems, how we social creatures pressure people to function, how when there is increasing anxiety things fall apart and then slowly, if one is lucky, we recover.

The apple does not fall far from the tree. If fortune allows, the apple can roll to find a bit of light and release its seeds to grow as best they can, away from the shadow cast by the past. After the deaths of my parents and grandparents, the family was fragmented and isolated. We were and to some extent still are, a sensitive and a somewhat cut off family. As one of my brothers said, "I like to see people on my own terms, which is seldom." We are not that different from most families.

Over the years, I have learned the most from my brothers, Butch and Drew. In my relationships with each of my brothers, the best approach for me was to be with them as individuals and just talk. We found ways to be with one another without fear and expectations. I have my bubbly way of trying to influence them, of course. They were willing to try the newest technology for calming self and integrating the brain, as it might help their golf game. The older of the brothers, Butch, thought the Zengar (neurofeedback) did help his golf game. It helps me when he is doing well playing golf or anything. The younger brother Drew had a bipolar episode after the death of our uncle Jimmy Maloney. So he and his wife Margie came up to my cousin Liz's Zen Farm to talk things over, have a good meal and laugh. We had these family reunions once a month for about five years before Margie's physical problems made the drive too difficult. Eventually these experiences were used to help other families with similar issues. Liz Eitt has continued to develop The Zen Farm (www.thezenfarm.com) as a center for families wanting to have a more stabilizing experience and an overview of the systems challenges they face.

Being calmer, more aware and emotionally available is one part of changing self in relationship to important others. But there is far more to do in dealing with the past and in taking responsibility for family problems. Dr. Bowen suggested I would benefit by getting to know as many people as possible in my extended family. Nothing would help me to grow up more than taking on that kind of a project. As I went out looking up distant family members, it was initially uncomfortable and eventually did change my life. Knocking on family doors in places as far away as Ireland and Norway, I found the people and their stories fascinating. Deep connections came alive. No one slammed the door in my face. A few wondered about what I wanted. A few worried about what I might say. To learn more about my part, I took the additional step of videotaping the relationships and the conversations to figure out "Who am I and who are you? What is emotional process? Where do I stand on this or that issue or problem?"

Looking back, I see these trips to far out of the way places, (like Elyria, Ohio, to see my very distant, great aunts,) lead to knitting my family relationships back together again. Part of this voyage of self-discovery led to forming very close relationships with my once distant family members. From my mother's side of the family, Cita Strauss and her daughter, Annie, (one of the editors of the book) have traveled with me as far away as Norway. Cita's mother, Dana, was my mother's best friend and may partially account for the closeness I have maintained with the Strauss family.

In my father's family, Liz Eitt has been like a sister. She and her husband Mark continue to provide great warmth and support. I lived with them when I moved to Washington, D.C. in 1980 to work at the Family Center. Liz and I were co-owners of our grandparents' family home for many years. In 2006, Liz and Mark opened their home as a meeting place for my brothers Drew and Butch and myself. My cousin, Charlie Crone and his wife Ginny were crucial in helping me stay connected to my brother Drew and his wife Margie in Williamsburg, VA. Charlie is a steady, responsible, and perhaps too kind and generous man. But he and Ginny make my life a joy and Williamsburg is a family home. My uncle Jimmy Maloney's wife Kim Maloney has carried on for my uncle. She went to visit Drew in the hospital and let the staff know she was upset with the conditions at the hospital and would take things up with anyone.

One of the most central and somewhat challenging family relationships is with my first husband, Marty Schara. His parents, Jo and "Captain" stood by me after Marty and I divorced. These relationships were crucial to my ability to raise children and not feel or be cut off. Our long-standing ability to remain friends through upheavals persists in my relationship with Marty's brother Charles and his wife, Ann. Divorce, like death, shows us the point at which living together ends. But in a divorce the relationships do not have to die. The stress and tension in a marriage can impinge on our ability to relate well or the challenge of relating can enable us to grow past these events and nourish the core of the family relationships.

Marty's and my marriage ended due to our ignorance of the inner workings of the emotional system following the increasing anxiety around the deaths of family members. After my father's death in 1967, I became more distant from other people without realizing it. This kind of emotional distance had not been there after my paternal grandfather died in 1964. Perhaps it was the early experiences with loss and then the multiple losses of both grandmothers and my mother in the early 1970s that lead to the distance and the eventual divorce. With that came the opportunity to redefine myself: who am I, what do I stand for, what is important and how will I take care of my children, find a job, a career and relate well to the remnants of my family?

We divorced in 1973, four months after my maternal grandmother died. My mother died the following year. Three days before my mother's death, my brother was hospitalized for mental illness. The center no longer held. What seemed to happen is that the relationship system got smaller and smaller and the intensity and expectations larger and larger. The few remaining folks were unable to cooperate well. I turned to psychiatry to learn all I could. With two years of college, I took a job at a psychiatric hospital. It made more sense than trying to go back to school to earn a degree. My very good friend, Ann Karnitchnig, M.D., worked at the same psychiatric hospital that I did. She suggested that Murray Bowen, M.D. come for a talk on alcoholism. He told the group that day; "I am looking for the family leader, the one who is willing to take responsibility for the situation. They will do it their way. They will come up with some kooky answers to get out of the mess. But if they are willing to be responsible for the family problem, I will be with them." I asked Dr. Bowen about taking a course for officially uneducated people and the rest is history.

After four years in the post-graduate program at the Georgetown Family Center, Bowen offered me a job there and I moved to Washington, D.C. Ruth Sagar was my boss. She was gracious and kind and laughed about my spelling issues. I spent the next ten years with Bowen before his death in 1990.

I continued to work at the Family Center until 2003, when I left Washington, D.C. and moved to Darien, CT, just four miles away from my daughter and her family. Michelle had invited me to come when her fifth child, Patrick was born. How fortunate for me to have a great life with this family. Michelle has been generous in providing me with warmth, enormous support and a few good-hearted challenges during these years. It was Michelle, who gave me the idea of reducing the complexity of Bowen theory down to four points on a compass, instead of bundling the eight concepts into multiple points on a compass. She is a wise woman.

This grandmother era of my life has been the best. I have been part of family life again and continue to learn and teach and coach motivated people and to follow my love of writing. To be a grandmother involved in the daily life of these grandchildren has had powerful effects on my happiness, health and well-being. None of this would have been possible without the support of Michelle's husband Michael. Somehow, he has been able to relate well to me and not make it a big deal. He has written four business books and is a source for a variety of systems ideas: the psychology of decision-making, complexity and evolutionary processes. I have learned a lot from Michael. One of his qualities is to quietly provide opportunities for all to think and question. Both Michelle and Michael are steadfast in the highest commitment to one another. Their children, Andrew, Alex, Madeline, Isabelle and Patrick, each provide me with unique interactions and with sustaining love. I am so grateful.

Perhaps, in being close to one child, it becomes harder to be close to the other. Perhaps, this is for the best. I know only that it is challenging. My son Martin and his family live further away, and the great distance requires acceptance. Often, I wish it were not so but it is. Still today, my son has a way of making me laugh and loosening me up with his different way of seeing the world. He is an oldest of oldests, always trying to do the right thing by those he loves. His two daughters with Nenie, Victoria and Bridgette, are strong people. Caroline, Martin's first wife, remains in Virginia Beach, where I grew up. Their daughter, Alexa, is in college where she enjoys expanding on her great love of art. She produced the cover for this book. I am also very fond of Caroline's husband, Louie Snyder, who has been a warm and generous stepfather.

Professional Life

I am most grateful to all of my clients who, over the past thirty-seven years, taught me firsthand about the challenges of changing self in various kinds of family systems, and to see over and over again just how my sensitivity relates to theirs. Best of all, the individuals I coached demonstrated the many ways one can rise up by taking a few outrageous ideas, and by risking, learn to be his or her best Self in an emotional system.

The colleague with whom I have had the longest and most enduring relationship with is Priscilla Friesen. She has an amazing ability to listen and laugh and to think deeply about complex problems. We are a good mix. She is organized and ordered as a left-brain person, and in her creative way has deeply understood my leaps and intuitive thoughts. We have both devoted a great deal of time to learning biofeedback and then neurofeedback.

Priscilla and I also work with our good friend and colleague, Kathy Wiseman. (http://www.workingsystemsinc.net/) She is a deep thinker, an amazing observer and very talented at teaching systems theory to those in family-owned businesses. What a challenge. Kathy loves to learn and you sense this in how she teaches us about emotional systems in work organizations. This has been Kathy's primary interest and she has been a trailblazer in understanding emotional process in family organizations. The three of us teach a course at The Learning Space in Washington, DC, for professionals titled, **Navigating Systems** [www.navigatingsystemsdc.com].

After Dr. Bowen died, Dr. Michael Kerr became my boss. As the audiovisual coordinator, I had taped Dr. Bowen for hundreds of hours. Eventually, I was able to have these tapes donated to the National Library of

Medicine in Bethesda, MD. This became an archival collection of all Dr. Bowen's papers and tapes for which his family took responsibility. I tried to retire in 1993 when Dr. Kerr was kind enough to put me on the faculty. Kathy Vlahos took over my audiovisual job in 1999. I remained at the Bowen Center until 2003 when I moved to Connecticut. As in any system, things fall in and out of balance, triangles arise, sides are taken, but the direction of the mission of bringing Bowen Theory to the world never ceased. When Dr. Kerr retired in 2011, he asked me to resign. I have deep respect for him and for our differences. Each of us persists in preserving and communicating Dr. Bowen's ideas. Currently, Anne McKnight has taken over the job as director of the Bowen Center and she keeps a clear head in rough seas.

Editors

During the process of writing I have had many talented editors, who have encouraged and disciplined me to keep my ideas well connected and to be as clear as possible. Judy Ball has been a fabulous and patient editor. She has worked with me since the beginning. I think that is now eight years. Her knowledge of Bowen Theory helped her question ideas leading to deeper analysis and to a more penetrating explanation of theory. She has encouraged me to offer more detailed explanations and more connections between ideas. I also asked people to read it for content. Bob Mathis encouraged me to write in my own voice. Then, for an overall edit from a professional, my third cousin Annie Chagnot worked on this book. How fortunate to have someone who knows the family and is willing to work with these ideas. She is artful, precise and sees the big picture, bringing an outsider's appreciation of these ideas. After I did my best with all the feedback, the final look over was given to Donna Troisi. She is another person with whom I enjoy working. She has been around Bowen Theory and is a natural born editor. Zane O. Adoum also worked on the index and reviewed the book. After it was published, as is common, errors were found. Donna went to work and has once again given the book and especially the index, a new life. Without all of these people I would never have been able to find all the errors or most importantly stick with the effort to be clear. You the reader will no doubt find other errors and, for sure, ways I can be clearer. Please do e-mail me at Arms711@aol.com and the next edition will be better.

Readers and Colleagues

The readers for the book include: Ann Bunting, Laura Havstad, John Engels, John Cammack, Eric Thompson and Laurie Lassiter. These are the people I have the most confidence in to give my work a reasoned review. Each challenged and gave me very useful feedback. Their comments enabled me to see the book in a different light as they focused on themes that I might not have highlighted. John Engels has an amazing way to use Bowen's ideas as a business consultant and he was the one who suggested the sub title - *Breakthrough Strategies for Managing Life Relationships*. Victoria Harrison has also worked with me over the years. She has been an inspiration in her effort to make Bowen Theory available to a broad audience, publishing a reader friendly journal, and directing the postgraduate training course at the Bowen Center.

I would include in the group of individuals who have been important contributors to my efforts: Robbie Gilbert, Katherine Guinnan, John Cammack, Frank Giove, Frank Gregorsky, Lee Kelly, Pat Comella, Paulina McCullough, Doug Murphy, Dan Papero, Marge Hottel, Bob Noone, Sydney Reed, Stephanie Ferrera, Carol Moran, Jim Smith, Cynthia Larkby, Ryuko Ishikawa, Regina Carrick, Glennon Gordon, Ann Curran Gordon, Kathy Kerr, Ann Nicholson, Peter Titelman, Lida Beth Cavanah, Charlie White, Ona Bregman, Susan Luff, Myrna Carpenter, Gary Emanuel, Mickie Crimone, Peggy Treadwell, Ted Beal, Larry Foster and Emlyn Ott. Another important person is Donna Willis, who was the first person to suggest I needed a web site. She and I spent an afternoon in 1998 outlining the ideas. That effort has grown in many directions but the main goal was to practice writing to further the effort to have my own voice. (www.ideastoaction.wordpress.com) And, of course, there are many others who have encouraged me. Over the years these people in particular have allowed me opportunities to be my best Self. Many have supported my efforts or been positive about or challenged my ideas, and this has made all the difference.

Others not involved with Bowen Theory include Candace Pert, Mark Flinn, Norman Johnson, and Mary Beth Saffo. Each has taken the time to consider how these ideas fit with other bodies of knowledge. Candace Pert worked with me on a project where one person in the family was diagnosed with HIV and had symptoms of AIDS. We hypothesized that having the "guts" to build an emotional backbone might produce more VIP hormones, an analogue for the drug she designed - Peptide T - which blocked the AIDS virus. Candace died September 12, 2013. She was a rare and bubbling optimist in our doubting world. I will always be grateful for her generous and energetic support over these years. Her husband, Mike Ruff, continues her work.

Bowen Family

The Bowen family has been part of this effort naturally. I am most especially grateful to Joanne Bowen, who has the vision of what the Bowen Archives can be. She and Judy Bowen are the most involved family members and they represent the investment the family maintains for the future of the archives. They are tireless workers in making sure that the Bowen Archives are preserved and in being there for all the people who would like to be helpful. For many years, Mrs. Bowen was the family leader in this important and unbelievably complex task and journey. She died in 2011, yet she is with me still. Thanks to all the efforts to collect the papers and other records of Dr. Bowen, the future will be far richer for any researcher or biographer.

The preservation efforts begun by the Bowen family are now the responsibility of Leaders for Tomorrow, Inc. (LFT) a non-profit. LFT was formed to archive the historical record of Murray Bowen, M.D. and to make it accessible to all. I have enjoyed working with many people in the organization. The person who has worked on the Bowen Archives the longest is Catherine Rakow. She has a deep and abiding interest in Bowen's life work and his theory and has been a willing collaborator for many.

Lastly, I would like to mention two very thoughtful and dedicate colleagues who died way before their time – Bobbie Holt and Monica Baege. Both were very strong contributors to Bowen theory and to my life. I am grateful to each of them.

The First Book Published in 2009

I began interviewing leaders in 2004 to see what I might learn from people who were contributing in some way to their community and family. I was approached by Maria Bustos to have my first book translated for a Spanish audience. I interviewed many fantastic leaders in Mexico about how they saw and understood the emergence of leaders in families. This book saw the light of day in 2009, thanks to my editors Deb Schwab and Judy Ball and producer for the project Maria Bustos and publisher Herberto Ruz. After that I decided to refocus on the social aspects of the pressure people innocently put on one another and the enormous challenges of being an aware leader. *The Mindful Compass* enables people to see what they are up against in a social system and what it takes to be for Self and for others.

Acknowledgements Summarized

All the individuals, mentioned above, gave freely their time and ideas. I admire each of them and their ongoing contributions to the development of Bowen Theory and/or to my life. I am deeply grateful for all those who have encouraged me to reveal and enlarge my ideas, and who have encouraged me to enjoy and live life as fully as possible.

REFERENCES

Allen, Sharon L., "Descendent of Strong Women," **The New York Times,** July 2, 2006

Allman, John, *Evolving Brains,* Scientific American Review (W. H. Freeman; March 27, 2000)

Ant colony, Art, from ***Britannica Online for Kids,***
http://kids.britannica.com/comptons/art-144467

"Are Ants Intelligent," http://quotations.hubpages.com/hub/Intelligent_Ants

Bowen, M.D., Murray, *Curriculum Vitae,* http://ideastoaction.wordpress.com/dr-bowen/curriculum-vitae-of-dr-bowen/

Bowen, M.D., Murray, *Family Therapy in Clinical Practice,* (Jason Aronson, Inc.; 2nd edition 1993, 1976)

Buffalo State University, "Triune Brain"
http://www.buffalostate.edu/orgs/bcp/brainbasics/triune.html

Buss, David, *Evolutionary Psychology: The New Science of the Mind,* (Prentice Hall; 4th edition, February 28, 2011)

Calhoun, John B., "Space and the Strategy of Life," *Behavior and Environment: The Use of Space by Animals and Men,* (Plenum Press; New York, London 1971)

Calhoun, J.B. "Population Density and Social Pathology," (**Scientific American** 206: 139, 1962). http://nihrecord.od.nih.gov/newsletters/2008/07_25_2008/story1.htm

Cialdini, Robert B. **Influence: Science and Practice** (Allyn & Bacon, 2001)

Damasio, Antonio R., **Descartes' Error: Emotion, Reason, and the Human Brain** (Penguin Books, 2005)

Darwin, Charles and Wilson, E.O. *From So Simple a Beginning: Darwin's Four Great Books (Voyage of the Beagle, The Origin of Species, The Descent of Man, The Expression of Emotions in Man and Animals* (W. W. Norton & Company; Reprint editions, June 17, 1994, Nov 7, 2005)

Desmond, Adrian and Moore, James, *Darwin: The Life of a Tormented Evolutionist* (W. W. Norton & Company; Reprint edition, June 17, 1994)

Ericsson, Charness, Feltovich & Hoffman. "The influence of experience and deliberate practice on the development of superior expert performance." in *The Cambridge Handbook of Expertise,* (2006)

Fields, R. Douglas, **Of two minds: Listener brain patterns mirror those of the speaker,** July 27, 2010. http://blogs.scientificamerican.com/guest-blog/2010/07/27/of-two-minds-listener-brain-patterns-mirror-those-of-the-speaker/

Friedman, Lawrence Jacob, *Menninger: the Family and the Clinic,* (Univ. Press of Kansas, 1992)

Garnett, Carla, "Medical Historian Examines NIMH Experiments in Crowding," *nih record,* http://nihrecord.od.nih.gov/newsletters/2008/07_25_2008/story1.htm

Gawande, Atul, *The Checklist Manifesto: How to Get Things Right,* (Picador; Reprint edition, January 4, 2011)

Gazzaniga, Michael S., "Decoding the Brain's Cacophony," **New York Times,** October 31, 2011 http://www.nytimes.com/2011/11/01/science/telling-the-story-of-the-brains-cacophony-of-competing-voices.html?pagewanted=all

Gell-Mann, Murray, *The Quark and the Jaguar: Adventures in the Simple and the Complex,* (St. Martin's Griffin; ILL edition; September 15, 1995)

Ghose, Tia, "Brain Size Didn't Drive Evolution, Research Suggests," March 26, 2013 http://www.livescience.com/28209-brain-organization-key-to-intelligence.html

Glieck, James, *Chaos: The Making of a New Science,* (Penguin Books; Revised edition, August 26, 2008)

Gordon, Debora, *Ant Encounters: Interaction Networks and Colony Behavior,* (Princeton University Press; March 22, 2010)

Jacobs, A.J., "Do I Love My Wife? An Investigative Report," *Esquire* http://www.esquire.com/features/mri-of-love-0609

Kagan, Jerome, *The Temperamental Thread: How Genes, Culture, Time and Luck Make Us Who We Are,* (Dana Press (April 15, 2010)

Lassiter, Laurie, "Others" in *Chimeras and Consciousness: Evolution of the Sensory Self,* Lynn Margulis, editor, (Massachusetts Institute of Technology, 2011)

LeDoux, Joseph, *Synaptic Self: How Our Brains Become Who We Are,* (Viking Press, 2002)

MacLean, P.D., *The Triune Brain in Evolution: Role in Paleocerebral Functions,* (1990)

Maren, Stephen, "Functional Anatomy of Neural Circuits Regulating Fear and Extinction," Texas A&M University, October 12, 2012. http://tamutimes.tamu.edu/tag/stephen-maren/

Mauboussin, Michael J., *The Success Equation: Untangling Luck and Skill,* (Harvard Press, 2012)

McLeod Saul, "Asch Experiment" http://www.simplypsychology.org/asch-conformity.html

Missouri Department of Social Services, "Diagramming Families for Assessment" in *Child Welfare Manual,* http://www.dss.mo.gov/cd/info/cwmanual/section7/ch1_33/sec7ch25.htm

Mlodinow, Leonard, *Subliminal: How Your Unconscious Mind Rules Your Behavior,* (Pantheon Books; April 24, 2012)

Newport, Frank, "Four in 10 Americans believe in Creationism," *Gallup,* Dec 17, 2010, http://www.gallup.com/poll/145286/four-americans-believe-strict-creationism.aspx

O'Toole, Kathleen, "The Stanford Prison Experiment: Still powerful after all these years," Jan 8, 1997, http://news.stanford.edu/pr/97/970108prisonexp.html

Panksepp, Jaak and Biven, Lucy, *The Archaeology of Mind: Neuroevolutionary Origins of Human Emotions,* (W. W. Norton & Company, Sep 17, 2012)

Paul, Anne Murphy, "Where Bias Begins: The Truth About Stereotypes," *Psychology Today,* May 01, 1998. http://www.psychologytoday.com/articles/199805/where-bias-begins-the-truth-about-stereotypes?page=3

Pennebaker, J.W., *Opening Up: The Healing Powers of Confiding in Others,* (William Morrow & Co; 1st edition, September 1990)

Pert, Candace, *The Molecules of Emotion,* (Simon & Schuster, February 17, 1999)

Pribram, Karl H, MD, *The Form Within: My Point of View,* (Prospecta Press, for the Washington Academy of Science, 2010)

Seeley, Thomas, D., *Honeybee Democracy,* (Princeton University Press, September 20, 2010)

Science Daily, "Critical Brain Chemical Shown to Play Role in Severe Depression" http://www.sciencedaily.com/releases/2010/03/100301102803.htm

Science Daily, "Structure deep within the brain may contribute to a rich, varied social life", 2010 http://www.sciencedaily.com/releases/2010/12/101226131603.htm

Sulloway, Frank J., *Born to Rebel: Birth Order, Family Dynamics, and Creative Lives,* (Vintage Press, September 2, 1997)

Toman, Walter, *Family Constellation: Its Effects on Personality and Social Behavior* (4th Edition Springer Publishing Company, November 15, 1992)

Tsien, Joe Z., "The Memory Code," June 17, 2007, *Scientific America* http://www.scientificamerican.com/article.cfm?id=the-memory-code

Weiner, Jonathan, **The Beak of the Finch: A Story of Evolution in Our Time** (Vintage; 1995)

Williams, Ruth, "Peer Pressure Starts Early," August 31, 2012, *Scientific America* http://www.scientificamerican.com/article.cfm?id=peer-pressure-starts-early&WT.mc_id=SA_DD_20120831

Zolli, Andrew and Healy, Ann Marie, *Resilience: Why Things Bounce Back,* (Free Press, 2012

INDEX

ENDNOTES

CHAPTER I

[1] Friedman, Lawrence Jacob, *Menninger: the Family and the Clinic* (Univ. Press of Kansas, 1992)

[2] Bowen, M.D., Murray, Curriculum Vitae. http://ideastoaction.wordpress.com/dr-bowen/curriculum-vitae-of-dr-bowen/

[3] Bowen, M.D., Murray, *Family Therapy in Clinical Practice*, (Jason Aronson, Inc.; 2nd edition 1993, 1976)

[4] Bowen, M.D., Murray, *Family Therapy in Clinical Practice*, (Jason Aronson, Inc.; 2nd edition 1993, 1976) p. 200

[5] Bowen, op. cit., p. 202

[6] Bowen, op. cit., p. 474

[7] Toman, Walter, *Family Constellation: Its Effects on Personality and Social Behavior*, 4th Edition Springer Publishing Company; 4 edition (November 15, 1992)

[8] Summary of Bowen Family Systems Theory Concepts written by Laura Martin and Andrea Schara

CHAPTER II

[9] Buss, David, *Evolutionary Psychology: The New Science of the Mind*, (Prentice Hall; 4th edition, February 28, 2011)

[10] Lassiter, Laurie, "Others," in *Chimeras and Consciousness: Evolution of the Sensory Self*, edited by Lynn Margulis (Massachusetts Institute of Technology 2011) p. 70

CHAPTER III

[11] Zolli, Andrew and Healy, Ann Marie; *Resilience: Why Things Bounce Back* (Free Press, 2012) pp. 123- 132

CHAPTER IV

[12] Paul, Anne Murphy, "Where Bias Begins: The Truth About Stereotypes," *Psychology Today,* May 1, 1998. http://www.psychologytoday.com/articles/199805/where-bias-begins-the-truth-about-stereotypes?page=3

CHAPTER V

[13] Pribram, Karl H, MD, "Freud's Project" in *The Form Within: My Point of View,* (Prospecta Press for the Washington Academy of Science, 2010) p. 237

[14] Sulloway, Frank J., *Born to Rebel: Birth Order, Family Dynamics, and Creative Lives,* (Vintage, September 2, 1997)

[15] Kagan, Jerome, *The Temperamental Thread: How Genes, Culture, Time and Luck Make Us Who We Are* (Apr 15, 2010)

CHAPTER VI

[16] Ericsson, Charness, Feltovich & Hoffman. "The influence of experience and deliberate practice on the development of superior expert performance" **The Cambridge Handbook of Expertise** (2006).

CHAPTER VIII

[17] Personal note: John B. Calhoun on March 31, 1973, wrote this quote on the first page of the book: *The Unconscious Before Freud,* by (Doubleday Anchor, 1962)

[18] LeDoux, Joseph, *Synaptic Self: How Our Brains Become Who We Are,* (Viking Press, 2002) p. 9

[19] Tsien, Joe Z., "The Memory Code," June 17, 2007, *Scientific America,* http://www.scientificamerican.com/article.cfm?id=the-memory-code

[20] Damasio, Antonio R., *Descartes' Error: Emotion, Reason, and the Human Brain,* (Penguin Books, 2005)

[21] Pribram, Karl, H., *The Form Within: My Point of View,* (Prospecta Press, Feb 19, 2013)

[22] *Science Daily,* "Structure Deep Within the Brain May Contribute to a Rich, Varied Social Life," 2010. http://www.sciencedaily.com/releases/2010/12/101226131603.htm

[23] Gawande, Atul, *The Checklist Manifesto: How to Get Things Right,* (Picador; Reprint edition, January 4, 2011)

[24] Ghose, Tia, "Brain Size Didn't Drive Evolution, Research Suggests," March 26, 2013 http://www.livescience.com/28209-brain-organization-key-to-intelligence.html

[25] Allman, John, *Evolving Brains,* (W. H. Freeman, Scientific American Review, March 27, 2000)

[26] Wikipedia

[27] Mauboussin, Michael J., *The Success Equation: Untangling Luck and Skill,* (Harvard Press, 2012) p. 132.

[28] Gell-Mann, Murray, *The Quark and the Jaguar: Adventures in the Simple and the Complex,* (St. Martin's Griffin, ILL edition, September 15, 1995)

[29] Gleick, James, *Chaos: The Making of a New Science,* (Penguin Books, Revised edition, August 26, 2008)

[30] O'Toole, Kathleen, "The Stanford Prison Experiment: Still powerful after all these years," Jan 8, 1997, http://news.stanford.edu/pr/97/970108prisonexp.html

[31] From Wikipedia: The Stanford marshmallow experiment[1] refers to a series of studies on delayed gratification in the late 1960s and early 1970s led by psychologist Walter Mischel, then a professor at Stanford University. In these studies, a child was offered a choice between one small reward (sometimes a marshmallow, but often a cookie or a pretzel, etc.) provided immediately or two small rewards if he or she waited until the experimenter returned (after an absence of approximately 15 minutes). In follow-up studies, the researchers found that children who were able to wait longer for the preferred rewards tended to have better life outcomes, as measured by SAT scores,[2] educational attainment,[3] body mass index (BMI)[4] and other life measures.

[32] Pennebaker, J.W., *Opening Up: The Healing Powers of Confiding in Others,* (New York: William Morrow. 1990)

[33] Bowen, M.D., Murray, "Family Reaction to Death," in *Family Therapy in Clinical Practice,* (Jason Aronson, Inc.; 2nd edition 1993, 1976) p. 321

[34] Zolli, Andrew, *Resilience: Why Things Bounce Back,* (Free Press, 2012) p. 126

[35] Leonard Mlodinow, *Subliminal: How Your Unconscious Mind Rules Your Behavior,* (Pantheon Books, April 24, 2012)

[36] Allen, Sharon L., "Descendent of Strong Women," *The New York Times,* July 2, 2006

[37]Fields, R. Douglas, "Of two minds: Listener brain patterns mirror those of the speaker," July 27, 2010, *Scientific America,* http://blogs.scientificamerican.com/guest-blog/2010/07/27/of-two-minds-listener-brain-patterns-mirror-those-of-the-speaker/

[38]Gazzaniga, Michael S., "Decoding the Brain's Cacophony," **New York Times,** Oct 31, 2011, http://www.nytimes.com/2011/11/01/science/telling-the-story-of-the-brains-cacophony-of-competing-voices.html?pagewanted=all

CHAPTER XI

[39] Bowen, M.D., Murray, Family Therapy in Clinical Practice, (Jason Aronson, Inc.; 2nd edition 1993, 1976) p. 363

[40] Ibid, p. 364

[41] Ibid, p. 366

[42]Bowen, op. cit., p. 365

[43] Bowen, op. cit., p. 371

CHAPTER XII

[44] Gordon, Debora, *Ant Encounters: Interaction Networks and Colony Behavior* (Princeton University Press, Mar 22, 2010)

[45] Seeley, Thomas, D., *Honeybee Democracy,* (Princeton University Press, September 20, 2010) p. 213

[46] "Are Ants Intelligent," http://quotations.hubpages.com/hub/Intelligent_Ants

[47] The GABA neurotransmitter and its receptors are critical to how humans think and act, Dr. Levinson adds. "We apply so many conscious and unconscious perceptions and judgments to our actions at every second, without even realizing that we are doing so," she says. "GABA is part of the brain system that allows us to fine-tune our moods, thoughts, and actions with an incredible level of detail." http://www.sciencedaily.com/releases/2010/03/100301102803.htm

[48]Jacobs, A.J. "Do I Love My Wife? An Investigative Report," *Esquire,* http://www.esquire.com/features/mri-of-love-0609

[49] Buffalo State University, "Triune Brain, http://www.buffalostate.edu/orgs/bcp/brainbasics/triune.html

[50] Jaak Panksepp and Lucy Biven, *The Archaeology of Mind: Neuroevolutionary Origins of Human Emotions* (Sep 17, 2012), p. 1

[51] Panksepp, Jaak, and Biven, Lucy, *The Archaeology of Mind: Neuroevolutionary Origins of Human Emotions* (Sep 17, 2012) p. 330

[52] Like an overwhelmed traffic cop, the depressed brain may transmit signals among regions in a dysfunctional way. Recent brain-imaging studies suggest that areas of the brain involved in mood, concentration and conscious thought are hyperconnected, which scientists believe could lead to the problems with focus, anxiety and memory frequently seen in depression. http://www.scientificamerican.com/article.cfm?id=the-depression-connection

[53] Returning from their geological excursion together in North Wales (Aug1831), he found a letter from Henslow urging him to apply for the position of naturalist on the "Beagle," which was about to start on a surveying expedition. His father, at first, disliked the idea, but his uncle, the second Josiah Wedgwood, pleaded with success, and Darwin started on Dec 27, 1831, the voyage lasting until the Oct 2, 1836. http://www.darwin-literature.com/l_biography.html

[54] Desmond, Adrian, Moore, James, *Darwin: The Life of a Tormented Evolutionist* (W. W. Norton & Company; Reprint edition, June 17, 1994)

[55] Darwin, Charles and Wilson, E.O., *From So Simple a Beginning: Darwin's Four Great Books (Voyage of the Beagle, The Origin of Species, The Descent of Man, The Expression of Emotions in Man and Animals,* (W. W. Norton & Company; Reprint editions, June 17, 1994, Nov 7, 2005)

[56] Newport, Frank, "Four in 10 Americans believe in Creationism," *Gallup,* Dec 17, 2010, http://www.gallup.com/poll/145286/four-americans-believe-strict-creationism.aspx

[57] Weiner, Jonathan, *The Beak of the Finch: A Story of Evolution in Our Time,* (Vintage; 1995)

CHAPTER XIII

[58] McLeod, Saul, "Asch Experiment" http://www.simplypsychology.org/asch-conformity.html

[59] McLeod Saul, op. cit.

Lightning Source UK Ltd.
Milton Keynes UK
UKHW02f1944030418
320469UK00016B/932/P